As Dr. Gerald Borchert writes, "The me. _ _ _ story available to us as humans." With that passion providing the momentum, Dr. Borchert provides a fresh expression of how we as followers of Christ can share the story of Jesus with the increasing number of people who are unaware of the kingdom of God and its king. With his experience, heart for God, and passion for sharing the story of God in Christ filtering through everything he writes, each of us should listen to what Dr. Borchert shares in this book.

—*Greg Henson*
President, Sioux Falls Seminary

Gerald Borchert shares his long experience as an expert teacher of the New Testament in the classroom and in the church to present the varying portraits of Jesus . . . . The result is an excellent guidebook that brings out the different emphases and nuances of these works. Highly recommended.

—*David E. Garland*
Interim President, Baylor University

In this important book Gerald L. Borchert writes, "following Jesus is not an easy task. We may not like the words or acts of Jesus in the portrait we are called to emulate." Our deep and often overly inculturated misunderstanding of who Jesus is has hamstrung, to an extent, the ministry of the Church in fulfilling its mission as the true mystical Body of Christ. Dr. Borchert advocates for a biblical literacy that clarifies and interprets the true, unique, multi-faceted, complex, even strange person of Jesus the Christ, the only Son of the Living God, revealed in different ways in the full counsel of New Testament Scripture. Ultimately, to know and love this Jesus more fully will lead us, as Dr. Borchert states, to ". . . a more dynamic life with God." What could be more important than that?

—*James R. Hart, D.W.S.*
President, Robert E. Webber Institute for Worship Studies, Jacksonville, Florida

Gerald Borchert masterfully combines seasoned biblical understanding with deep pastoral awareness to lead the reader on a life-changing walk with Jesus. Just as the disciples' eyes were opened to see the resurrected Jesus as they ate with a stranger in Emmaus, so will those who read this book encounter Jesus in all the challenging richness the biblical writers intended. I commend this book to those who long to know and walk with the Jesus of the New Testament.

—*Eric W. Bolger*
Vice President for Academic Affairs
College of the Ozarks

Dr. Borchert's book is a holistic approach not only to describing the counter-cultural, upside-down kingdom values that Jesus espoused during his earthly ministry but also to defining biblical illiteracy not just as a lack of knowledge but as a lack of applied knowledge. He invites the reader to see in the Gospel portraits of Jesus a way forward for his body, the church, to become the gospel. He invites us to become living gospel portraits in our everyday worlds.

—*Ralph Korner*
Dean and Associate Professor of Biblical Studies
Taylor Seminary, Edmonton, AB, Canada

Were Jesus to walk into our churches today, as He did the Temple, would tables remain upright? Would pews? Pulpits? Can we say "Yes" to God in worship and "No" to the poor? If we want to be Christlike, we must know what Christ is like. Professor Borchert shows us Jesus Christ.

—*J. Randall O'Brien*
President, Carson-Newman University

Portraits of Jesus for an Age of Biblical Illiteracy is a highly personal and engaging study reflecting Borchert's perceptive insights on the intents of the New Testament texts based upon his many decades of research and teaching along with the cogent analysis of his legal training. He carefully explicates the essence of the New Testament message with his lucid "portraits of Jesus" as the New Testament writers meant to convey Jesus to the people of their era. By extension, Borchert explicitly demonstrates how these original portraits in the Gospels and Epistles are appropriate for our present age where the original understanding of Jesus has been obfuscated and is not easily discerned. Thus, the book addresses the relevance of the "transforming" New Testament portrayals of the "authentic" Jesus to the troubling conditions of our current world situation. Highly appropriate for any person's journey with Christ, this book is essential reading for both lay and clergy in showing how we should both understand and communicate the biblical meaning of Jesus for our present generation. As such, this book serves as an essential antidote to our modern biblical illiteracy.

—*Charles W. Weber*
Emeritus Professor of History
Wheaton College (IL)

GERALD L. BORCHERT

Portraits of **Jesus** for an **Age** of **Biblical Illiteracy**

Smyth & Helwys Publishing, Inc.
6316 Peake Road
Macon, Georgia 31210-3960
1-800-747-3016
©2016 by Gerald L. Borchert
All rights reserved.

Library of Congress Cataloging-in-Publication Data

CIP Information on file.

Selected Works Also by Gerald L. Borchert

Today's Modern Church

Dynamics of Evangelism

The Spiritual Dimensions of Pastoral Care

Assurance and Warning

The Crisis of Fear

John 1–11 (NAC, vol. 25A)

John 12–21 (NAC, vol. 25B)

"Galatians" in Mohrlang and Borchert, *Romans and Galatians*

Worship in the New Testament: Divine Mystery and Human Response

The Book of Revelation

Jesus of Nazareth: Background, Witness, and Significance

Assaulted by Grief: Finding God in Broken Places

Lands of the Bible: Israel, The Palestinian Territories, Sinai and Egypt . . .

Lands of the Bible: In the Footsteps of Paul and John

A Translator of Galatians and Romans (New Living Translation)

Dedicated to the Mission of the Living Jesus

Acknowledgments

I wish here first to acknowledge what has been for me a very special privilege of writing about the portraits of Jesus.

Then I have been very blessed by the support of my dear wife, Dr. Doris Borchert, and our two sons, Drs. Mark (a communications professor) and Tim Borchert (a pastor), and their wives, Karen and Phyllis (both chaplains).

I am grateful to my students and the Methodist pastors at Lake Junaluska for the encouragement to put my ideas concerning the portraits of Jesus in writing. I am also grateful to Rich Gorsuch for giving me permission to use his graphics at the beginning of each section of the book.

Finally, I am exceedingly grateful to Keith Gammons and his superb staff at Smyth & Helwys for assisting me in bringing this work to publication.

GLB

Contents

Journeying with the New Testament Writers in an Era of Growing Biblical Illiteracy

This book on the challenge facing Christians and the church in an era of growing biblical illiteracy arises in large part out of my recent experiences of teaching the New Testament to undergraduate university students. It also arises from the fascinating invitation by United Methodists to address their ministers at Lake Junaluska, North Carolina, on the subject "Communicating the Gospel in an Age of Biblical Illiteracy." While I have taught seminary and graduate students for many years throughout the world, I have been challenged by and grateful for both these new opportunities. The intersection of these two tasks has caused a seething in my mind that has forced me to focus on the crucial issue of trying to understand and communicate the message of the New Testament to the bright but bewildered people of our era. This challenge has been reinforced by debates and statements made by presidential hopefuls who have provided stark examples referring to the Bible and God with little genuine understanding of the meaning and context of their biblical references.

This summons to address biblical illiteracy has also reminded of Jesus' stirring words that the people of his generation were like sheep who were lost in a confusing wilderness of reality, who did not know where they were going, and who were desperately seeking their way out of bewilderment.

Namely, they longed for authentic meaning and the genuine resources for life (cf. Mark 6:34). In the process of writing this book, I have been forced once again to consider the early Christian community that, as Luke tells us (Acts 1:1-10), Jesus continued to direct after his death and resurrection in the crucial task of understanding the implications of his coming. I have also been more keenly aware of my colleagues who minister to their anxious people, many of whom attend church on a regular basis yet do not know how to listen for the Good Shepherd's call on their lives. Indeed, they scarcely even think about "shepherds" in our computer-oriented generation.

Addressing biblical illiteracy has also made me wrestle with why I would even talk about "journeying" or "walking" with the New Testament writers in this era of space travel when we contemplate inter-planetary flights. But as I will suggest in this work, the term "walk" (as a way of life with God) is crucial for the biblical writers and for the problems that can arise from a foundational misunderstanding of that biblical concept.

I have been challenged by and grateful for the response of the North Carolina ministers to my presentations, some of whom suggested that my initial ideas should be shared with a wider audience. Thus, in the succeeding months I have given my attention to writing this work for my students as well as for some of my colleagues in ministry. My hope is to help ministers (both current and future) who seek to lead their people in how the portraits of the authentic Jesus and the power of his transforming grace can communicate a living reality of Jesus' presence to people in our struggling generation.

To introduce myself briefly, I have been a "Neuatestamentlicher"— a New Testament professor—for many years, but over those years I have also been given the opportunity to teach many subjects, including preaching, counseling, evangelism, and worship. Although I make no claim at being an authority in those fields, I count it a privilege to have collaborated with well-known professors of preaching, evangelism, worship, sociology of religion, and counseling in teaching various seminary courses and ministry seminars. Moreover, although I have written books in a number of ministry fields,[1] I would not begin to suggest that I am an expert in those areas. But I do know a little concerning my own field of the Bible. And I firmly believe that the Christian Scriptures, which have been passed down to us under the guiding hand of God's Spirit, can powerfully confront our sophisticated but very lonely generation.

It is a generation that may have heard about but often does not really understand the magnificent Story of the Seeking God—the one who has been in the process of working out hope and new life in the world for centuries. I firmly believe that this message, which centers on Jesus, can be unpacked more clearly in the process of walking or journeying with the New Testament writers. It is a message that every Christian leader and witness should long to understand more deeply and to impart to others who are searching for the meaning of life.

This world that God graciously created, however, is suffering from intense pain and agony. Half of its six billion-plus people live on the edge of starvation and death, and countless individuals are being uprooted daily and cast into poverty. Many are wracked by war, violence, injustice, and economic imbalance and suffer from all types of disease, some of which can be treated with simple pills if we had the economic will to make them available to the poor. The *anawim* (Hebrew for "the very poor and helpless") of our world, like all of us, are in desperate need of new encounters with the mind-blowing Jesus who announced that he came to fulfill God's promise of bringing regenerating hope to the oppressed, the blind, the captives, and those who are encompassed by grief and mourning (see Isa 61:1-3 and Luke 4:18-19 for the coming of the time of Jubilee).

While we have proclaimed this Jesus and his message for centuries, I think it is necessary that we should ask again, who is this Jesus about whom all Christians have been called to witness, and what is his transforming message? Is he really God's answer to the traumas of the world? And who is this Messiah who offers hope especially to those whom my former classmate, Tony Campolo, has consistently reminded us do not even use the future tense in their speech? The reason, he argues, is that they do not expect to have a future. Many of us in the diminishing middle class hardly ever encounter such people and scarcely realize that they exist—even in America.

Unfortunately, because of the tragic situations around the world, a huge number of people live only for the current day and for a few sparse necessities of life. Their present bankrupt reality is all they know. Some have dismissed the concept of the future as they seek to exist in the present. Others are willing to commit suicide or kill others in their quest to escape from their unhappy present in exchange for the promise of a phantom future.

On the other side of the economic scale, a lesser number of people also live only for today and the convenient luxuries of life. They too have little thought of the future except perhaps to provide for their children and grandchildren. They hope that possibly some others will remember them and their existence after they depart this present realm. They may even be existing in our world like present-day Scrooges and say, "Bah, humbug" to the possibility of receiving a transforming vision. Some of these people may be sitting in the pews of our churches or in the classes of our institutions listening to our proclamations and instructions. They may know in their heads about Jesus, but they don't know how this Jesus applies to their daily lives.

Many of us pass the poor as we rush to work or other activities of life. When we travel the world, we are conveniently not shown such people. Of course, most of us would rather not be reminded of their existence. Yet if we are truly Christian, we cannot live, teach, and model the message of Jesus and ignore the suffering of people who are regarded as the rejects of society. It is imperative for us to be reminded that these people are the kind who heard Jesus gladly (cf. Mark 12:37)! The "religious," however, were the ones who sought ways to discount Jesus and his message because he made them realize that they were irrelevant or made them uncomfortable. It was these others, these so-called proper ones, who ultimately sought to eliminate him.

Many of us who are not among the poor and rejects of society are honestly seeking to be genuinely Christian, but we struggle to understand the plight of those on the margins. We wonder what Jesus would think of us. Would we be categorized as the irrelevant "religious" of today? Where would we fit into the harsh statements of Jesus concerning the Pharisees (cf. Matt 23:1-36), especially if we have heard the stories concerning Jesus in our churches for years?

I wonder, to what extent do we who call ourselves Christians perceive the incredible implications in the coming of Christ and the message of the New Testament? Is it possible that our personal portraits of Jesus have become slightly skewed so as to fit our life patterns? Have we conveniently "touched up his image" in such a way that the reality of Jesus is judiciously masked from us and our friends in church? Does our portrait of Jesus challenge us today, or have we conveniently neutralized him into our cultural patterns so that he no longer troubles us?

In thinking about the New Testament writers and their messages for people in an era of growing biblical illiteracy, I have wrestled with wrenching questions. Accordingly, I think it is imperative for us as Christians and leaders of Christian faith communities to be reintroduced to the strange and shocking nature of this Jesus who is portrayed in fascinating ways in the New Testament. My recent assignments have, therefore, caused me rethink a good deal about the messages of the New Testament and what the ancient writers were trying to communicate about Jesus and his purpose in coming to planet Earth.

I know that many teachers and ministers have tried to be faithful to the task of presenting authentic portraits of Jesus in their ministries, and this study is in no way intended to be a critique of others. Instead, I have been challenged to ask myself: How much do people I encounter know about this Jesus? Do they know the Jesus of Mark who shocked people? Do they know the Jesus of Matthew who forced people to confront their longstanding religious traditions? Do they know the Jesus of Luke who challenged people to reexamine their lack of concern about the marginalized of society? Have they really met the Jesus Christ of Paul who confessed that "for me to live" is to follow the self-giving Christ and indeed to die or be killed? Do we recognize what such an experience with the eternal God would mean (cf. Phil 1:21)? Finally, I am forced to ask with John, would our people be ready to be faced with the presence of the divine reality in human flesh?

And what do these questions say about people's understanding of the theological significance of the coming of Jesus for our church practices today? If Jesus walked into our churches, what would be our reaction? If he started to speak as he did in Nazareth (see Luke 4:16-30), would we become incensed? It is crucial at this critical time in our world for followers of Jesus to ponder these questions. We need to ask ourselves anew, do we live in the light of this Jesus who is portrayed in the New Testament, or is it possible that our living portraits of Jesus—our embodiments of Christ— are adding to or promoting contemporary biblical illiteracy?

The people who attend our institutions of learning or come regularly to worship and study in our churches are God's wonderful gifts to our faith communities. But have those dear people been aided in grappling with the reality of Jesus and the fact that his early followers were condemned by others for "turning the world upside down" (cf. Acts 17:6)? This question has haunted my thinking recently, and it should stir all of us as teachers, ministers, and laypeople in all denominations that claim to be Christian. Indeed, it should force all of us as Christians to reexamine our life rationales, perceptions, and responses to the New Testament writers concerning the Jesus we proclaim as Lord.

This book then is an attempt to address some of the crucial questions that revolve around the significance of what we are doing when we read the New Testament. It is not meant to introduce some new "quick-fix" program; we already have far too many of those. Instead, this study is intended to offer suggestions concerning how we are thinking about and communicating who Jesus is and what his world-altering message is to the people of our generation. In doing so, I have also reflected briefly on the changing nature of our society, especially in the light of an American Values Survey that was conducted in November 2012.[2]

I trust that through this work, we all might be better enabled to grasp the incredible meaning in the coming of God's amazing son—Jesus, the Christ! It is my prayer that this reflection will serve as a helpful and empowering tool as we are challenged to reread the New Testament with less cluttered and adorned lenses so that we all might encounter more fully the fascinating and life-altering Jesus of the New Testament.

As you read, I would ask that you have a copy of the New Testament with you. My goal is not to highlight what I have to say but to help you understand more clearly what our God-touched authors have to say concerning their portraits of Jesus.

I want to thank all those who have provoked a spark in me to ponder again the coming of Jesus. I am grateful for the work of those who wrote their missives concerning the Son of God. I likewise express my gratitude to God for my dear wife, Doris, a professor of Christian education, who continually spurs me on to represent Jesus as authentically as possible. And I thank God for my two sons—Mark, the chair of communications at Carson-Newman University, and Tim, the senior pastor in a wonderful church—both of whom remind me constantly of our important task in communicating the gospel to others in a way that does not engender theological fog on the pretense of our being erudite or bright.

A Note about the Images

I am deeply indebted to my longtime friend Richard (Rich) Gorsuch of Sioux Falls, South Dakota, now of Canon Beach, Oregon, who out of his concern for the continuing work of Jesus and the extension of Christ's church has given me permission to use without fee eight of his strategic graphic art pieces concerning the gospel. These eight pieces are presented in a slightly different order and focus than were included in my 1976 book *Dynamics of Evangelism*, which was published by Word Books, formerly of Waco, Texas. No further reproduction of Rich's work in this book shall be made without my express written permission and those of Richard Gorsuch or his heirs and legal assigns.

I would add that I have cherished the times in the past when Richard and I discussed at length our Christian life concerns and service for Jesus, and I have sought to honor him and our Lord by using his incisive artistic messages here.

—Gerald L. Borchert
Palm Sunday 2016

Introduction: "Walking" with the New Testament Writers and Discovering Their Portraits of Jesus for Our Generation

The Importance of Walking

Why do I focus on "walking" when it comes to the New Testament and its writers? The reason is because buried in the idea of "walking" is a crucial secret to understanding the nature of the New Testament and indeed all biblical theology. I have told my students repeatedly that the study of the Bible sets one on a journey. It is an *experience* with God. Reading the New Testament and the Bible is not so much about reading words. It is more about entering into a series of stories. These stories are in fact part of God's story. And "walking" seems to be the way the biblical writers describe those experiences.

The Hebrew word for "walk" is *halak*. The verb is used repeatedly to describe a relationship between God and humans. Among those whom Genesis designated as having walked with God are Enoch (5:22, 24), Noah (6:9), Abram/Abraham (17:1; 24:40) and Isaac (48:15). God promised the people in covenant to walk among them if they were obedient (Lev 26:12) but said that judgment would surely fall if they walked contrary to his will

(26:27-28). This alternative is a striking reminder of the fact that God is described as walking in the cool period of the day looking for the humans that had been created after they disobeyed the command concerning the forbidden tree of knowledge. Instead of walking with God, they tried to hide because their relationship with God and with each other had been fractured (Gen 2:8-13). Both David (see for example Pss 26:3; 116:9) and Hezekiah (2 Kgs 20:2; Isa 38:3) knew that walking with God was foundational to divine blessing, and they relied on that covenant promise as the answer to their survival in the face of impending danger. Walking with God was what God expected of the covenant people.

This concept of *halak*, however, was twisted slightly by the later rabbis who replaced the verb with its parallel noun *halakah*. Accordingly, instead of focusing on walking with God, the emphasis was shifted to focusing on rules. This seemingly slight alteration was a tragic, major shift away from the journey and experience with God toward words. Both are concerned with obedience, but the shift to rules and laws became for the people a convenient substitute for a living relationship with God.

This pattern of substituting rules for a relationship is crucial to our understanding of the coming of Jesus. To describe this shift in another way, one could say that Jesus and Pharisees both spoke of the "Law of God," but it is where they put the emphasis that made all the difference. The Pharisees spoke of the *Law* of God, and Jesus emphasized the Law of *God!* The centrality of a relationship with the unseen God is often sacrificed for words, rules, and institutions. This substitution is what Stephen, like Jesus, charged the Jews with doing. Thus, parallel to Jesus, Stephen was executed because the Jews had committed themselves to their substitutes of Torah and temple (cf. Acts 6:13-14). And this type of shift has happened repeatedly with humans who seem to choose rules, books, and institutions over a relationship with the living God.

As a mature rabbi, when Paul became a Christian, he clearly recognized this fundamental difference between Jesus and the rabbis. For this reason, Paul took a strong stance against legalism (see Gal 3). What is even more important at this point is that he returned to the use of the concept of "walking" (*peripatein* in Greek) to describe the Christian life and abandoned the rabbinic notion of *the walk* as a series of rules to guarantee acceptance by God.

There is no question, as I indicate later in this work, that Paul expected Christians to live authentic moral lives, and accordingly there are many moral instructions or ethical injunctions in his letters. But such instructions are expected to flow from a prior authentic relationship with God in Christ. They are not the basis for the transformed life or for living a "new morality" in Jesus. God in Christ Jesus invites people into a *divine-human journey* or encounter in which humans "walk" in Christ (cf. Col 2:6), in the Spirit (cf. Gal 5:16; Rom 8:4), by faith (cf. 2 Cor 5:7), and in newness of life with God (cf. Rom 6:4)—to mention only a few of Paul's expressions.

The New Testament writers invite us to join a journey or a walking with God in the risen Christ—not a covenant with a set of rules. And I invite you now to a journey with these New Testament witnesses. But before we begin, let me explain my thought process in creating this book.

The Purpose of this Book

I often ask myself, how am I communicating the Jesus who is God's answer to the problems of the world? Am I presenting an authentic picture of Jesus? Wrestling with that question is the purpose of this book. If you want to know what is behind my thinking—what makes me tick—you will want to read the rest of this chapter. But if going behind the scenes seems a little too heavy at this point, please skip it for now and continue reading what I say concerning Mark and 1 Peter. Then you can come back to this chapter after you have caught a sense of my vision.

I am a descendant of German immigrants and also a professor. Knowing these two facts should let you in on a secret. German professors by nature seem to be committed to writing "introductions" or mapping out their process before they get to the task of writing the content of their books. So if you want to have my rationale for this work—which I think is quite important—then here it is. In chapter 2 you will begin to visualize what I am doing and why it is crucial to rethink how we understand and communicate Jesus to those who live in this time of growing biblical illiteracy.

The message of the Bible is the most exciting story available to us as humans. Our task as Christians then is to invite people into this amazing story of God. Believing in the incredible power of God's actions in this story is and always has been a key to the effective communication of the gospel, especially for a generation that simply doesn't have the biblical foundation of earlier ones. We have been given the priceless opportunity of following in the footsteps of the early evangelists, who after encountering the risen Jesus burst onto the world's scene as a remarkable group of witnesses to a divine reality. They were, indeed, merely human agents, yet they were without doubt bold and unafraid in the face of the most powerful human authorities and hostile forces of their day.

As members of the current company of those who have been called by God into the power of God's story, I say to you, welcome! I know that you now understand that to be part of this important company necessitates a personal "walk" (*halak*) with the Divine Author of this story, the one who is the most powerful force—the *pantocrator* (Greek for the "Almighty")—in the entire universe!

Mark and the other Gospel writers clearly indicate that when the first followers met and "walked" with Jesus, they had little understanding of what the messianic coming of this person would mean for the world. After their gripping encounter with the resurrected Lord, they were transformed into an explosive team of witnesses to God's story of change and new life. Getting inside this dynamic story and communicating it to others is the God-given task of every serious Christian.

The Apostle Paul was not one of the first of Jesus' followers, but when he came to know and to walk with the resurrected Christ, he stunned even the earlier disciples with his commitment and enthusiasm for communicating the amazing message of God in Christ ("Immanuel") to those beyond his earlier fence of Judaism. The life and messages of Saul/Paul are a strategic part of this thrilling story of God touching humanity. And such is also the case for you and me who are the contemporary messengers of God in the world.

This amazing story begins with God, who is said to have graciously created the world "good" (*tov* in Hebrew). But the story is *not* all "good." It leads through the tragedy of sin and involves the selection of people descended from Abraham who were to bless the world (Gen 12:2). Their pilgrimage through history, however, was not marked by a series of unmitigated successes. Instead, what has been recorded is a series of repeated human failures and frustrations involving experiences of both freedom and slavery, victory and defeat, obedience and disobedience, entry into the promised land and banishment from it through the exile. Then the story reaches its climax with anticipating the messianic era and tragically missing its coming!

This dramatic interaction of the divine with humans reached its focus in the coming of God's only Son, who touched the world in the historic "incarnation" (or in-fleshment) of Jesus. But this Jesus was soundly rejected by most of the descendants of Abraham, who united with the mighty Gentile military force of Rome to execute their Messiah in a ghastly crucifixion in which they sought to blot out his memory from the face of the earth. Yet these heirs of Abraham and their cohorts hardly understood that their ugly act involved much more than disposing of someone who did not fit their religious ideologies or concepts of power.

Indeed, we now know that God was in this story! This fact makes all the difference! Yes, God responded and transformed the heinous murder of Jesus into a cosmic sacrifice for anyone who genuinely believes in him and seeks to follow him. Moreover, this story continues to unfold even in our world today as people come to understand the real significance of the coming of Jesus and the fact that the destiny of all humanity is encompassed within the divine story.

But the question for all people remains: Who is this Jesus? And to that question may be added the following: Do most contemporary Christians know and follow him? Have they experienced the excitement of knowing his incredible transforming power? In these questions lies an important key to recognizing the power of this story and communicating it in an era of growing biblical illiteracy.

As Christians, therefore, we are duty-bound to ask: What are we trying to communicate to people about God today? What is the key to our understanding and sharing this message? And how convinced are we in God's transforming power through this message? In listening to my seminary students preach and teach over the years, I have often pointedly asked them in reviewing their messages, "What in the world were you trying to do?" When they have recovered from the immediate shock of my question, my repeated response has been, "Your task is *not* to prove your intelligence. Your task is to be a living messenger!" So, repeatedly, I must ask the same question of myself and of you, my readers: are we correctly focused as we form our understandings and communications concerning Jesus?

Where is Jesus in relation to our lives, our possessions, and our conversations as well as in our church sermons and lesson plans? The answer to these questions is the correct starting point for dealing with the messages of the New Testament writers in this era. We may have access to enormous amounts of information on our cell phones and computers, but that does not mean we have internalized the biblical message.

Having pondered these questions, I turn now to what may be an unsettling reality for Christian leaders in our era. The Public Religion Research Institute gave us significant insights into our American population after the presidential election of 2012.[3] While the study was concerned with that election and its political implications, I want to focus on the implications for our understanding of religious commitment. The findings are as follows:

Unaffiliated: In the 18 to 29 age group, the study showed that 35% were *unaffiliated religiously*. Compare that number to the unaffiliated in the 65 and older group at 8% and in the 50 to 64 age group at 11%. The differences are revealing.

Affiliated and Identified: The above numbers can be contrasted with those in the 18 to 29 age group who are affiliated and identified with a denomination: the numbers are 12%, 9 %, and 5% (total =26%) for those who were white Evangelicals, mainline Protestants, and Catholics respectively. Compare those numbers with those in the 65 and older age group at 28%, 19%, and 22% (total = 69%) for white Evangelicals, mainline Protestants, and Catholics. Also important is the fact that in the 50 to 64 age group, the numbers were 29%, 13%, and 19% (total = 61%) for white Evangelicals, mainline Protestants, and Catholics.

If we have learned anything from such a comparison, it is the fact that the number of those who are affiliated with Christianity, especially in the white population, is dwindling rapidly. But such a fact should not surprise anyone who has been an observer of the trends in churches over the last two decades.

My purpose in citing this study, however, is not to pursue the matter further but to remind us of a crucial reality in our day. When we talk about an increasingly biblically illiterate generation, we are not imagining a potential situation or playing games with words and statistics. The younger generation that is on the scene now needs the concerted attention of those who are currently in all forms of Christian ministry; indeed, it needs the *concern* of all Christians. We cannot afford to pretend that a problem does not exist today. We are called to *present Jesus to a growing biblically illiterate generation!* It is a generation that needs to know the magnificent story of God in Jesus.

The Organization of this Work

Welcome then to a different way of understanding and communicating Jesus in this study. I have tried to help us recognize the reality of various portraits of Jesus that emerge from the New Testament. Understanding these portraits can provide us with a framework for reading the New Testament and applying the implications to our lives.

Pictures, of course, can be as varied as people. We need to recognize that all the portraits of Jesus presented in the New Testament do not need to be identical. In fact, the differences provide a basis for understanding the incredible breadth of the gospel writers in explaining both God and Jesus. This perspective can assist us in seeing how the divine has impacted our world in the past and continues to impact it today.

The Nature of the Portraits

Let me challenge us to reflect for a moment on pictures. First, a picture may be a photograph that catches subjects or objects in a single time frame. A series of photographs may be joined together to form a running picture that is popularly known as a movie or its derivatives such as a television story, video, or some other form of visual media. Second, a picture may be the result of a drawing or painting, and it can take several forms, from a catchy cartoon to abstract art that challenges the observer to make a mental connection between the reality of a subject or object and the crafted image on a canvas or lithograph. Such a picture provides an impression for the imagination that may or may not seem to have much relationship to a direct observable form. Third, a picture may be a portrait, a painting or drawing that usually bears a close connection to the person being represented and yet, because it is painted by an artist, also represents what catches the artist's attention as the important features of that person. In other words, a portrait goes through the mind and feelings of the artist before it appears on the canvas. A portrait is both similar and yet quite different from a photograph or a video.[4]

Accordingly, when Mark sketched out our first Gospel account of Jesus, he was not simply writing a direct history or creating a photo account about Jesus. He was doing something far more significant than running a videotape. He was providing a testimony about the figure he believed was the most important person who ever lived on the face of planet Earth— namely, the Son of God! The other Gospel writers followed his lead and penned their testimonies as well. These evangelists did not use all the information they had at their disposal (cf. John 20:30), nor did each of them use the stories and messages of Jesus in the same order. They organized what they used so that it would fit their presentations or testimonies. Each Gospel writer had his own organizing principles, and the result is that each portrait of Jesus has a slightly different emphasis. But each testimony is a *legitimate portrait or account* of who they believed Jesus to be.

Our task then is to read each Gospel carefully and discover what type of portrait emerges of Jesus. This issue is crucial to our task of being messengers—or witnesses—of Jesus. The portraits of Jesus in the New Testament are not all alike, and that means the authors' use of the various pericopes (segments) or patterns of theologizing on Jesus may be different. These differences in the presentation should never be viewed as mistakes or errors. They are instead the result of different foci in the Gospels and the other books of the New Testament.

We must try to grasp if possible the *entire argument* of each biblical book so that we do not misrepresent the use and meaning of a single pericope (or section) in that book. Particularly in the Gospels, it is imperative to see the full picture of Jesus that is being portrayed so that we do not misinterpret the point of any particular pericope (a story, a teaching, or a question) in its context. Many believers and seekers who listen to our presentations hardly think about variations in this manner. Many think that presentations about the Gospel stories should be exactly the same, and if not, then something must be wrong with the presentations. And perhaps some Christian presenters have given biblically illiterate listeners this impression.

Note that what I have said about the Gospels also applies to the New Testament epistles, the book called Acts, the sermon designated as Hebrews, and the book of Revelation, which may seem strange or daunting to many in the task of explaining its meaning. Unfortunately, Revelation has been badly handled by many interpreters who have turned it either into a contemporary chart of the future or a Western schismatic document.

My Hope

Without further delay, then, let me describe what I hope to accomplish in this book for helping those who are trying to communicate a better understanding of biblical texts in a meaningful manner to people in a generation that is becoming increasingly biblically illiterate.

Since Jesus is the focal point of the New Testament, I intend to help you find some important keys to who Jesus is in each of the books I have selected for review. In doing so, I have sought to assist you in identifying the primary focus or foci of a book so that understanding and communicating its message is easier. Grasping an author's unique pictures of Jesus in each book is important for arriving at an adequate interpretation of that book. Other interpreters may choose other foci, but the ones I have chosen should help in providing understanding.

In approaching this task, I do not intend to cover all the books of the New Testament as I did in my work *Worship in the New Testament* because my goal was different there.[5] In the present case, what you will soon discover is that I am using some representative books and comparing them to provide models for understanding Jesus and for interpreting our biblical texts.

Before I begin my analysis with the portrait of the strange and shocking Jesus in the Gospel of Mark, however, I must ask, why did Mark so pointedly present Jesus in a startling manner? This type of question forces us to confront the issue of *purpose* not only for Mark but also for all the books in the New Testament. When we begin to analyze the purpose of a book like Mark, we have moved beyond simply using a pericope in the Bible as the starting point for a favorite topic or as fodder for argument, discussion, teaching, or preaching what otherwise might come randomly into our minds.

Confronting this issue concerning an author's goal means that we have an important task in understanding a biblical book. That task is to try to lay open, if possible, the book's purpose and organization to find unifying patterns within that book and enable us to remember and communicate its content to others. Following this procedure will be quite different than the usual flat pattern of many Bible readers who assume that words and ideas mean the same thing throughout the Bible. Words and ideas in one book, though, may not necessarily mean the same thing in another book— a custom not understood by Christians who love to do word studies. Such people scarcely realize, for instance, that the word "law" in Paul has multiple meanings depending on the context in which it is used.

Moreover, helping people understand the purpose of a book and the place of a pericope in the book's organization can open minds to read the Bible in a new light. I am a firm believer in the fact that we can assist each other in the realization that the Bible is far more than a book of inspired golden nuggets that can be lifted out of their contexts without reference to the argument of the entire book.

This latter point reminds me of an experience I had as a younger professor when I delivered a series of Bible studies on the West Coast and was invited to a Bible study on Romans the Monday morning before my plane departed. For the Romans study, each person took one verse and explained what it meant to him or her. The experience was undoubtedly meaningful to the people, and I support Christians meeting together and sharing. But unfortunately, most of what they found in the text of Romans was inserted into it and had little to do with what Paul was saying. In this era of growing biblical illiteracy, Christians need to use resources that help them understand the meanings of our foundational texts so that the applications become more significant.

Hopefully we can help people begin to do some important relearning in which they reevaluate inadequate notions like (a) all the Gospels are saying the same thing, (b) these Gospels are merely history reports, (c) the red letters in some Bibles are more important than the black letters, and (d) each author is merely a secretary for God and does not have anything special to say, especially about the Triune God and about Christ Jesus our Lord.

Indeed, I believe our task in leadership is to help people grow in their realization that (a) each book is addressing particular issues, and the way they are addressed is not the same for each book; and (b) there is a reason we have four Gospels and not one.[6] Taken as a whole, then, these books have become the standard for judging authentic Christian thinking and practice throughout the centuries since the time of Jesus, and all the books of the New Testament are not to be treated in the same way.

I believe that we as Christian leaders are up to the task of reeducation and that, in the process of instruction particularly about Jesus, we can help the people in our faith communities discover a significant development in their understandings of the New Testament. In this process, I want to be clear that I do not intend to diminish our people's commitment to God's inspiration of Scripture. Instead, my goal is to help them understand how marvelous is the multi-dimensional nature of God's gift of the biblical witnesses to humanity. This gracious gift provides us with a glimpse into the magnificence of the one whom the biblical writers designated the "Almighty." But I would quickly remind you as I remind my students that when we use terms that are prefixed with "all" (omni-) or "not" (im-/in-), we are recognizing that such ideas are beyond our human experience and understanding.

My Method

It may come as a surprise to you that in presenting portraits of Jesus, I have attempted to link each Gospel with at least one other representative book in the New Testament. I have purposely made these connections not with other Gospels but with other books that may not be linked by other contemporary commentators. The reason is to try to show how each picture of Jesus affects the way the message of one author is being presented. It is my intention to provide you as a reader with representative examples so that you will have models for continuing to develop your own approaches to understanding how the New Testament writers formulated their works.

In beginning with Mark, I have linked that Gospel with 1 Peter so that you will ponder the implications of how Mark's surprising Jesus might relate to or contrast with the purpose of the powerful first epistle of Peter and the reality of Christians who felt displaced as they suffered for their faith. In making this connection, we must not forget the tradition that tells us Mark served not only with Paul but also, and more importantly, with Peter.

Next, I turn to the Gospel of Matthew, often designated as the one written for the Jews, and ask, what kind of Jesus did Matthew present? Then, I look at the sermon called Hebrews and see what implications can emerge from comparing the Matthean picture of Jesus with another book that is clearly Jewish in its orientation. Asking about the pictures of Jesus in these books is quite revealing and provides significant theological insights, especially concerning how we deal with matters of tradition.

Third, I analyze the Gospel of Luke, whose author was clearly a Gentile, and yet I ask, why did he, a Gentile, make Jerusalem and the temple so important in this Gospel? What kind of Jesus is portrayed in Luke, and how does that picture affect our understanding of what is being presented in his other work, the fascinating book of Acts? The comparison is revealing and instructive. It may suggest for us a rationale for why Acts is such a dynamic work.

Fourth, I tackle the Apostle Paul, and I have selected for our study Galatians, the detailed work called 1 Corinthians, and Colossians. The task of summarizing Paul is a momentous one, but I have chosen these three texts for review: one from the beginning of his writing (Galatians[7]), one from the midpoint of his career (1 Corinthians), and one from the later period (Colossians, which some scholars consider was written not by Paul but by a follower of Paul). How does the Pauline picture of Jesus impact the way the author thinks? Do the pictures of Jesus in these epistles have anything to say about how Pauline theology is formulated? Does the view of Jesus affect the advice given to the churches, especially in the dialogical work of 1 Corinthians?

Fifth, I turn as a climax to John, which has been a major emphasis in much of my writing and teaching. What picture of Jesus is presented in the Gospel of John? While this Gospel is easy for the beginning Greek student to read, it is clearly one of the most sophisticated theological works in the entire New Testament. Because it does not follow our Western patterns of thinking, it can be poorly understood. In fact, even in the matter of Johannine chronology, I believe that most people are a little confused.[8] The question, therefore, is, how does John's picture of Jesus influence his overall theological thinking, and how does the Johannine Jesus relate to the thinking in the book of Revelation? These questions are significant for our understanding of Jesus. Since these two books have been foundational in formulating the church's various portraits of Jesus, I have given extended attention to them.

Finally, I close my work with general reflections derived from this study. It is my hope that by analyzing Jesus in this manner and following the method of seeing how the various pictures of him emerge and are inter-related within the New Testament, I will be able to assist you, the reader, in gaining a greater grasp of the theological content and structure of each book discussed. Moreover, I believe that by offering these portraits of Jesus to people in our churches, study groups, and classes, we can give those who are unfamiliar with the content of Scripture a framework for absorbing and integrating the stories in the Bible that are presented in their churches and faith communities. By using this method, I hope we will better be able to assist people to grow in their understanding of the exciting nature of the Christian message and its significance for life.

Issues in Communicating the Gospel to a Biblically Illiterate Generation

Having reviewed the purpose and organization of this work, I turn now to some things I have discovered about communicating Jesus to this generation.

First, I would remind us that many people have an underdeveloped understanding concerning the jargon of the church. Even words like "incarnation" (meaning Jesus was both human and God) may leave some people in a fog. Therefore, we must make sure our hearers understand our terms—such a suggestion can make us uncomfortable because we like our terms. They carry the theological weight of history as well as our sense of precision in definition.[9] Our task, however, is communication. I recognize that I also use jargon such as "pericope" (a segment, story, etc.), but I hope I will explain it well and not overuse it. I remind myself continually to be ready to use words that can better communicate with others.

Second, I believe that, with the growing problem of biblical illiteracy, we need to be aware of what we have learned from neuropsychology and the California Institute of Technology, which pioneered the field in the

1960s. We now know that people learn in different ways depending on the priority of their brain hemispheres. While all people use both hemispheres, some are more oriented to the left or verbal hemisphere whereas others are oriented more to the symbolic or right hemisphere.

The God of the Bible communicates to both hemispheres. In the Western world, we have normally given preference to the left brain, but God's story is clearly communicated in both verbal and symbolic ways so that it affects both hemispheres of our brains. God not only speaks but also acts. The Bible not only provides theological reasons for believing but also clearly communicates in stories concerning actions that involve the glory and the dread of God. When God spoke in Genesis 1, creation came into being. When Gabriel came to Zechariah in Luke 1, the angel not only told him of the forthcoming miraculous birth of a son but also, in light of his reaction to his own prayers, demonstrated the power of God by making Zechariah unable to speak until he named that son.

Accordingly, communicating the message of Jesus to people today should not involve us merely telling them about the transforming power of Jesus; it should also involve our embodying or demonstrating the life-changing power of Christ in us as transformed messengers. So, as Christian communicators, we must be prepared to employ symbolic means as well as words in the process of communicating the reality of Jesus.

Symbolic actions such as baptism and the Lord's Supper should never be viewed as subordinate means of communicating the presence and power of God in a faith community. The recent Worship Renewal Movement with its emphasis on the symbolic is a corrective to left-brain patterns in some circles where the Lord's Supper is viewed as a "tack-on" to the so-called more important aspect of preaching. On the other hand, solid biblical instruction is a corrective elsewhere when we encounter the ritualistic view that Communion is the main reason for worship. But I will deal further with what I see as the four minimal dimensions or expressions of our Christian heritage that should be evidenced in an authentic faith community when I treat Acts 2:42 (below).

What I am concerned to emphasize here is the fact that while the story of God may seem to be focused on "words," that story involves much more than words. It concerns the "God who acts" to redeem a fallen and rebellious humanity. The God of the Bible uses many means to accomplish the divine purposes, and the presence of God is experienced in far more than a verbal message. In working out the divine purpose in the world, God is neither Western nor Eastern, neither left brain nor right brain, neither male nor female. God, the creator and redeemer, is the master of all means of communication and calls people to resist divisive patterns that separate us into categories (cf. Gal 3:28) such as race, sex, economic position, or indeed ways of learning. Instead, even though we differ in many ways including nationality, position in society, education, and ways of achieving understanding, we all—by God's grace—become one in Christ Jesus, who is the Lord (3:25-29). Recognizing our differences is crucial to the ways we understand who Jesus is and communicate his work on earth to others.

Third, also important is our task of providing others with an adequate contextual framework for our messages. This issue is particularly important for we who are Christian leaders and who have not always given people the best framework for what we say, perhaps because we may not have had an adequate framework ourselves. It takes work to provide people with a framework for receiving biblical messages. I long ago realized that many of my students—even my seminary students—do not know the Bible well. Indeed, I have encountered doctoral students with only a vague framework of understanding the biblical texts and who used a few key verses over and over again. Such a pattern may be sufficient at times, but it is hardly a pattern to be advocated for ministry. The students in many schools where I have taught were often bright and logical, but they didn't necessarily know the Bible. That was one reason I wrote my earlier study on *Worship in the New Testament: Divine Mystery and Human Response* (noted earlier). My goal there was to help them see that the New Testament is a worship book, that worship is not confined to a few verses such as Isaiah 6 and John 4, and that worship is not a mere activity or part of a church service. Instead, worship involves an entire way of life!

As leaders in the church, we are partly responsible for this increasing biblical illiteracy. Even some denominational Sunday school materials have not always provided an adequate contextual framework for the lesson material being discussed. The big picture was not always there for students, and sometimes it was also not there for teachers. The result was that a chosen pericope (a story or section in a book from a unit) was often treated like a general wisdom saying or a theological concept given in a vacuum. Accordingly, the people in our churches often view the biblical texts as a series of wise sayings or a chain of eternal truths devoid of the great contextual framework of God's story, to say nothing about how a specific pericope fits into that story.

A framework is foundational to any pericope. But I hasten to add that the situation has greatly improved with the influx of many new commentaries and other biblical resource materials. All one needs to do is compare the first *Interpreter's Bible* with the second or the "New" edition to see the change that has taken place. I purchased the first edition when I was in my first year of seminary studies, thinking I had obtained a great resource for preaching and teaching only to discover later that I would hardly use it. Many excellent commentary series are now available and are great tools that not only provide excellent exegetical and interpretive understandings but also aptly apply the messages to life.

The danger is always present that in our communicating the message of a particular text, the biblical context may be overlooked or minimized. In dealing with each book I have reviewed in the following chapters, I have tried at the beginning of each discussion to provide a footnote that indicates important resources for studying that book.

Fourth, a similar criticism can be made of preaching from the lectionary. The lectionary (or the set of texts prescribed for preaching from a year to three years) has the advantage of forcing preachers and worship leaders to focus on a number of topics during the year. It also has the benefit of expecting them to tie the Old and New Testament texts together. It clearly implies that they will supply worshipers with the overall contextual framework for linking the texts, which doesn't always happen, so preaching from the lectionary can often be a problem for a generation that does not know the Bible. People today generally lack the basic contextual framework to connect two or three different texts that are used in church worship experiences. Providing the growing number of biblically illiterate people with an adequate framework for these diverse passages, then, is essential if they are to understand why those texts are read and used together. I would be remiss if I did not acknowledge that providing such a framework is hard work for a minister. We as leaders must be aware of the real difficulty that is faced by our people who are receiving our messages.

For the above reasons and others, I have often challenged my students to learn how to preach a single sermon on an entire book. The point is that I want my students to become keenly aware of the development in a biblical author's train of thought throughout the book. Preachers also need to learn how to integrate the flow of the scriptural argument from a biblical book into their homiletical reasoning patterns. Once a person can preach a single sermon on a book, that book can become far more focused for them, and the pericopes (stories or selected texts) should then hang together much better. Such a suggestion is not a cure-all for poor preparation in preaching and teaching, but it can be an important pattern for the communicator to adopt when studying and learning how to deal with an entire book.

I realize that it takes intensive work to be able to summarize one's thoughts so that the logic of a biblical writer becomes transparent to the hearer. I recognize that we as seminary professors have not always done well in teaching future ministers how to get the heart out of the biblical books, yet it is important for all of us to begin employing such a pattern in study so that the Bible becomes the foundational text for ministry.

Fifth, I come to a very real problem. It is the problem of *time* for preparation. Ministers are so busy today that preparing sermons is for many a task that is done "on the fly." They are swamped with counseling, staff, and parish meetings, dealing with organizational problems, and putting out burning fires among the membership. The result is that they often reach for any help they can find to get the task of sermon and Bible study preparation done. Accordingly, many sermons and lessons are not a minister's own work. They have not gone through the process of personal acquisition, adoption, and digestion before proclamation. Inherently, ministers know the problems of preaching undigested sermons, but deadlines never end and crises seem to be ongoing so that they feel robbed of the freedom for study and adequate readiness for the time of delivery.

Please hear me clearly at this point. I do *not* want to place on preachers and teachers of the Bible a painful critique of their ministries. They are usually critiqued more than enough. Instead, this book is written to encourage them to reflect on the importance of the divine story that underlies or is foundational to their study, preaching, and teaching. Each book of the New Testament has an individual identity and offers a contribution to our understanding of God's great story. Thus, I wish to suggest that Christian leaders should begin to redesign their sermon and lesson preparations in such a way that the big picture of each book emerges for this contemporary generation.

Biblically illiterate people need to gain big glimpses of the differing portraits of Jesus in each of the Gospels and other books. When Mark wrote his Gospel, he was not merely writing a "historical" account. He was providing a testimony about who he understood Jesus to be. *That testimony is far more important than the individual pericopes or stories about Jesus.* In like manner, we need to try encapsulating for our people the focus of each epistle, the exciting book of Acts, the intense sermon called Hebrews, and the dramatic work we designate as Revelation in order that they can see the big picture and integrate it into their lives. The communicator may indeed understand what is being said, but the receiver of the communication needs the overall picture as well.

Each of these books is quite different. We, of course, need to present the unifying nature of the Christian gospel, but we also need to help our people understand the differences in the books that make them unique in our inspired canon. When we concentrate on the primary focus or foci of each book, the organization and the argument should become clearer so that our people will not be as likely to conceive of the Bible as a book of snippets of truth that do not hang together. We need to help them integrate the texts we present in a holistic pattern for meeting the challenges to their lives.

To conclude this introduction, I pray for each of you as you read this book and as you ponder its ideas. May this reading experience be of assistance to you as you organize, integrate, and communicate what you already know in a thrilling manner. May those you encounter understand who you are as a Christian, and when you seek to communicate your understanding of God in Christ Jesus, may people grasp that your witness flows from a genuine sense of what the biblical witnesses are saying. If you are a minister, may your people be better enabled to carry with them the main foci of your sermons and biblical messages as they leave our churches and schools and transition into the world where they live and work.

It is my heartfelt prayer that this book may in some small way help you and those you encounter become more convinced that the Jesus who lived so many years ago really did bring a powerful climax to the great story of God in human history. May we all come to realize more intensely that this Jesus continues to provide the people of our generation with a living hope for their present lives and a destiny far beyond anything the world can offer them.

Questions for Reflection

- As a Christian communicator, do you try to get a focused picture of Jesus when you read and study a biblical text? How might such an approach to Bible study change the way you communicate the message of the text?
- What pictures of Jesus do you, as a witness, carry in your mind? How do those pictures affect the way you live and communicate the message of Christ?
- What pictures of Jesus are currently being evidenced in your faith community? What impact have you had in helping formulate those portraits?

Notes

1. See for example Gerald L. Borchert, *Dynamics of Evangelism* (Waco TX: Word, 1976) and *Worship in the New Testament: Divine Mystery and Human Response* (St. Louis: Chalice, 2008); Edward E. Thornton and Gerald L. Borchert, *The Crisis of Fear* (Nashville: Broadman,1988); Gerald L. Borchert and Andrew D. Lester, *Spiritual Dimensions of Pastoral Care* (Philadelphia: Westminster, 1985); David E Crutchley and Gerald L. Borchert, *Assaulted by Grief; Finding God in Broken Places* (Jefferson City TN: Carson-Newman/Mossy Creek, 2011).

2. Please see my comments on the Values Survey in chapter 1.

3. See the Post Election American Values Survey, November 2012 (N=1410) by the Public Religion Research Institute, http://www.prri.org/wp-content/uploads/2012/11/AVS-2012-Post-election-Memo-Part-1-2-Layout1-1.pdf

4. For further discussion of this idea, please see Gerald L. Borchert, *Jesus of Nazareth: Background, Witnesses and Significance* (Macon GA: Mercer University Press, 2011) 73–76. Hereafter *Jesus of Nazareth*.

5. See Gerald L. Borchert, *Worship in the New Testament: Divine Mystery and Human Response* (St. Louis MO: Chalice Press, 2007). Hereafter *Worship in the New Testament*.

6. In the second century the historian Tatian tried to put all the Gospels together into one harmony (the *Diatessaron*) because he was troubled by some of their variations or differences. He was a typical Westerner who wanted to resolve what he thought were problems. Similarly, we have multiple epistles and multiple prophetic messages in our "canon" or biblical collection—not just one exemplar. For my further comments on Tatian and the canon, see the final chapter of this book.

7. Please see my comments on the dating this epistle in Borchert, "Galatians," in Roger Mohrlang and Gerald L. Borchert, *Romans and Galatians*, vol. 14, Cornerstone Biblical Commentary (Carol Stream IL: Tyndale House, 2007) 248–51.

8. Please see my discussion in Gerald Borchert, "Passover and the Narrative Cycles in John," in *Perspectives in John: Method and Interpretation in the Fourth Gospel*, ed. R. Sloan and M. Parsons (Lewiston NY: Edwin Mellon, 1993) 300–16, and Gerald L. Borchert, *John 1–11*, in New American Commentary, vol. 25A (Nashville: Broadman & Holman, 1996) 134–35, 230, etc.

9. In the Western world, we define "ideas" primarily by separation or distinction, whereas "story" is a much more encompassing method of communication.

Chapter 2

The Portraits of Jesus in the Gospel of Mark and the Epistle of 1 Peter

The Dynamic Gospel of Mark[1]

We begin our review of the portraits of Jesus with the power-laden Gospel of Mark. Journeying with the evangelist through this portrait is a truly thrilling experience of gaining biblical understanding.

As the early Christians were organizing the New Testament, however, they partially buried this exciting document by placing it second in our Christian testimonies about Jesus, even though it was likely the first Gospel to be written. Among the probable reasons for its position is that it seems to have lost its beginning and end. In addition, since Matthew seems to pick up more clearly where the Old Testament ends (at least in the Protestant canon[2]) and mentions the church, the Gospel of Matthew was positioned by the editors of our canon at the start of our New Testament. Given these realities, however, please do not jump to the conclusion that the Gospel of Mark is a second-rate or inferior work. It is one of the most electrifying books in the New Testament.

I love to reflect on how Mark must have pictured Jesus as his superhero! Can you imagine what his portrait implied for an early Roman reader?[3] As his writing stands now, Mark loses no time in getting past John the Baptist to Jesus, the one who is quickly introduced as God's "beloved Son." Then, in a mere two verses (Mark 1:12-13), this Jesus is sent into the wilderness where we are informed he was tempted by the superhuman foe known as Satan. The mention of the forty-day wilderness encounter along with wild beasts suggests that the experience was like the barrenness of sin when Adam and Eve were excluded from the garden; it was not an easy encounter for Jesus (cf. Gen 3:22-24). Yet Jesus' victory is asserted by the angelic affirmation he received (Mark 1:12). Then Mark presents Jesus as "immediately" (*euthys*)[4] ready for his divinely appointed assignment. Jesus in Mark is definitely a "man of action"!

But he is more than an activist. He is also a man who irritates people and takes them by surprise. He begins his work by calling four fishermen who are at the bottom of the Jewish religious spectrum—the *am haeretz* ("people of the land"). The first action pericope in Mark (1:21-28) presents Jesus as healing a man in a Capernaum synagogue on the Sabbath (*Shabboth*, the Jewish holy day). In Mark, Jesus is repeatedly ready to work on the Sabbath—a pattern that greatly frustrates the religious leadership, undoubtedly because they think that perfectly keeping the Sabbath is a strategy for hastening the coming of their Messiah.

As the story is presented, Jesus liberates the man who has been captured by an evil spirit. He does so by merely commanding the spirit to leave the man and quit talking (I think "Shut up!" would be a better translation). The spirit knows who Jesus is and responds appropriately. The reaction by those in the synagogue, however, is one of stunned amazement, and as a result the haunting questions of Mark begin: What is going on here? Who is this fellow?

The obvious response is that Jesus is a very unusual person because his words carry incredible power. He reminds us of the God who, in the first chapter of Genesis, spoke what was formless into an ordered reality and created the world. Do you sense where Mark is going? To make sure the reader knows this story of healing is not an unusual event for Jesus, Mark continues by supplying a series of other stories in which Jesus confronts demonic activity and human illness. And Mark's Jesus does not allow the demons to speak (1:34). Moreover, Mark adds another pericope in which a healed leper is likewise instructed not to talk about Jesus (1:44). Notice, however, that whereas the spirits or demons obey Jesus (because they know who he is; 1:24), the healed man does not follow the instructions of Jesus (1:45).

The next story brings a synthesis to the opening presentation of Mark's mysterious Jesus. The friends of a paralytic attempt to bring their invalid colleague to Jesus but are unable to reach him because of the crowd. So they take part of the roof off the building above where Jesus is teaching and let their friend down on his bedroll just in front of Jesus. When Jesus sees "their" faith (notice it is not "his" faith), he says to the invalid, "Your sins are forgiven." People had earlier been shocked at his power, but now the religious leaders are stunned by his words. They charge him with blasphemy because in their religious teaching they know that only God can forgive sins (2:7). Jesus is not surprised by their human patterns of splitting life and religious thinking. So he asks them, "Which is easier to do: heal a bedridden person or forgive sins?" For Mark, the answer is obvious. But sadly, those judgmental religious leaders do not understand that in Jesus divine reality is in their presence. He is not just another human being! He is God come to earth as a real man.

Did you notice that "their" faith was important in the story? Sometimes in our individualistic, narcissistic society, we think everything depends on "me." We need to remember that there is great power in the community faith. Individual faith is essential, but we should never discount the impact of community prayer and action.

As Mark's portrait of Jesus continues to unfold, Jesus is thrust into a series of conflicts over religious practices such as fasting and observances epitomized in Sabbath obedience. Thus, as early as the beginning of chapter 3, the religious leaders (Pharisees) and the political powerbrokers (Herodians) have teamed up and are prepared to kill him (3:6). Eliminate him at this point in the Gospel? It is only chapter 3! Think about the picture. What do you think Mark is trying to say about people accepting Jesus?

While Jesus continues with his healing and teaching ministries, more people begin following him, so the religious leaders seek to destroy his character. They want to discount his work by characterizing him as an agent of the evil demon leader Beelzebul, an ancient Satanic figure (3:22). Jesus counters that such thinking is illogical since good is not the activity of evil workers. Then Mark reminds his readers of the actual reality of blasphemy—namely, that according to Jesus there is no forgiveness for those who purposely twist the truth of the Holy Spirit (3:29).

Although Mark does not spend a great deal of time outlining the teachings of the wonder-working Jesus, he includes in chapter 4 a number of parables that point to the hidden or mysterious nature of the kingdom of God. The real nature of Jesus is hidden from humans, and so are the ways of God's kingdom. They are a mystery to the world. Yet even though God's realm is hidden, its secret pattern of growth means that it will ultimately become evident, just as light cannot remain hidden in the darkness.

As Mark continues to paint his portrait, he focuses on two strategic miraculous stories that take place on the Sea of Galilee. Through them, he skillfully reminds us that God's power in Jesus was supreme not merely among humans but even over chaos in the natural realm.[5] In the first story (4:35ff.), Jesus is comfortably asleep on a pillow in the stern of a boat when a great storm blows through the pass into the Kinneret Valley (the mountainous bowl surrounding the Sea of Galilee). The stormy waves nearly swamp the boat, so Jesus is quickly awakened by his terrified disciples. When he is aroused from his sleep, Jesus shouts to the storm, "Shut up!" (the Greek is "Be muzzled!"—hardly our gentle English "Peace, be still"). Immediately, the storm stops. Likewise, in the second story (6:45ff.), the disciples are in the boat while Jesus is on a nearby mountain praying, and a storm again blows in through the pass now known as the Valley of the Pigeons, threatening the terrified disciples. Jesus appears, confidently walking on the water as though he is out for a midnight stroll. Indeed, he seems ready to pass them by because they think he is a ghost. But Jesus quickly turns to them, tells them not to be afraid, and enters the boat. The storm stops immediately.

These magnificent stories portray a person of incredible power. But watch for the punch lines. In the first case, the disciples are so stunned that they ask each other, "Who is this guy?" In the second, they think he is spooky! He does not fit any human categories. They are utterly traumatized by the actions of Jesus. The disciples in the second story have experienced him feeding a multitude, but stopping storms hardly computes for them. Do you start to get the picture? In the academic world, we call these types of experiences encounters with the *mysterium tremendum*. It is a fancy Latin expression indicating that "we don't understand what's going on." The Latin designation is certainly descriptive, but I prefer "He's spooky!" What about you? Do you recognize where Mark is going? This Jesus is strange—very strange![6]

I turn next to a few more stories to complete this brief portrait of Jesus. Mark is famous for his so-called Marcan Sandwiches in which two stories are woven together so that they help us interpret Mark's point. One example of these combination stories is at 5:21-43, which involves the religious leader, Jairus, and a pathetic unnamed woman who has suffered a blood hemorrhage for twelve years. Jairus wants Jesus to heal his daughter, and they are on the way to the girl when the woman who is insignificant in the Jewish religious system enters the picture and *in faith* touches Jesus' cloak, thinking that by merely touching it she will be made well. As the story unfolds, her touch in fact leads to her healing, and Jesus affirms that her faith is a decisive aspect of her getting well. Then a messenger comes to Jairus and tells him his daughter is dead. But Jesus assures Jairus to *have faith* because the situation is only temporary. When they arrive at the house, the religious family laughs at Jesus for his insistence that the daughter will be okay. And then Jesus calls her back to life. The point of course is that being religious does not necessarily mean having faith and trusting God.

While there are other sandwiches in Mark, I mention here a second and crucial one that follows the so-called "triumphal entry" in Mark 11. The sandwich involves the cursing of the fig tree and the cleansing of the temple. In this combination of stories, Mark shows Jesus and the disciples passing a fig tree in full leaf on their way from Bethany. But since the tree has no figs, Jesus declares that it will never again bear figs. In the next pericope, Mark describes how Jesus throws over the business tables of the temple merchants and proclaims that the original intention of the temple—to be a house of prayer for all people—is badly profaned. This incident, of course, greatly angers the religious authorities, who are convinced that Jesus should die for his acts. Then, in the final segment of this sandwich, the disciples are once again passing the fig tree. This time they note that the tree is dead. Jesus reminds them of both the mountain-moving power of faith and the fact that God hears human prayers.

In interpreting this latter sandwich of stories, there are several points to note. First, the main force of the comparison is that, like the leafy fig tree, the Jewish temple had in fact become merely a show place; its real purpose had been lost in its activities and merchandizing. It was indeed dead! But the second point is that this message moves beyond the irrelevance and death of the temple to the incredible power of God that is available to trusting humans. If you think God is powerless or unable to deal with human rebellion and wickedness, think again!

I would add two additional comments about interpreting these sandwiches. First, many of my students have not liked the story of the poor little fig tree. They focus on the cursing of the tree for not having figs, saying the tree was not at fault because the season for figs had passed (11:13). Unfortunately, some of them miss the significance of this episode. For Mark, the tree is a symbol that the temple and the priesthood are not prepared for the coming of the Messiah.

Second, I have a long-standing question about Matthew's use of the same materials as Mark. I have no doubt that Matthew was a fine writer, but his presentation is not as vibrant and sophisticated as Mark's use of sandwiches. Concerning the first sandwich, Matthew briefly summarizes each event, but without Mark's strong contrast of two people concerning their faith (cf. Matt 9:18-26). And with regard to the second combination, whereas Mark beautifully interweaves the two stories, Matthew presents them separately. Thus, Matthew does not achieve the exciting force of the temple irrelevance as evidenced in Mark's second sandwich (cf. Matt 21:18-22).

Of course, there are other less obvious sandwiches in Mark involving the significance of child-like faith, the ambition of the disciples, and the attempt on John's part to exclude some people from participating in the work of Christ (cf. Mark 9:33-49). We could also add Jesus' blessing of the children who lacked riches and understanding and that story's link to those of the rich man and the disciples being called children (10:13-31).

But much more can be added concerning Mark's picturing of Jesus. As interpreters of Mark, we should always keep in mind that while the people in general are told not to speak about their healings and the disciples are instructed not to talk about Jesus' power—at least not until after the resurrection (cf. Mark 9:9)—the spirits are bound to silence. There is, however, one person in Mark who is specifically commanded by Jesus to tell his neighbors about Jesus' vested power. He is a Gentile from the Decapolis (the Greek-speaking independent cities) who has experienced the amazing power of God after being healed from the "legion" of evil spirits (5:19-20). I realize that the disciples are commissioned to preach and cast out demons (6:7-12), but in relation to these texts about being silent, Mark is obviously making a point. The question is, why is a Gentile allowed to witness? Try to imagine a possible answer.

Scholars have designated the theme of silence in Mark as the "Messianic Secret." By writing in this manner, Mark is calling the reader's attention to the supernatural power of Jesus in his healings. When a person is told not to speak, it immediately raises questions like "Why?" and "Who is he?" The reader is thus forced to wrestle with such questions because they point to Mark's unfolding purpose about who Jesus is. The answers to these questions involve Mark's purpose. Hasn't he painted a great portrait of an awe-inspiring Jesus and the world-wide intent of the gospel?

As Mark proceeds, Jesus predicts the end of the temple era. So, when the disciples are marveling at the beauty of those buildings (13:1-2), Jesus stuns them by announcing that they should be prepared for the temple's destruction. Yet the shock of the temple destruction is not all he predicts. He also warns them to be ready for the coming of their own rejection

(13:9). Persecution is their destiny, as death is for Jesus. Mark also makes a point that the proclamation of the good news is in their future as well. Indeed, Jesus indicates that the gospel will be taken to all nations (13:10) before he will return with immense power and glory (13:26).

There is no doubt in Mark's mind that Jesus understands beforehand that he is destined to be condemned, mocked, and brutally executed (9:31; 10:31; 11:33-34) and that he will give his life for the salvation (ransom) of humanity (10:45). He goes to the cross with such a realization, accepting an anointing for his burial ahead of time (14:8-9) and instituting a new covenant in the bread and the cup concerning the coming kingdom of God (14:22-25). But the Marcan Jesus also knows that his death is *not* the end.

The sham trials before the Jewish high priest and the Roman governor and the excruciating crucifixion that sap almost everything out of Jesus only show the immense power of evil. But the story also reveals the incredible significance of Jesus' self-giving death. The Roman centurion at the cross summarizes Mark's stellar portrait of Jesus by identifying him as "truly" the "Son of God!" (15:39).

Little more needs to be said about this magnificent portrait of Jesus. It is a priceless piece of literature and a moving testimony. But I must tie a few knots before I conclude. Those matters involve the beginning and ending of Mark.

I have taken issue with Norman Perrin and others[7] who have suggested either that Mark ended at 16:8 or that the ending was ripped off because it was heretical. On the contrary, I firmly believe that both the ending and the beginning are missing. I am convinced that both were lost at an early stage and must have been consistent in style with the rest of the Gospel of Mark.[8] Moreover, I believe that there was at least one resurrection appearance story that would have completed the book and that there was a better introduction to the book. Yet we must let silence be silent because we cannot fill in the ending as some later scribes attempted to do (see two of the proposed endings in most Bibles, and particularly the longer reading of Mark 16:9-20). While some scholars argue that 16:8 is the ending Mark intended, I have argued repeatedly that ending a book, let alone a paragraph, with the Greek post-positive *gar* makes no sense. But I do not want to speculate on what the ending would be. It is simply not there!

This does not dismiss all the discussion concerning Jesus' resurrection, though. What we have in the extant chapters is a majestic portrait of Jesus whom people clearly believed was raised from the dead (cf. 8:31; 9:9, 31; 10:34). Moreover, Mark makes it clear that while Jesus was on earth, he was a unique figure who not only shocked people with his incredible power and amazed them with his mind-stretching words but also called a group to follow him. Those disciples were mostly from the *am haeretz* (the lowly people of the land). But those lowly folks later became exceedingly powerful witnesses to the reality of God who had touched the world through the "beloved Son"—a Son who was absolutely "pleasing" to God (1:11).

What a great portrait! The Marcan Jesus is truly awesome.

Questions for Reflection

- In what ways does Mark's portrait of Jesus catch your attention?
- How awesome is Jesus to you and your faith community?
- Mark's portrait of Jesus forces us to consider more than mere words about Jesus. What feelings do you have when you think about Jesus as Mark reveals him?
- How can you help your faith community discover a more living portrait of Jesus?

The Gripping Epistle of First Peter[9]

Now let's explore how Mark's portrait of Jesus is related to the epistle of 1 Peter. First Peter is a remarkable book. It literally throbs with the painful sufferings of the early Christians. Yet it pulsates with an amazing sense of confidence in the face of opposition and death. It is a book that every Christian who longs to be a faithful witness to Christ's mission in world should read and inwardly digest. It is a book that truly captures the spirit of the powerful Marcan Jesus who backed down to no one, yet understood fully the huge cost of Christ's mission on earth.

As I indicated above, the action-oriented Jesus of Mark appealed to the Romans and was uniquely identified at the cross by a Roman centurion as the "son of God" (cf. Mark 15:39). Now as we move to the epistle of hope called "1 Peter," we note that the writers were Peter, Silvanus (also called Silas; cf. Acts 15:22, 40), and Mark (see 1 Pet 1:1 and 5:12-13). Do not miss Mark! These missionaries dispatched their dynamic letter of advice to the suffering and persecuted Christians in Asia Minor from the capital city, Rome (called "Babylon" at 5:13).[10]

Like the Marcan Jesus who staunchly confronted the spirit world and silenced the evil forces (e.g., Mark 1:25-26), so too the Jesus of 1 Peter forcefully confronts the spirit world in his resurrection and ascension. He proudly proclaims to the imprisoned spirits that he is very much alive (cf. 1 Pet 3:18-19), that he has taken his place in heaven, and that all authorities and powers are now subject to him (3:22).

But as the Jesus of Mark predicted that his followers would soon suffer persecution (cf. Mark 13:9), the recipients of 1 Peter are portrayed as undergoing severe persecution, vividly identified here by the expression of "the fiery ordeal" (cf. 1 Pet 4:12). In the midst of this painful suffering, however, Peter's Jesus is portrayed as the great caretaker of persecuted and displaced Christians who live and witness in the world. Indeed, in providing readers with a superb analysis of this epistle, John Elliott titled his important study on 1 Peter *A Home for the Homeless.*[11]

This epistle does not treat the persecution of Christians lightly nor does it predict its elimination; instead, it recognizes that these new disciples of Jesus Christ are like displaced people, aliens or exiles in the world (1:1). Yet they are also the ones chosen and destined by the Triune God[12] to experience a vital hope through the outworking of power evidenced in the resurrection of Jesus. And they are guaranteed to receive God's imperishable, pure and changeless heavenly inheritance (1:3-5).

Their ultimate destiny is secure because they are following in the "footsteps" of their Lord—Jesus, the Christ—who provided them with the ultimate example or model for life (2:21). His suffering and consequent revelation of glory should not have been unexpected because, as Peter clearly asserts, it was predicted by the prophets and was clearly anticipated in the angelic realm (1:10-12).

Understanding this divine reality and pattern then should supply the followers of Jesus who suffer like their Lord with the foundational rationale for reflective thinking and transformed living according to the model of Jesus. Using the language of the slave market, Peter exhorts his readers to remember that this Jesus, who "ransomed" (saved) his followers from their sinful and rebellious human ways, did not "pay" for their freedom and transformation with mere money. The cost of their salvation was very dear—namely, the cost to the Triune God was the life ("the precious blood") of Christ (1:13-19).

As a result, Christians are called to a new way of living. They have been "born anew" (1:23) and should no longer conceive of themselves in mere earthly terms like perishing grass (1:24). Rather, they should earnestly desire to follow the Lord's leading and mature into the way of salvation (2:1-2).

To emphasize this process of new life and salvation, Peter uses a number of important images. With the well-known "rock" image from the confession at Caesarea Philippi (cf. Matt 16:13-20), Peter, whose nickname could be rendered "Rocky" ("stone," cf. John 1:42), makes it indelibly clear that the foundational rock or "living stone" is not Peter himself but is Jesus. Likewise, Christians are to be viewed as little "living stones" who follow the pattern of Jesus and are being built into a spiritual temple for God's purposes. Then shifting the image slightly, these Christians are also likened to a consecrated, royal priesthood as well as a chosen, holy people who serve God through their relationship with Jesus (1 Pet 2:4-5, 9). But there is no doubt in Peter's mind who is really the foundational rock of the people of God. That chief rock is Jesus, who was rejected by his nation, the Jewish people, but has now become the marking or "cornerstone" for the entire structure known as the people of God—Christ's followers (1 Pet 2:6-8; cf. Mark's use of this same Old Testament text at Mark 12:10).

Having thus defined his understanding of the people of God, Peter next reviews the various responsibilities of Christians in following Jesus. He first exhorts them to be a model for the Gentiles (those who are outside the church), an example in holy living by refraining from worldly passions (2:11-12). Then he counsels them as followers (1) to treat all people including those in the government with respect; 2) to love all those who belong to Christ; and (3) to fear God (2:13-17). I have purposely delineated the categories of *respect, love,* and *fear* here so that we see that Peter in no way puts honoring government authorities (see 2:17) or anyone else on the same level with obedience to God. The terms in the Greek are purposely differentiated.

But like similar Pauline statements (Rom 13:1-7; Eph 5:21), Peter desires Christians to be models of submission to Christ in everything they do (1 Pet 2:13). Such a pattern of submission is often misunderstood even by Christians who import worldly patterns of authority and subjection into the thought patterns of the New Testament. The basic concept in 1 Peter is that the supreme authority in all things must be Christ!

With these thoughts in mind, Peter turns to focus briefly on a couple of segments concerning Christian household codes. In the Hellenistic world, the codes were always given by authority figures to their underlings. It is crucial to understand that in non-Christian ancient codes, we do not find instructions for the authority figures. They give the rules for others! But the Christian codes are different. There are often instructions in the Christian codes for both the so-called authority figures and the underlings. Ephesians 5:21–6:9 is an excellent example of expanded codes that patently lay the greater onus or burden for obedience on the authority figures rather than on those who might be regarded as underlings. The code in 1 Peter is brief, and in the first section it focuses only on slaves (2:18-20). But in the section on wives and husbands (3:1-7), the code is slightly more expanded and provides an example of how the big stick of warning falls on the husbands. If husbands do not honor their wives appropriately, they will not have an authentic relationship with God because their prayers will be short-circuited and not be heard (3:7).

In the midst of this section on the codes, Peter inserts a powerful discussion concerning following Christ who, in the pattern of Isaiah 53:4-12, is described as the model for authentic life. Although this Jesus/Christ was sinless and never deceived anyone, he was nonetheless humiliated and berated as an evildoer. Yet he did not retaliate against his persecutors (1 Pet 2:22-23). Instead, he took into his own self (his body) our sins so that we might be healed and become righteous through his death ("his wounds," 2:24). Moreover, despite the fact that we may have strayed like unruly sheep from God, our good Shepherd, we have been enabled through Jesus to return to the guidance of the Lord (2:25). As the result of this restoration, Christians are exhorted to build communities of harmony, empathy, love, tender-heartedness, and humility while they live in a hateful and evil world (3:8-12).[13] Although Christians often suffer for righteousness, they are instructed to keep their consciences clear in Christ and their behaviors above reproach so that their opponents might be put to shame when they see the integrity of Christians (3:13-17).

Then in vindication of righteousness and in support of Christians who are suffering in this world, Peter announces that Christ has proclaimed to the entire spiritual realm that he is the victor over evil. This declaration of vindication and victory was *not* done during some strange descent into the nether glooms (as is assumed in some theological speculations and creeds) but took place in Christ's powerful resurrection and ascent (3:19).[14] Similarly, Peter pictures Christian baptism as representative of how we should understand our powerful union with Jesus and his transforming resurrection power (3:21-22).

In confronting the horrors of persecution, Peter does not paint a rose-colored picture of life but instead reminds his readers that, like it was for Christ, the possibility of Christians dying for their faith is very real.[15] Indeed, death seemed very close for them. While we might not find this picture of death as a friend very inviting, in Peter's context this "friend" freed Christians from the possibility of further sin (4:1). Moreover, Peter wants to remind believers that the amazement exhibited over their transformative life by their former friends—who have continued in immoral lifestyles—should not surprise them (4:2-4). But he firmly adds that judgment on the sinful ways of their former friends, like all humanity, is inevitable.

Instead of concentrating on the imminent possibility of death, however, he advises his readers to focus both on prayerfully upholding their Christian brothers and sisters in love and on glorifying God through Christ (4: 5-11). By doing so, he asserts, they can put the prospect of death in its proper perspective. They will be able to rejoice in the fact that, as the authentic household of God, they are sharing in the sufferings of Christ while entrusting their destinies to the great Creator of the universe (4:12-19).

What a perspective! Do you understand why early Christianity was able to confront the power of imperial Rome? To follow Jesus Christ was life, and to die for him was to be set firmly in the hand of God (cf. Phil 1:21). If you bear these thoughts is mind, I believe you will be able to read the final chapter of this amazing book with a discerning perspective. So to the last chapter we turn.

When Peter addresses the elders of the churches of Asia Minor as a fellow elder who is both a witness of the sufferings of Christ as well as a partaker of his glory (5:1), he is not talking about a comfortable life. He is also not talking about some vague theory of suffering. He has in his mind his own suffering and coming death. When he instructs the elders to "take care of God's flock" (5:2), one can hear echoes of the last chapter of the Gospel of John where Jesus asks Peter three times after his betrayal if Peter really loves him. Then Jesus tells Peter not only that his future involves caring for Christ's sheep but also that Peter will follow his master in death (cf. John 21:15-19).

Being a follower of Jesus and a Christian leader was and is from Peter's perspective a calling to be done willingly in self-sacrifice, not out of human pressure for attention or financial remuneration and certainly not because one is interested in the prestige of being a bishop or a chief executive officer (1 Pet 5:2-3). Instead, being a minister or Christian leader must grow out of a commitment to follow in the footsteps of the exemplar, the self-giving Shepherd (5:4). Humility is the key to Christian service, and it is not something that comes naturally to humans (5:6). Accordingly, when we quote the often-repeated statement, "Cast all your cares upon Christ" (5:7), we must remember that we are not focusing primarily on the little troubles in life (though they may be included). Instead, Peter has in mind the context of suffering and death!

Such a context involves facing the onslaughts of the devil as he prowls the world and seeks to eliminate Christians and their work for Christ (5:8). Like Mark's report concerning Satan tempting Jesus (Mark 1:12-13), the devil for Peter was no figment of the human imagination that needed to be demythologized, as some people today might suggest. Moreover, the agents of the devil were the fierce powers in the world that were aligned against the church and Christ's servants. These minions of evil, under their satanic leader, take up the task of opposing Christ's mission on all fronts (5:9). Engaging the devil, therefore, is hardly an easy assignment for Christians. It can involve genuine suffering (5:10). But the Petrine promise continues even today—that those who stand with and for Christ will be made whole, will be given gracious support, and will be strengthened in their divine commission to the glory of God (5:10-11)!

Here then is the message of the epistle called 1 Peter. It is a book that is desperately needed in an era of growing biblical illiteracy and weak Christianity. It is a book that all believers need to read and reread until the portrait of the suffering Christ and the challenge of the early Christians who followed "in his steps" (2:22) becomes absorbed into Christ's contemporary disciples. Like the Gospel of Mark, this gripping letter of 1 Peter is a book that must be studied, taught, and preached in our faith communities today without hesitation or compromise.

Questions for Reflection

- How do you think the message of 1 Peter compares with what is usually taught and preached in our churches today? How would you summarize the differences?
- In what ways does Peter's message carry us beyond mere verbal statements of faith?
- Have you considered the possibility that you might someday be called to endure a period of intense suffering for Christ? How well would your commitment stand in the face of persecution?
- In three sentences, how would you describe Peter's portrait of Jesus and his disciples? How do you think your description compares to one you would do for Mark?

Notes

1. A helpful book for understanding the narrative development of Mark is David Rhoads and Donald Michie, *Mark as Story: An Introduction to the Narrative of a Gospel* (Philadelphia: Fortress Press, 1982). A helpful commentary on Mark for preaching is David E. Garland, *Mark*, New Application Commentary (Grand Rapids MI: Zondervan, 1996). See also Robert Guelich, *Mark 1:1–8:26*, Word Biblical Commentary (Dallas: Word, 1989); C. A. Evans, *Mark 8:27–16:20*, Word Biblical Commentary (Nashville: Thomas Nelson, 2001); Pheme Perkins, *The Gospel of Mark*, The New Interpreter's Bible, vol. 8 (Nashville, Abingdon, 1995) 507–733; Robert H. Stein, *Mark*, Baker Exegetical Commentary on the New Testament (Grand Rapids MI: Baker, 2008); Mark L. Strauss and Clinton E Arnold, *Mark*, Zondervan Exegetical Commentary on the New Testament (Grand Rapids MI: Zondervan, 2014); and Ben Witherington III, *The Gospel of Mark: A Socio-Rhetorical Commentary* (Grand Rapids MI: Eerdmans, 2001). Other works include Ernest Best, *Following Jesus: Discipleship in the Gospel of Mark* (Sheffield: University Press, 1981); Werner Kelber, *The Kingdom in Mark* (Philadelphia: Fortress, 1974); and Grant R. Osborne, *Mark*, Teach the Text Commentary Series (Grand Rapids MI: Baker, 2014).

2. The Hebrew canon concludes with 2 Chronicles. Note that in referring to the entire Jewish canon, Matthew cites Jesus as adding to his listeners' condemnation the judgments from the blood of Able to Zechariah—namely Genesis to Second Chronicles (cf. Matt 23:35).

3. Although it is difficult to be precise about dating and authorship questions, Mark was probably written by a bilingual Hellenistic writer named John (Hebrew name) Mark (Greek name) who was an understudy of Peter (1 Pet 5:13), knew Paul (Acts 12:25; 13:2-3; Col 4:10; Phlm 24) and was a relative of the Cypriot Barnabas (Acts 4:36; Col 4:10). The book was probably written from Rome ("Babylon") in the 60s CE when Mark was with Peter (1 Pet 5:13) around the time of Peter's death in 64 during the reign of Nero. For further information, see the quotation of Papias in Eusebius, *Hist.eccl.*, 3.39.36.

4. The concept of "immediately" is a recurrent theme in the early part of the Gospel, e.g., 1:18, 20, 21, 23, 30, etc.

5. Note that in Jewish thinking the sea was understood as "the depth" (the *tahom*), the abode of confusion and disharmony (cf. Gen 1:2). It also became associated with evil (cf. Ps 98:7 and Jonah 2:6).

6. Throughout his Gospel, Mark uses questions and other means to force readers to ask, "Who is this Jesus?" Wilhelm Wrede at the beginning of the twentieth century noted this phenomenon and designated it as a purposeful secret. See the English version as *The Messianic Secret*, trans. J. C. G. Gregg (London: James Clarke, 1971). For an analysis of the significance of this work in the history of scholarship see Albert Schweitzer, *The Quest for the Historical Jesus* (repr., New York: Macmillan, 1964).

7. See for example Norman Perrin, *The Resurrection according to Matthew, Mark and Luke* (Philadelphia: Fortress Press, 1977) 16–31.

8. See G. Borchert, *Jesus of Nazareth*, 78. See also my *Worship in the New Testament*, p. 240, note 3.

9. For helpful works on 1 Peter, see J. John H. Elliot, *A Home for the Homeless: A Sociological Exegesis of 1 Peter, Its Situation and Strategy* (Philadelphia: Fortress, 1981); Ramsey Michaels, *1 Peter*, Word Biblical Commentary (Waco: Word, 1988); and Scot McKnight, *1 Peter*, New International Version Application Commentary (Grand Rapids MI: Zondervan, 1996). See also David Bartlett, *The First Letter of Peter*, The New Interpreter's Bible, vol. 12 (Nashville Abingdon, 1998) 227–319; Peter H. Davids, *The First Epistle of Peter*, New International Commentary on the New Testament (Grand Rapids MI: Eerdmans, 1990); Wayne A. Grudem, *1 Peter*, Tyndale New Testament Commentaries (Leicester: InterVarsity; Grand Rapids MI: Eerdmans, 1988, 1999); Karen H. Jobes, *1 Peter*, Baker Exegetical Commentary on the New Testament (Grand Rapids MI: Baker, 2005); Thomas R. Schreiner, *1, 2 Peter, Jude*, New American Commentary (Nashville: Broadman & Holman, 2003); and E.G. Selwyn, *The First Epistle of Saint Peter* (London: Macmillan, 1958).

10. While there is debate concerning the Petrine authorship of this letter because of (1) the high quality of Greek, (2) our lack of information that Peter knew the churches of Asia Minor to which this letter is addressed (see 1 Pet 1:1), and (3) the fact that some have thought that the reference to the author as an "elder" among other elders is demeaning of his apostleship (1 Pet 5:15), it is important to recognize that Christian tradition is strong that the letter was written by Peter and, as noted in 1:1 and 5:12-13, it was written with the assistance of Hellenistic writers Silvanus (Silas) and Mark. The dating of the letter is probably prior to Peter's death in 64 during the reign of Nero when hostility against Christians in Rome was growing.

11. See John H. Elliott's extended discussion of *paroikos* ("Homeless Strangers") in *A Home for the Homeless*, 21–58.

12. Note the early order of the Trinity of Father, Spirit, and Jesus at 1 Peter 1:2. Cf. Rev 1:4-5.

13. Three of these words are "hapax," namely, they appear only here in the Greek New Testament.

14. For my further discussion of "preaching to the spirits in prison," see Gerald L. Borchert, *Worship in the New Testament*, pp. 194–95 and 247, note 2. For the concept of imprisoned evil angels, see 1 Enoch 18:12-14; 21:10. *Sheol*, the place of the dead, is not generally described as a prison.

15. For my further discussion on this subject see Gerald L. Borchert, "The Conduct of Christians in the Face of the 'Fiery Ordeal' ([1Pet] 4:12-5:11)," *Review and Expositor 79* (1982): 451–62.

Chapter 3

The Portraits of Jesus in the Gospel of Matthew and the Sermon Called Hebrews

If you were on trial for being a Christian would there be enough evidence to convict you?

We come now to two intriguing portraits of Jesus. Having taught at several theological schools throughout the world, I have become aware of the fact that Jesus is portrayed quite differently in various settings. Indeed, I have collected pictures and cards of Jesus from many places in the world, and those portraits are as varied as the people who inhabit planet Earth. Similarly, we should recognize that the portraits of Jesus in the various books of the New Testament are not all alike. While there is a commonality in the general presentations, there are some striking differences that provide us with important perspectives on our Lord and on our role as Christians.

This chapter should give readers powerful examples of the differences as we compare the two previous portraits of Jesus with the two in the present chapter. Let us turn from the dynamic, vital messages presented in chapter 2 and focus here on the tradition-oriented Jews who needed to be convinced that Jesus was Israel's intended Messiah and the hope of the world.

The Intriguing Gospel of Matthew[1]

Studying and communicating the message from the Gospel of Matthew can be a delightful yet mind-stretching experience. It can be enhanced significantly if people have some understanding of Jewish rabbinic patterns of thinking. Delving deeply into the rabbinic arguments of the Tannaim,[2] however, is not a necessity for the average student, minister, or general layperson unless he or she wants a more thorough understanding of rabbinic thought processes. But certainly, a review of concepts such as promise and fulfillment and a substantial understanding of the framework of the Old Testament will be helpful. Without further introduction, then, we turn our attention to the task of understanding and communicating the message of Matthew in our era of increasing biblical illiteracy—a task that challenges most of us to a new level of commitment and study.[3]

What better way was there for the Matthean writer to introduce Jesus as the promised Messiah to the Jews than to start with a genealogical table as proof that Jesus was descended from Abraham and from the historic royal line of David, their heroic king (Matt 1:1, 6)? But Matthew has another goal in mind as well. That goal is the issue of the Gentiles—a concern that unfolds throughout his Gospel. He wants to remind the Jews that the blessings promised to Abraham are likewise intended to include Gentiles (see Gen 12:1-3). So he begins immediately by showing his readers that this prized genealogical table of the Davidic line is not purely Israelite. Accordingly, he purposely mentions that in the Davidic male lineage, four women are outsiders (Tamar, Rahab, Ruth, and the wife of Uriah [the Hitite], cf. Matt 1:3, 5, and 6).

Having thus cared for the genealogical question, Matthew next inserts into his Gospel story of Jesus the first of many fulfillment statements. These fulfillment statements are intended to support his overall thesis that Jesus is Israel's promised Messiah. The initial fulfillment statement pointedly proclaims that "a virgin will conceive and bear a son and his name will be called Emmanuel." Then Matthew reminds his Greek-speaking readers that the name means "God with us" (1:22, cf. Isa 7:14).

I often tell my students that when they read a Gospel, it is vitally important to read both the beginning and the end because it should help them discover the purpose of the book. With that idea in mind, we note that the Gospel of Matthew concludes with the promise of Jesus that "I am with you until the end of time" (28:20)! It would not be too much to assume that an aspect of Matthew's purpose was to make sure his readers realized that Jesus, the Messiah, was none other than "God with us." Pointedly, this Jesus of Matthew, as God with us, was not some far-off *Deus absconditus* (a hidden or absent God). Accordingly, Matthew is at pains to make sure the Jews are reminded not to focus on the fact that during the traumas of the intertestamental period, the rabbis regarded God as so transcendent, holy, and remote that out of fearful reverence they even ceased speaking the divine name (the tetragrammaton—the four-letter name YHWH, often translated as Jehovah).

While many people in our churches have probably been taught that Matthew was written to the Jews, it is crucial to help them realize that Matthew sought to stretch the Jewish mind to recognize that God's intention was to use the Jews to include the Gentiles (as far back as Abraham in Gen 12:1-3) in the divine purpose of reversing the tragedy of sin and rebellion in the world. Notice then how this issue impacts Matthew's selection of the materials in his birth story of Jesus.

He says that Jesus was born in Bethlehem in fulfillment of the prediction of Micah (Mic 5:2). But the only people in Matthew who seem ready for God's timing in the coming of the Messiah are some Gentile stargazers. These astrologers who come to see the baby Jesus probably journeyed from faraway lands of Mesopotamia like Abraham, the Jewish forefather (Matt 2:1; cf. Gen 11:31-12:1). These stargazers have likely assumed from casting their horoscopes on the sign of Pisces (the fish) that a significant new king or messianic figure has been born in a palace in the Roman province known as *Palistina*. So naturally they come to Jerusalem in their quest. But Jerusalem is the seat of the megalomaniac Herod the Great, who readily kills anyone who threatens his position, including his relatives and even his son by his favorite wife, Mariamne.[4]

When these foreign astrologers (not kings) come to Jerusalem, their message upsets the scheming Herod (Matt 2:3). Any uneasiness in Herod produces great anxiety among the residents of Jerusalem because they know about his death threats and past actions. So, when Herod summons the Jewish religious hierarchy and demands information concerning the coming of the Messiah, whether they know his intentions or not, they readily accede to his request and provide him with the prediction that Bethlehem is the place of the probable birth (2:4-5; cf. Mic 5:2). After these Gentile stargazers complete their visit and understand better the scheming nature of Herod, however, they do not return to the king but quickly leave his territory (Matt 2:12).

In typical Herodian fashion, therefore, after waiting for further information and not receiving it, he responds and dispatches his soldiers to eliminate the threat to his rule. The strategy, however, fails because the parents of Jesus have escaped to Egypt, thus fulfilling for Matthew another typological prediction to the effect that God called his son out of Egypt (Matt 2:15; cf. Hos 11:1).

The slaughter of the Bethlehem infants that follows is a tragedy, but even in that event Matthew finds another fulfillment of the prediction in Jeremiah 31:15 concerning the weeping in Ramah of Rachel for her children (Matt 2:17-18).

These fulfillment references continue throughout the Gospel as proof-texts or confirmations that Jesus is indeed to be regarded as Israel's true Messiah. When Herod dies, Jesus' family returns to Palestine from Egypt. But since they fear Herod's most ruthless son, Archelaus, they move to Galilee instead of settling in Bethlehem. In this move north to the tiny nondescript town of Nazareth, Matthew again discovers a fulfillment of some unclear prediction that Jesus will be known as a "Nazarene."[5] Then in the call to repentance by John the Baptist, the forerunner of the Messiah's mission, Matthew (3:3) finds a fulfillment of Isaiah's "comfort" expectations (40:1-3). Likewise, the beginning of Jesus' ministry in Galilee is noted by Matthew as the fulfillment of a couple of other texts from Isaiah (cf. Matt 4:14-16 with Isa 9:1-2 and 42:7). Some interpreters have even suggested that the number of these fulfillment texts reaches the religiously significant number of fourteen,[6] although the actual number is difficult to ascertain because of some vague statements in Matthew, such as at 26:54 and 56.

But there is much more in Matthew for the faithful Jew to consider in reflecting on the messianic nature of Jesus. Matthew organizes Jesus' teachings into five sections, all of which end with the specific notation that at that point, Jesus had "finished" his teaching (see: 7:28; 11:1; 13:53; 19:1; and 26:1). Why are there five specifically designated teaching sections? Could the reason for five sections be that Matthew was indicating to the Jews that Jesus should be understood as bringing a New Torah or a new set of instructions from God? Any Jew would recognize the implications because Moses had been God's agent in delivering the five Torah books (the law or foundational instructions) to the people of Israel. Moreover, this image of Jesus providing a New Torah is enhanced by the fact that Jesus is pictured as sitting down to deliver the first and last segments of these teachings (5:1 and 24:3 make an *inclusio*[7]). This picture of the sitting Jesus is symbolic of a majestic ruler who, like Solomon or indeed God, delivered his wise counsel from the throne—the basis for the idea of *ex cathedra* pronouncements.

The symbolic importance of Jesus' teaching is even further enhanced by the fact that Matthew identifies these two pericopes as having taken place on mountains (the Sermon on the Mount in 5:1–7:28 and the Olivet Discourse in 24:1–26:1). Such a context would hardly have escaped the notice of a Jew who was familiar with the fact that Israel's history was intimately intertwined with mountains and the presence of God. Witness for example the call of Moses on Mount Horeb (Exod 3:1ff.) and the receiving of the Ten Commandments on Mount Sinai (Exod 19:16 ff.) as well as Elijah's victory over the priests of Baal on Mount Carmel (1 Kgs 18:20 ff.) and his re-commissioning on Mount Horeb (1 Kgs 19:8 ff.).

Because mountains were so important to the Jews, Matthew focuses a good deal of attention on mountains. He not only highlights the teaching of Jesus with respect to mountains but also notes that after Jesus climbed the hills/mountains, he "sat down" and dispensed healing there (Matt 15:29-31). Yet Matthew's concern with mountains goes much further. In Matthew's temptation account, after being without food for forty days, Jesus has his final temptation encounter with the devil on a mountain,[8] where the satanic enemy challenges him to compromise his messianic mission to achieve his goal. But Jesus does not succumb to such a short-circuited strategy. Matthew also uses the well-known transfiguration story on the Galilean mountain (probably Mount Hermon) with the two Old Testament mountain men (Moses and Elijah) but enhances it slightly by picturing Jesus as gently touching the terrified disciples and rehabilitating them after their traumatic encounter with the holiness of God (17:7). Then, as one might guess, Matthew concludes his Gospel with the final resurrection appearance occurring on an unnamed Galilean mountain (28:16).

Do you begin to get the picture of Matthew's Jesus? Do you also understand why our growing biblically illiterate generation may need assistance in reading this Gospel to grasp more fully the implications of this unique portrait of Jesus?

Matthew, like Luke, was also eager for his readers to realize that authenticity with God involved care for other people. For Matthew, Jesus focused much of his ministry among the *anawim*: the poor and the dispossessed who normally had no one to take their side. The Beatitudes in Matthew 5:1-12 reflect this concern in highlighting those who are poor, those who mourn, the meek, the hungry, the persecuted, and also those who are merciful, pure, and who seek to bring about peace among people.

In Matthew, Jesus is patently opposed to all forms of inauthentic religious piety (6:1–7:23), and he calls on all people to depend on God and treat others as they want to be treated (7:7-12).[9] But Jesus is not suggesting that obedience to God should be understood in terms of the Jewish *halakic* rules that formed the basis for rabbinic legalistic thinking and involved endless distinctions. Such legalistic patterns of interpreting obedience led to stern condemnations by Jesus (see the harsh woes on the Pharisees in Matt

23:1-36). Instead, as I indicated in the opening chapter, Matthew's Jesus expects people to honor without hesitation the way of humbly walking (*halak*) with God while rejecting the picky rules and patterns (*halakah*) of the rabbis.[10]

Clearly, the reader should sense the holistic spirit of Jesus as over against the rabbinic pattern when he responds to the six well-articulated Antitheses (views of the "men of old"—see Matt 5:21, 27, 31, 33, 38, and 43). He refocuses their approach to commandments from the mere acts of murder and adultery to God-like thinking patterns for humans; from the permissible arguments for divorce to the nature of marriage and concern for others; from the hierarchy of oaths to the integrity of speech; and from patterns of strict justice and rules for retaliation to authentic self-giving living. Of particular importance for our attention is the focus of the Sixth Antithesis, which may have been advocated by some rabbis— that one should love one's neighbor (namely other Jews) but that it was quite appropriate to hate one's enemy (contrast Jesus' pronouncement at 5:43-44). Jesus' response to such a view is that it reflects mere human morality, common among even the Gentiles, and is hardly from God. God calls us to love even enemies as the perfect (or mature) way of life modeled on the pattern of God's dealing with humanity (5:44-48). This pattern can be summarized in what is commonly known as the "Golden Rule" of positive action (7:12).

There is, moreover, no question that Matthew believed Jesus had the divine authority to confront and reconfigure the legal and religious rules of the scribes and the Pharisees. The reason is that Jesus was none other than the Lord of rules and regulations. He was the indisputable Lord even of Shabboth (the Sabbath; see 12:1-8), which for the rabbis was without doubt one of their central rules because they held that even God obeyed the Sabbath (their interpretation of Gen 2:2-3).

Because of his perspectives on these prized rules of the religious leaders, Jesus was marked as being diametrically opposed to the Jewish establishment. Thus, the Jewish hierarchy was convinced that to maintain their authority, Jesus had to be eliminated from the scene (Matt 12:9-14). So, like Mark, Matthew details the fact that opposition to Jesus continues to grow (12:22 ff.; 16:1 ff.; 21:33 ff.; 22:15 ff.) and is epitomized in Jesus' lament over Jerusalem—the city that became a sad symbol because its people had repeatedly killed the prophets and stoned the messengers God had sent (23:37-39).

The disposition of this antagonistic relationship between Jesus and his opponents is summarized in the conclusion to the Olivet discourse when Jesus indicates that upon his return in power, the Son of Man will separate the sheep from the goats. He will then deliver the rejected ones to the curse of "eternal fire"—the same punishment assigned to the devil and his assistants (cf. Rev 19:19-20; 29:10). Those, however who respond appropriately to Jesus and the way of God will be blessed with the gift of "eternal life" (25:31-46). The division is here clearly articulated.

The stage is thus set for the horrendous death story of Jesus. From Matthew's perspective, Jesus was never powerless. His betrayal and arrest—which one of the disciples tries to forestall with his puny sword—and his subsequent death could easily have been halted by the powerful Son of Man, who had at his disposal a superhuman force of "twelve legions of angels" (26:53). But such a move would not have fulfilled the scriptural predictions (26:54, 56) and thus did not conform to God's intention for the salvation of humanity. Such a route would have more appropriately fit the short-circuit pattern of Satan and therefore had to be rejected.

Instead, the story of hostility continues with the sham trial before the high priest, which goes nowhere because Jesus remains silent through the proceedings until Caiaphas is exasperated. Thereupon, with a solemn oath the high priest demands that Jesus declare openly whether he is "Christ [the Messiah], the Son of God" (26:63). In response to this oath, Jesus not only acknowledges that fact but also declares that he is the expected Son of Man who will be seated at "the right hand" of divine authority ("Power," 26:64). The high priest forces a self-confession and then symbolically tears his robe as a show of defilement and condemns Jesus to a predetermined sentence of death.

A cacophony of events follows—including Peter's denials (26:69-75), Judas's suicide (27:3-10), the manipulative trial before Pilate with his attempted substitute of Barabbas (27:11-26), and the pathetic mocking and the ghastly crucifixion with the charge indicating that Jesus is "the King of the Jews" (27:27-44) —all of which are encased within the definitive declaration of the centurion that he was the "Son of God" (27:54).

But from Matthew's point of view, much more is going on than the heinous death of Jesus. Pilate's wife, a Gentile, is warned in a fitful dream that her husband is dealing with a "righteous man," but her husband refuses to take her advice (27:19). The temple curtain that keeps people from the presence of God is ripped from top to the bottom, as in Mark—indicating the displeasure of God. The earth in Matthew is also shaken in a powerful earthquake, cracking open tombs and enabling holy people of the past to emerge from the dead as walking symbols of the catastrophic death of Jesus (27:51-53). And the puny soldiers set to guard the tomb by the Jewish establishment (27:62-66) are stunned and immobilized by the appearance of an angel during the resurrection of Jesus (28:4).

Human ingenuity and power have confronted Jesus, the Messiah, and sought to eliminate him and his mission from the face of the earth. But mere humans have not understood the mission or the power that resides in God's messenger. In Matthew, the only recourse left to the Jewish establishment is to bribe the guards and create a convenient myth by accusing the disciples of stealing Christ's body (28:11-15). But God supplies the response. Those same traumatized disciples who fled in terror from the presence of a band of soldiers at the betrayal of Jesus are transformed by the power of God in the experience of the resurrection and receive the irrevocable commission to (1) go forth, (2) disciple all people, (3) baptize them into the Triune God, and (4) teach them to obey all that Jesus has instructed.

This risen Jesus, however, does not simply leave them with a commission. He promises them that his presence will be with them always until the end of time (28:18-29).

The Gospel of Matthew is thus complete! The God who promised the coming of Immanuel in Isaiah (7:14; cf. Matt 1:23) reasserted that promise through the risen Jesus for all Christians (Matt 28:20).

God truly answered the hopes of Israel. But that answer was unfortunately missed by most of those for whom the promise was originally given. Yet it is being worked out today in the lives of Christians through the presence of the risen Christ. Those who hear and respond in obedience to the proclamation of Jesus can expect to hear the hearty welcome of God in Christ: "Come, you blessed of my Father, inherit the kingdom which has been prepared for you from the foundation of the world!" (Matt 25:34).

Well, dear reader, do you not agree that understanding and communicating this Jesus from the Gospel of Matthew can be a stimulating experience? The book is a great resource for challenging those who wrestle with the significance of the coming of Christ in this growing biblically illiterate era. It not only assists us today in understanding how the early Christians came to recognize that Jesus fulfilled the expectations for the coming of God's Messiah and the salvation of all people but also helps us recognize that obedience to God is not to be understood in terms of keeping mere rules.

Moreover, Matthew makes it clear that in sending Jesus, God was not concerned with visible demonstrations of piety but instead summoned followers to build authentic relationships with the Lord and with other people. Wholeness or maturity (5:48; 19:21) is the goal of the Christian life, and humility is the pattern of those who would inherit the kingdom of God (18:4).

May all Christians accept the summons to live authentic lives and share their understanding of Matthew's mind-stretching portrait of Jesus with others!

Questions for Reflection

- How would you summarize the main aspects of the portrait of Jesus in Matthew? What aspects are most in line with the Jewish expectation of the Messiah? Why do you think most Jews have rejected Jesus as their Messiah?
- What aspects of this portrait do you think might speak most forcefully to a biblically illiterate generation?
- What do you think is the role of apologetics (using arguments to prove your case) in sharing your faith (witnessing, preaching, and teaching)? Does this presentation in Matthew offer clues for better proclaiming Jesus? What clues can you identify specifically?

The Fascinating Sermon Called Hebrews[11]

As I have indicated elsewhere,

> Hebrews is a unique book in the New Testament. It is not a letter like Romans, nor an historical work like Acts, nor an apocalypse like Revelation, nor a Gospel presentation about Jesus like Mark. It most resembles a sermon—a very special sermon that calls the Christian reader to proceed beyond elementary matters of faith and discover a mature level of Christian life (Heb 6:1).[12]

This special sermon called Hebrews, however, has not always been regarded highly by Christians, partly because of the severe warnings found in its pages. Many ministers avoid preaching from it except for the famous chapter 11 on "faith" and other selected passages that do not seem to upset people.

Martin Luther was greatly troubled by some of its statements, particularly on the idea of "falling away" or what has often been called apostasy (see Heb 2:11; 3:12; 6:6; and 10:26-29). Accordingly, he consigned Hebrews along with James and a few other books to the second level of his New Testament canon—which meant that it could be helpful for spiritual growth but hardly used as a standard for Christian doctrine like Romans. Many interpreters from the Calvinist position likewise either effectively dismiss its harsh exhortations (especially in chapters 6 and 10) or else seek to argue that the people who might be envisaged in these exhortations were hardly ever real Christians.

But dismissing the warnings of Hebrews is a tragic example of a poor pattern of biblical interpretation. It generally represents the inclination on the part of readers of Scripture to allow personal doctrinal presuppositions to determine what they believe must be the meaning of texts. To study, preach, and teach the message of Hebrews, therefore, means that the interpreter is duty bound to understand and communicate the true and full message of the writer. To refocus and employ here an expression drummed into me while I was in law school, our task is to seek "the truth, the whole truth, and nothing but the truth."

This writer of Hebrews was hardly the Paul of the epistles, as is noted in most King James Bibles. The language is a neo-classical style of Alexandrian Greek, and as I have often indicated to my students, they may be able pass a Greek test in Paul's Koine Greek, but that hardly assures them that they can pass a similar one in Hebrews. Moreover, the portrait of Jesus in Hebrews—as a priest after the order of Melchizedek (Heb 5:6; 7:1-3)—is very different than the one of Jesus in Paul who seems to be modeled on a Davidic Messiah (cf. Rom 1:3).

The question then is, who wrote Hebrews? There have been many suggestions but the best response remains, "Only God knows at this point." Nevertheless, I would speculate that the writer was an educated Jew who must have been oriented to the priestly traditions and the cultic patterns of the Jews. He was a convinced Christian and may have formerly been a priest or a rabbi himself.[13]

Hebrews is an important testimony concerning early Christianity, and it desperately needs to be taught in this era of increasing biblical illiteracy. Scholars have recognized the book not as a letter but as a magnificent sermon. William Johnsson for example has appropriately noted that it alternates between sections that are primarily expository or informational in nature and other parts that are hortatory or focused on warnings and applications.[14] Accordingly, readers are challenged throughout the course of the entire sermon to "pay attention" or "take care" (e.g., 2:1; 3:12; etc.), and they should give heed to the repeated use of expressions such as "therefore" so that they will bring their lives into conformity with the patterns of Christ.

This Jesus Christ, the Son of God, is portrayed in Hebrews as "superior" to every aspect of Judaism. In contrast to the presentation in Matthew, however, the logic or argument of Hebrews does not primarily use fulfillment statements (though they are present) to advance the author's goal. Instead, one could say that the contrast in Hebrews presents Jesus as so far beyond the thinking of Judaism that the faith Christ has brought to the world far surpasses Judaism. Indeed, the Preacher of Hebrews would argue that Christian faith has rendered Judaism as no longer viable—or, to be more specific, it has become obsolete (cf. Heb 8:13)!

In light of such an evaluation, the question must be posed: What brought on such a forceful conclusion? The answer, I believe, is found in the contextual situation that is evident in the book. The book indicates that the setting was one of intense persecution in which the property of Christians was being plundered and they were suffering and being killed for their faith (10:32-34). Under such conditions, the likelihood of some Christians giving up and forsaking their earlier commitment to Christ was a genuine possibility (10:35).

The exhortation not to give up in the context of shedding one's blood (of dying; 12:4), I believe, is key to understanding the message of this intense sermon. Perseverance in the face of devastating and debilitating conditions is the framework for the exhortations or the basis for the summons in this gripping homily (cf. 12:1, 12-13). In communicating the message of Hebrews, it is crucial not to read into the sermon a Western or American context of freedom or religious liberty. The Christians addressed in Hebrews were "living on the edge," and they knew they might soon hear a knock on the door that could end their freedom and even their lives.

Did the "Preacher" of Hebrews have anything meaningful to say to these followers of Christ amid such a traumatic context? The answer is a resounding "YES!" And many years later we are given the opportunity to read and inwardly digest this crucial message to his people.

He starts his sermon by reminding his listeners that God had spoken to his people through the prophets in times past in many ways, but now God has communicated ultimately to them through a Son who reflects the authentic glory and character of God. Moreover, this Son is now seated at the right hand of divine authority (1:1-3). With such a beginning, one would guess that everything else in all of creation would pale in comparison to Jesus.

And that is exactly what follows. What better way was there for the Preacher to achieve his goal of presenting a high christological portrait of Jesus than to compare this Son of God to angels (1:5 ff.)? During the inter-testamental period, angels were regarded as the intermediaries between a transcendent God and mere human beings. In that period, angels were viewed as semi-divine figures, and super angels were even introduced with special assignments and special names such as Gabriel, Michael, Uriel, Raguel, etc.—note that all their names ended in "el," the Hebrew name for God. The reason was that they were viewed as closely associated with God and understood as agents of the divine.[15] But in the book of Hebrews, the angelic host is lowered in the hierarchical structure so that these spiritual beings are merely assigned the tasks of serving Christians (1:14).

The Preacher not only reduces the significance of angels but also, in chapter 3, he treats Moses similarly in the illustration of the house. Christians are compared to a house. Moses is viewed as a servant in the house. But Jesus, who is the apostle and high priest, is proclaimed to be the builder of the house and the one who exhibits the greatest glory (3:1-6). Accordingly, Jesus is clearly "superior" to Moses and thus his message is superior to the earlier covenant of God with Israel (cf. 8:6).

A comparable argument is likewise offered in chapters 5 and 7 concerning the Jewish high priesthood. A high priest, like Aaron, was appointed to serve the people, but it was obvious that no high priest was perfect. Therefore, each one who assumed that role had to offer sacrifices not only for the people but also for himself since he too was a sinner (5:1-4). But according to the Preacher, Jesus was different. In his obedience, Jesus proved himself to be "perfect"—the Preacher's meaning for "being made perfect" through obedience and suffering (5:8-9). Indeed, in chapter 7 this Jesus is understood to be "holy, blameless and clearly unstained by sin." Thus, he is completely different from sinners (7:26) and must be judged as "perfect" (7:28).

Yet the Preacher had a minor problem in using the comparison of Jesus to the high priest. The reason was that Jesus had not been born into a priestly family; nor was he even from the tribe of Levi. Jesus was from the royal tribe of Judah (7:14)! The Preacher, however, was a skillful Jewish interpreter and his solution involved a typical type of Jewish rabbinic exegesis. In Hebrews 7:1-28, he builds his argument on the brief note in

Genesis 14:18-20 about Melchizedek who was a priest of *El Shaddai* ("God Most High"). This Melchizedek offered Abram/Abraham "bread and wine" and "blessed him" (cf. Heb 7:6). The typological significance of this statement, with its connection to the "Supper of the Lord," could hardly be missed by a Christian thinker like the Preacher.

The problem was thus resolved by establishing another viable priesthood appointed by God. Indeed, the Preacher interpreted the fact that Abram gave a tithe to this otherwise unknown figure—who represented God—as the basis for declaring that all the descendants of Abram/Abraham (even the contemporary Jews) are now subject to this new priest who is to be considered in the order of Melchizedek (7:5). And I should add here that since Melchizedek was identified as the king of "Salem" (Gen 14:18; cf. Heb 7:1), one should not miss the further typological connection with "Jerusalem," which means "Yahweh's peace."

Then, to bring this part of his argument to a conclusion, the Preacher cites Psalm 110:4 (a messianic Psalm) in Hebrews 7:21, which indicates that—under "oath"—the Messiah is to be identified as an eternal priest in the pattern of Melchizedek. The dots are thus connected and, behold, the Preacher has the matter proved—namely that the unknown priest of "God Most High" is none other than a model for the coming Messiah. This Messiah is clearly Jesus, the one who delivered the New Covenant (Heb 7:23). Although we in our contemporary world might not be convinced by the Preacher's logic, it was for him, as an ancient rabbi, a perfectly legitimate way of thinking.

Having thus introduced Jesus, the Preacher next asserts that this Jesus is the initiator of the new covenant. And then he compares the new covenant to the old one, which was oriented to animal sacrifices. The new one is far "superior" because it is based not on mere animal sacrifices but on the sacrifice of the eternal Christ (9:15-22). In this discussion, there are important references made to "law" that may be confusing to contemporary readers (see, e.g., 7:11-12, 28; 8; 4; 10:28; etc.). I will pause for a moment and explain them. The concept of law for the Preacher of Hebrews should not be interpreted in terms of obeying rules as, for example, in Paul's letter to the Galatians (cf. ch. 3). Rather, the focus here is on rules for temple observances, offerings, and Levitical sacrifices such as the blood of goats and bulls or calves and the ashes of a heifer. For him, these sacrifices are obviously far less effective than the offering of Christ's blood (9:11-14).

Recognizing this difference in the meanings of "law" in Hebrews and Paul is crucial to understanding the logic of Hebrews, especially for many who may have been taught a single meaning for "law" in Paul's thinking. For the biblically illiterate, however, this distinction will be even more difficult to assimilate since they will probably have no framework for conceiving of "law" as being associated with rules that pertain to a sacrificial system. Having attended the celebration of the Samaritan Passover in the West Bank (Israel) just outside of Nabulus, I will not soon forget that experience, which reminded me of a synthesis between a rock festival and visiting a slaughterhouse. I readily realize the difficulty of communicating such information to contemporary Western people who have had little experience with blood sacrifices. They would no doubt fully agree with the Preacher that it was appropriate for the old covenant to become obsolete (8:13).

But I would not want us as contemporary readers to dismiss the pattern of sacrificing animals for sin and overlook the crucial idea that is being communicated in Hebrews. For the Preacher, the point is that "without the shedding of blood, there is no forgiveness" (9:22). The cost of human wholeness or salvation was the death of God's Son! That sacrifice of Jesus can only be viewed as an event in history that took place "once" for all time and for all people. That sacrifice is not repeatable (9:12)! God was not playing games in the death of Jesus. Taking the sacrificial death of Jesus seriously is the goal of the Preacher.

Deliberately playing loose with the death of Jesus and turning away from his salvation "after having received the truth" has eternal consequences (cf. 6:6). The reasoning in Hebrews is clear. There is "no other sacrifice that can cover our sins" (10:26). Readers are therefore warned to take the death of Jesus seriously. But the Preacher is also quick to add the assuring note that he is convinced his readers will not turn back from God. Instead, he believes that they will be among the "faithful ones" (10:19, 35-39; cf. 6:19).[16]

This reference to the "faithful ones" provides the Preacher with his springboard to introduce into his sermon the well-known chapter 11 with its illustrations concerning the faithful ones from the past. "Faith" for him is not merely some good characteristic listed in a Hellenistic set of virtues as over against vices. "Faith" or better "faithfulness" is in fact the quality of consistency that is represented in the "steadfastness" or "truthfulness" of God. Faithfulness is not an attribute in a vacuum. It is a way of life modeled on the way God deals with humans. Thus, as the Preacher argues, "faithfulness" is best defined not in words but in examples of human consistency. Understanding and communicating this idea from the eleventh chapter of Hebrews then should be done in full recognition of the contextual framework of Christians who were experiencing intense suffering and persecution.

When one recognizes the reason for these examples, one can better visualize why the Preacher conclusively reaches his announcement that his readers are "surrounded by a huge company of witnesses" who have preceded them in their life struggles (Heb 12:1). He does this to follow his announcement with an athletic-type summons to take off the training weights and persevere in running the marathon of life, following the model of Jesus who died on the cross and is now portrayed as "seated at the right-hand of the enthroned God" (12:1-2)!

To copy this Jesus, however, is not easy. Achieving true holiness and divinely endowed peace demands a disciplined life (12:10-11). So he challenges his readers like athletes in training to strengthen their muscles (hands and knees), to set out a straight path for themselves from which they will not deviate, to act like Christians in matters of peace and holiness, and not to succumb to patterns of life that result in the forfeiture of their goal, like Esau did when he lost his rights of inheritance (12:12-17).

Then, calling the attention of his people to the frightfulness of God's actions at Mount Sinai, he reminds them that this awesome God will shake the entire structure of our cosmic reality once again in the finale of the world. Accordingly, he warns them that only what is true and authentic will survive the coming judgment of God (12:18-29). And he concludes his sermon with practical advice concerning their responsibilities as Christians to care for strangers, their families, their personal finances, and their leaders in the Christian fellowship (13:1-7), bearing in mind that their model of Jesus is unchanging (13:8). This Jesus, who gave his life for them, beckons them as a holy people to join him in his rejection outside the camp or as he suffered in his sacrificial death outside the city (13:10-16).

This captivating sermon is thus finished except for the exquisite benediction that proclaims the power of God in the resurrection of Jesus Christ (our caring shepherd). Through his covenantal self-giving death (blood), he has equipped Christians with inner strength to face everything that comes their way. This Jesus who is "superior" to all other realities has provided the wonder of salvation for Christians and thus should be praised forever (13:20-21)!

Friends, do you not agree that the Preacher has formulated a truly magnificent portrait of Jesus? To focus on the superiority of Jesus and the resulting superiority of Christianity is a brilliant strategy for proclaiming the gospel. In the face of intense suffering and persecution, this sermonic letter must have instilled a great sense of confidence into early believers. Most of us in America and in the Western world today hardly understand how long-term persecution can be a debilitating experience, and yet somehow in such circumstances God seems to raise up spokespersons who can inspire Christians to faithfulness and endurance.

We do not know if we will be called to undergo such traumas, but there are Christians in our world today who are being severely tested. We must not neglect to pray for those people and their plights. May they be given the peace that can come only from God, and may they be granted a vision of the "Superior Christ" who hears their painful cries. Moreover, may we as contemporary Christians be found faithful. May we who seek to communicate with this generation recognize the seriousness of our calling because those who are the recipients of our testimonies and proclamations may not know the future contexts they may face.

In closing the discussion in this chapter, I would hastily remind all of us who are Gentiles that Jesus was not born a Gentile. He was born a Jew, and he first sent his disciples to the lost sheep of Israel (cf. Matt 9:5-6). But his goal was *not* to create an exclusive club. His goal was to reach all the people of the world (28:19). As his followers of today, we must therefore constantly be alerted to the fact that our calling is not simply to witness, teach, and preach to those who are just like us. Our summons as Christians is a universal one. The writers of the Gospel of Matthew and the sermon called Hebrews (like most of the other authors of the New Testament) were also *not* Gentiles. They were Jews who revered their heritage, but they were powerfully touched by Almighty God to use their skills in communicating the transforming message of Jesus to others. They knew that God's Beloved Son was sent not only to bless the descendants of Abraham through Jacob/Israel but also to include the people of the entire world (cf. Gen 12:3) with God's wonderful gift of salvation.

We should be exceedingly grateful for their willingness to accept their divinely inspired vocation. And we should covenant with the God who called them to a universal gospel that we will also accept the challenge to communicate this marvelous message to others and particularly to our growing biblically illiterate generation.

Questions for Reflection

• How would you summarize the main message of Hebrews?
• When have you struggled to proclaim this message?

• How seriously do you take the writer's affirmations of the superiority of Christ? What does that message of Christ's superiority mean in a world obsessed with struggles for power and wealth?
• For people today, how can you communicate in a meaningful manner the Preacher's thinking concerning Jewish ritual, covenant, and sacrifice?
• In your understanding, how do you handle the severe warnings of Hebrews?

Notes

1. For some helpful works on the Gospel of Matthew see W. E. Davies and D. Allison, *Matthew*, International Critical Commentary (Edinburgh: T. & T. Clark, 1988); Donald A. Hagner, *Matthew 1–13* and *Matthew 14–28*, Word Biblical Commentary (Dallas: Word, 1993, 1995); M. Eugene Boring, *The Gospel of Matthew*, The New Interpreter's Bible, vol. 8 (Nashville: Abingdon, 1995) 87–505; Craig Blomberg, *Matthew*, New American Commentary (Nashville: Broadman & Holman, 1992); Ben Witherington III, *Matthew*, Smyth & Helwys Bible Commentary (Macon GA: Smyth & Helwys, 2006); Robert Gundry, *Matthew: A Commentary on His Literary and Theological Art* (Grand Rapids MI: Eerdmans, 1981).

2. For a helpful discussion on the literature of the Rabbis also known as Tannaitic Literature see E. P. Sanders, *Paul and Palestinian Judaism* (Philadelphia: Fortress Press, 1977) especially at 33–238.

3. While the Gospels are in fact anonymous, Christian tradition links this Gospel with Matthew, who is also known as Levi (cf. Matt 9:9 and Mark 2:14) and who was one of the twelve who followed Jesus (Matt 10:3; Mark 3:18; Luke 6:15; Acts 1:13). Eusebius (*Hist. eccl.* 3.39.16) quoting Papias referred to this Gospel as having been written first in Hebrew; such a suggestion is unlikely, although one might argue that its thought patterns could be Hebraic. The book probably comes from a time when Christians were debating the issue of whether one needed to be a Jew to be a Christian. Thus, one can understand the "Jewishness" of dialogue that seems to be inherent in the Sermon on the Mount and elsewhere in the Gospel. As far as dating is concerned, it is difficult to say whether Matthew was written before or after the fall of Jerusalem, but probably before 75 CE.

4. For a brief review of Herod the Great, the Herodians, and the Roman provincial system see my discussion in G. Borchert, *Jesus of Nazareth*, 22–36.

5. It is not entirely clear to which text Matthew was referring or if he was building a theological construct associated with the concept of Nazarite. The long hair that is usually associated with pictures of Jesus and that is part of movies involving his life on Earth may also be part of this theological construct.

6. I would point out that in the genealogical list, the number fourteen is significantly tripled, but that in counting there seems to be one name short between the second and third lists. That so-called discrepancy for Westerners would hardly have troubled a Jewish writer

since the last name in the second list could be duplicated in the third list and then viewed separately as well (here Jechoniah, see 1:11 and 12).

7. When the first and last sections in a list or group are parallel, the two form what in biblical and literary studies is known as an *inclusio*. Such patterns are important for interpreters because they not only identify the list but also indicate when the list is complete. See for example the first eight beatitudes, which form an enclosure or an *inclusio* in Matt 5:3-10. While there is a ninth beatitude, readers should be alerted to the fact that there is something different in the ninth one that gives it an extra emphasis by changing from the third person to the second person.

8. In connection with the Lucan Gospel, I will later discuss the summary temptation in Luke that takes place in the temple area in Jerusalem and why the place for that final temptation is important to Luke.

9. I have purposely not discussed in much detail the so-called Sermon on the Mount because that text would expand this section to be again as long as the rest of Matthew. Indeed, I have taught an entire course devoted to those three chapters. For those who would wish to pursue them further, the following works should be helpful: Robert Guelich, *The Sermon on the Mount: A Foundation for Understanding* (Waco: Word, 1982); W.D. Davies, *The Setting of the Sermon on the Mount* (Cambridge: University Press, 1963); John Stott, *Christian Counter-Culture: The Message of the Sermon on the Mount* (Downers Grove IL: InterVarsity, 1978); Donald A Carson, *The Sermon on the Mount* (Grand Rapids MI: Baker, 1978); David Lloyd-Jones, *Studies in the Sermon on the Mount*, 2 vols. (Grand Rapids MI: Eerdmans, 1959–1960).

10. Readers should note that the term "Torah," which is normally translated "Law" in English, did not originally mean a set of rules but a way of living with God, namely "walking with God." Accordingly, it is important to understand the significance of the difference between *halak* and *halakah* (see my comments earlier).

11. For further information on Hebrews see Fred Craddock, "The Letter to the Hebrews," *New Interpreter's Bible*, vol. 12 (Nashville: Abingdon, 1998) 1–173; William Johnsson, *Hebrews*, Knox Preaching Guides (Atlanta: John Knox, 1980); Craig Koester, *Hebrews*, Anchor Bible (Garden City NY: Doubleday, 2001). See also Gerald L. Borchert, *Assurance and Warning* (Nashville: Broadman, 1987), 153–202; Borchert, "A Superior Book: Hebrews," *Review and Expositor* 82/3 (Summer 1985): 319–32; Luke Timothy Johnson, *Hebrews*, New Testament Library (Louisville: Westminster/John Knox, 2006); William Lane, *Hebrews 1–8* and *Hebrews 9–13*, Word Biblical Commentary (Dallas: Word, 1991); Edgar McKnight, *Hebrews*, Smyth & Helwys Bible Commentary (Macon GA: Smyth & Helwys, 2002). For an excellent survey of the literature on Hebrews see Robert Gundry, *A Survey of the New Testament*, 3rd ed. (Grand Rapids MI: Zondervan, 1994) 421–30.

12. See G. Borchert, *Worship in the New Testament*, 176.

13. As one might expect, since it is difficult to identify the author of Hebrews, it is also difficult to be precise on the time of the writing and the recipients. Some have argued that it was prior to the fall of the temple (70), but the Jerusalem temple is not the focus of the message, although "outside the gate" (Heb 13:12) may give some clue. Some have suggested that it was written to those in Rome (13:24) and others to those in Palestine or Syria and

even Jerusalem, but the references to leaders (13:17) and the "you" of 13:19-25 is so general that only speculation is possible.

14. See William Johnsson, *Hebrews*, 2.

15. For a better understanding of this phenomenon in Judaism, one should read works like 1 Enoch among the Jewish Pseudepigrapha. The best source for these works is James Charlesworth, ed., *The Old Testament Pseudepigrapha*, Apocalyptic Literature and Testaments, vol. 1 (Garden City NY: Doubleday & Company, 1983) 5–89, especially 22–24 and 31–32.

16. I must pause here for those Christian readers who find it difficult to imagine that the New Testament would envisage the possibility that a Christian might be able to commit apostasy, even though warnings are given throughout the New Testament and especially here in Hebrews. Because of such contemporary misperceptions, I wrote my earlier book, *Assurance and Warning* (noted above). We, as Christians, rejoice in the biblical assurances, but we often cringe at the warnings as though they do not apply to us. Or we simply forget them. But I would remind everyone that life with Christ is not a rigid theological formula. We can either live by faith or we can say to God, "I do not want to listen to you and I will walk my own way." Accordingly, we must remember that one of our popular theological formulas—"once saved always saved"—is not in the New Testament and is simply a formula that attempts to express many people's convictions about our security in Jesus. It is important, however, to remember that the formula is nowhere stated in the Bible. The Bible does, however, assert the idea that Christians ought to persevere in their faith and that God will be with them in their lives. For that reason, the preacher of Hebrews includes two (!) impossible statements in Hebrews 6 not just one (6:4 and 6:18). God is certainly a judge, but God is also like an anchor who holds the Christian both in good times and in the time of storms. God desires the children of God to reach their promised land, but they may not want to follow and walk with God. Similarly, it is for that very reason that the Apostle Paul also warned Christians not to fall in the wilderness like the Israelites (cf. 1 Cor 10:6-12). Yet he likewise also gave his Christian children the assurance that God would help them to escape devastating loss if they would be steadfast and consistent in the work for the Lord (see my further comments below in 1 Corinthians).

Chapter 4

The Portraits of Jesus in the Gospel of Luke and the Book of Acts

We turn now from the portraits and messages concerning Jesus that were written especially to the Jewish people and begin to discuss the portrait of Jesus and the story of the early church that were both penned by the Gentile writer named Luke. This author, who addressed both his Gospel and the book of Acts to his Greek patron Theophilus,[1] is without doubt one of the best storytellers in the ancient world. I have often told my students that when you hear a Lucan story you will likely not forget it. You may forget its source but you will generally remember the story. Luke seems to have been endowed with the incredible capacity to grasp and encapsulate the magnificent storytelling perspectives of Jesus, and he detailed his reflections on the early church in an unforgettable manner.[2] His wonderful stories of the early Christians in the book called Acts have inspired countless readers to follow the model of Jesus willingly as well as in the footsteps of the early believers—even to the point of martyrdom!

If you have forgotten Luke's captivating ability, just ponder some of his marvelous stories such as the good Samaritan (Luke 10:25-37), the rich man and Lazarus (16:19-31), the story of Mary and Martha (10:38-42), the "little" Zacchaeus who climbed the sycamore tree (19:1-10), the Pharisee and the tax collector (18:9-14), the rich fool (12:13-21), the widow and the unjust judge (18:1-8), the widow's tiny offering (21:1-4), the trilogy of the prodigal son along with the lost sheep and the lost coin (15:3-32), and Jesus praying in Gethsemane (22:39-53). And do not forget the shepherds, the angels, and the baby Jesus (2:8-20), as well as the exquisite Emmaus story (24:13-35). These stories are *only* found in the Gospel of Luke.

Add to these the exciting episodes like the "fiery tongues" of Pentecost (Acts 2:1-17), the healing of the lame man when the disciples had no silver or gold (3:1-10), the curse on Ananias and Sapphira (5:1-11), the death of Stephen (6:8-7:60), the conversion of the Ethiopian eunuch (8:26-39), the strategic Cornelius story that began to alter Christian perspectives (10:1-11:18), the gripping accounts of Paul in healing the slave woman at Philippi (16:11-40), Paul's address on the Areopagus in Athens (17:16-34), his bold encounters with the political authorities named Felix, Festus, and Agrippa in Caesarea (24:1–26:32), the incredible shipwreck off the island of Malta (27:27-44), and even his dealing with a poisonous viper (28:3-6), to name only a few of Luke's amazing stories in Acts.

Luke was a master at storytelling, and if you are attempting to share the gospel with people who tend to be biblically illiterate, you dare not fail to tell these Lucan stories. But remember that Luke's stories are not merely stories. Each story has a powerful point, and it is our task as Christians to help others discover the implications of these exciting stories in their contextual framework. Never forget to ask about the point of a Lucan story; when you ask, you should arrive at a fuller flowering of Luke's portrait of Jesus and his overall intentions for communicating to people the marvelous message of the coming of God's Son into the world. God bless you in your pilgrimage with Luke!

The Caring Gospel of Luke[3]

To gain perspective on Luke's writing, we first should ask, how do his books begin and end? It may surprise you, but this Gospel begins in Jerusalem in the temple and ends in Jerusalem in the temple. Why would a Gentile write in this way? And what about the book called Acts? It begins in Jerusalem and ends in Rome. Luke's goal was to get the good news from what he considered the religious center of the world to the political center. But there is much more to his purpose.

As we examine his gospel, I would ask, why did Luke focus on the temple in Jerusalem? And let's notice how the temptations of Jesus end in Luke. The third and final temptation does not follow the Matthean pattern of ending on a "mountain" wherein the devil challenges Jesus to compromise and receive all the territories of the world—which of course were not his to give in the first place (Matt 4:7-10). In Luke the final temptation takes place with the devil challenging Jesus to attract people by showmanship from nowhere else than the pinnacle of the temple (Luke 4:9-12). Why the temple? In the Lucan portrait of Jesus, the temple is crucial to who Jesus is and to the focus of his earthly ministry. The reason is that the temple was understood to be the house of God, the earthly throne room of God, and had been regarded as the worship center of the world. Of course, the derivative question in this context is, are people attracted to God through showmanship in worship? I suspect you know that this question still haunts us in the church today.

As we continue, notice that the birth of Jesus' forerunner is announced by the angel Gabriel to the old priest Zechariah in none other than the holy place next to the inner sanctum—the most holy place—of the temple (1:13-17). Then, just after Jesus is born, he is brought by his parents to the temple for his dedication, and there they receive the prediction of the old man Simeon that Jesus will be a light to the Gentiles and the glory of Israel. But this "good news" is shattered by the prediction that a piercing sword will also be present (2:32-35). Next, note that at the time of his *bar mitzvah* (his admission to adulthood), Jesus is once again brought to the temple for a defining moment with his mother because he is destined to be in his "Father's House"—namely, about his Father's work (2:49). One of the great focal themes in Luke's thinking is Jerusalem and the temple.

In the large central portion of this Gospel (the section we designate as the major journey), Jesus sets his face like an arrow to return to Jerusalem for his closing period on earth—his death and resurrection (9:51). When he finally arrives in Jerusalem, he is joyously welcomed as he enters (19:28-40). But Jesus knows it is not to be a celebration time. Instead, he mourns/weeps over the city not just once but, in Luke, a second time. He knows the city and its citizens are doomed because the people there fail to recognize the time of their visitation by the Messiah (19:41-44; cf. 13:33-35). Indeed, the temple no longer correctly functions as a place of prayer and of meeting with God. Rather, it has become nothing but a den of thieves. Therefore, Jesus drives out those merchants so that he can focus on teaching the people who are gathered there (19:45-48).

Then while he carries his cross to the crucifixion many wail, but Jesus turns to the crowd and announces, "Daughters of Jerusalem weep not for me, but weep for yourselves" (23:27-28). He knows they are about to experience a tragedy of such proportions that they will cry for the mountains to fall on them and hide them from the coming wrath (23:29-31).

I am convinced that Luke knew that time, which came in AD 70, because he clearly defines that tragedy as "when you see Jerusalem surrounded by armies then understand that the desolation has come near" (21:20). He wrote his Gospel after the fall of Jerusalem and wanted his readers to understand that the failure of Jerusalem was a symbol of failing to recognize who Jesus is.

In the death scene of Jesus, Luke notes the symbolic termination of the temple's role in forgiveness, as in Mark, so he announces to his readers that the temple's future usefulness has been shattered when the temple veil "was torn in two"—at the very time when Jesus breathes his last breath (23:44-47)! But at that point Luke is still not finished with Jerusalem and the temple because he must bring its significance to a conclusion. He does so by indicating that Jesus ascended to God from the Mount of Olives, the place looking eastward across the Kidron Valley from the temple to the rising sun and the hope of human resurrection. Finally, the disciples return to Jerusalem and the temple, awaiting the time when they will be enveloped with the power of God (24:44-53). With this understanding of the importance of Jerusalem and the temple in mind, we turn to reflect on a few other important issues in Luke.

To begin, let us return to some of the fascinating stories of Luke. Did you notice that most of these stories have a similar theme? Who were the shepherds? The "good" Samaritan? The prodigal? The tax collectors? The widows? And Lazarus? They were people whom the religious leaders in the time of Jesus regarded as the rejects of society, the *am haertez* (the people who work with their hands) or worse! Indeed, the Pharisees often viewed them as either impure or irreligious. Yet they are the people in the stories of Luke who are commended by Jesus. Accordingly, it is imperative to note that it is *not* the so-called righteous that Jesus says are blessed by God.

What is Luke trying to tell us? For whom did Jesus come? Who accepted Jesus? It certainly was not the so-called religious! Paying attention to this fact can provide us with an important perspective concerning Luke's focus in the ministry of Jesus. The Lord did not come to call the so-called "righteous" but sinners to repentance (5:32; cf. Mark 2:17; Matt 9:13).

That comment brings me to one of the truly magnificent stories of Luke that is often read quickly and forgotten unless one is sensitive to what is taking place between Jesus and the rulers of the synagogue. That story involves a crippled or bent over woman who is unable to straighten herself. In the Jewish categories articulated by the rabbis as the lowest type of people, she would be viewed near or at the bottom of the list. She is not only deformed and therefore regarded as cursed by God but she is also a woman and therefore has little status. To make the situation in this story even more intense, Jesus heals this virtually insignificant person on Shabboth—the Sabbath! The leader of the synagogue is indignant and publicly condemns Jesus in the presence of the people of the town.

Jesus immediately counters with an exceedingly sharp judgment: "You hypocrites!" These so-called righteous men have no problem taking care of their animals on the Sabbath. Their neat little rules allow them to do so, but they piously condemn Jesus for healing this helpless woman who has been bound by Satan for eighteen years (Luke 13:16). It is a top-level face-off, and the people are waiting to see what will happen.

Then Jesus says the almost unthinkable. He calls her a "daughter of Abraham"! (13:16). No, no, no! They would have argued. Talk about "sons of Abraham," sure. But not a "daughter of Abraham"! Daughters do not really count. They are for birthing children and doing housework (cf. 11:27)! But that is not the perspective of Jesus in Luke. Thus, he also must correct Martha for her criticism of Mary when she expresses a similar perspective (10:38-42). Friends, these three texts in Luke are indeed *revolutionary*. The Lucan Jesus strikes a note for egalitarian humanity that would hardly be realized until the twentieth century and still it is not fully recognized in many places—including some churches that take the name of Jesus! This Gospel penned by Luke clearly provides a portrait of Jesus as the author of a Christian's declaration of "no discrimination" for all people! And it came many centuries before the British Knights forced the monarchy in the Magna Carta to open the path for recognizing even the rights of the nobility. This Gospel is not a book to put on the shelf. It is a book that can lead the church to a new vision for humanity.

If you are a woman or someone who lacks status or have been regarded as second-class by society, then please recognize that this Gospel of Luke was written especially for you. And that statement fits perfectly with Luke's introductory story of Jesus when he begins his ministry in the synagogue at Nazareth. At the outset of his ministry Jesus is handed the scroll of Isaiah and he reads, "The Spirit of the Lord is upon me" (Isa 61:1-2). It must have seemed to those listening as though Jesus was reading about himself and his task—namely, to preach to the poor, to proclaim freedom to the imprisoned, to open the eyes of the blind, and to offer new hope to the oppressed. Luke understood that Jesus was officially proclaiming that the Year of Jubilee[4] had arrived with him (Luke 4:18-21). The sad story is that from this very first encounter, Jesus was rejected by most of those who considered themselves to be righteous and faithful to God. But they were badly mistaken.

Luke's Jesus is clearly portrayed as a servant who was sent to serve and who called his disciples to follow his model and become servants to others. Did they readily adopt such a calling? Luke's answer before Jesus' death and resurrection is a resounding "No!" In the final days of his ministry on earth and immediately following the climactic experience of the Last Supper in which Jesus seeks to symbolize his self-giving role as their Savior, the disciples are still arguing about who will be chief among them (22:24-27). At that point, they—like the religious authorities of their day—are not much different than most of humanity.

Indeed, Jesus understood that the Jews, like most people, were fundamentally "self-righteous," yet he did not avoid seeking all of them. The question that lies just below the surface of Luke's Gospel is, do people want to know Jesus? Do they want to obey God? That question continues to confront the church today. It is at the heart of the well-known story about the man usually referred to as the "rich young ruler," which is in all three of the Synoptic Gospels. That man comes to Jesus asking what more he needs to do to attain eternal life. It is a pertinent question. But we are also left with the question, does this man who considers himself among the religious elite want to learn the answer? Jesus' response that the man should sell all that he has and give the proceeds to the poor is exactly what he does not want to hear. The man has clearly stated that he has kept the second ledger of the Decalogue, but what we learn is that he has another "god"— wealth—and that he does not keep the first ledger, the one about honoring the true God of Israel (18:18-30; cf. Mark 10:17-31 and Matt 19:16-30). He is on the boundary, but he cannot take the step leading to authenticity. His encounter with Jesus is the tipping point.

Then Luke has another story that makes the focus much clearer. In the story of the rich fool, the man thinks he is in control of his life's destiny and that he can build huge barns to collect all his goods and then relax and eat, drink, and be merry for the rest of his life. But he quickly learns that his life is required that very night (Luke 12:13-21). He assumes that he does not have to answer to God for his life. It is a tragic mistake that many in this world still make today.

From the perspective of Jesus, those who think they are in charge of their destinies and treat others like the scum of the earth are in for a huge surprise. The rich man in another story discovers that the beggar Lazarus is granted the reward of entering the bosom of Abraham, whereas he, the respectable one, receives a sentence of enduring the tormenting fire from which there is no escape. Moreover, that man cannot even send a warning to his kinfolk to reform their lives because they already have sufficient knowledge from Moses. Indeed, the portrait of Jesus in Luke makes it clear that humans do have someone who has crossed over the chasm of life and death and has come back from the dead (16:19-31). Knowledge is not the major key to entering heaven—obedient response is! Humans tend to follow the mistaken way of mere *gnosis*—"information." But information alone does not rescue them from damnation.

And this concern for heaven brings me to an important point concerning the song of the angels and the birth of Jesus. Unfortunately, many people in our churches have developed their understanding about the birth of Jesus from Christmas cards and Christmas plays rather than from insightful teaching and biblically clear sermons. We should all be clear that the wise men (stargazers) and shepherds are not in the same story, even though those stories are harmonized and brought together in Christmas cards, nativity sets, and Christmas pageants. The Gentile stargazers who are in Matthew and the despised, smelly shepherds who are in Luke both fulfill important roles in each of their Gospels. The stargazers represent Matthew's concern for the rejected Gentiles and the shepherds represent Luke's concern for the dispossessed people who are overlooked by most proper people.

At this point I want to go beyond the shepherds and focus on the message of the angels to those shepherds. We now know that the best translation of the angelic message is *not* the way the King James Version renders the text: "Glory to God in the highest and on earth peace, good will toward men." It should instead be something like this: "Glory to God in the highest and on earth peace among humans [men] with whom God is well pleased" (2:14). The peace on earth is not promised to all humans but to those on whom the favor of God will rest.

Yet there is something more crucial to be noticed in Luke's Gospel, and it involves Luke's story of the triumphal entry. In this second story when Jesus officially enters Jerusalem as God's promised Messiah, he knows he is being rejected and so Luke alters the earlier message of the angels. That change is very telling because "peace" is moved from earth to "heaven" and "glory" remains "in the highest" (19:38). Why did Luke make this subtle change? I suspect he wanted every reader to understand that the promised peace on earth that should have come to the city of Jeru-"salem" (God's peace) would still have to await the coming of another era. Now I would affirm that we should all pray for peace to come not only to Jerusalem (Ps 122:6-7) but also to the whole world. Yet we should recognize where the source of true peace resides—not in human effort but in accepting the mission of the rejected Son of God!

Do you begin to understand why Jerusalem is so crucial to Luke's story? It is a turning point. Jerusalem is the place of promise, but it is also the place of the rejection and the death of Jesus. Yet it is also the place of the resurrection of Jesus—the symbol of expectation for which the disciples were commanded to wait (Luke 24:49). And it is the place where Pentecost would occur, the new symbol of hope for the early church. Indeed, it is from Jerusalem that the gospel would spread to the entire world. And that statement brings me to Luke's second volume—the book we call the Acts of the Apostles.

Questions for Reflection

• How do Luke's unique stories carry powerful messages concerning our responsibility for those who are among the marginalized of our society?
• How comfortable is your church with communicating this Lucan portrait of Jesus?
• How can we better impact our faith communities with a holistic presentation of the gospel? What might be the cost? What might be the possible results—both positive and negative?
• What does Jerusalem mean to you as a communicator of the gospel? How ready are you to commit to such a symbolic place as Jesus did?

The Captivating Book of Acts[5]

If any book in the New Testament could be labeled as thrilling reading, the book of Acts would win that prized designation. It is a fascinating episodic work, and even if Luke had not written his beloved Gospel, Acts would have marked him among the elite group of superb ancient classical authors. That evaluation can be made completely apart from the fact that this book is a crucial part of the Christian's inspired canon and has been used by God repeatedly to challenge countless evangelistic enterprises and "missional" movements throughout the centuries since it was penned. There is little doubt that God has placed his personal imprint on this book, and it is a work that should be read and inwardly digested by anyone who aspires to be an authentic Christian witness. It is also a book that can electrify and transform a blasé, biblically illiterate person into a passionate follower of

Christ, if such a person discovers that Jesus is truly alive and active in and through his followers.

If you did not catch what I just said, I strongly believe that the key to understanding the book of Acts is realizing that it is the Living Jesus who is acting through his followers. As Paul painfully discovered when he persecuted Christians, he was in fact persecuting Jesus (Acts 9:5)! Grasping that understanding can lead Christians to live with miracle—a concept almost lost and forgotten in our contemporary world. But for twenty-first-century Christians I would firmly emphasize: do not ever think that Jesus has abandoned this world and left it to the devil and the servants of evil. God in Christ Jesus is the agent of human transformation and authentic positive change on planet Earth. Miraculous change or transformation is the foundation for the stories in the book of Acts, and such can be the secret of our stories today in this era of growing biblical illiteracy. Jesus is very present on earth in you and me. So I welcome you to the book of Acts and to rediscovering the "Living Jesus." In your reading of this book, however, if you want to discover its secrets, I recommend that you read it with a prayer that God will visit you with his mighty power as you once again review the testimony to the Living Jesus in Acts!

The book is thrilling as the good news concerning Jesus explodes outward from Jerusalem to Rome. And if it were not enough for the book of Acts to be the most exciting document in the New Testament, one can add that it is also without a doubt among the most organized works in the Bible. It is a literary jewel. It can easily be divided into twelve sections with each section clearly designated by a concluding summary. Accordingly, it is not difficult to follow the development of Luke's incredible story of God at work in the early church.[2] But even more intriguing is the fact that each section (apart from the first and seventh) contains a defining speech that gives focus to the incidents in that section.[3] For the Western mindset with its formulaic pattern of thinking, such a tight pattern of organization is exceedingly appealing. Naturally, then, Western readers are drawn to the book for examples of witness even if they have not understood its fascinating organizational structure. Try studying it again, my friends. You'll like it!

But now I turn to the unfolding of Luke's second fascinating work. Some books can be summarized rather easily, but the stories of Acts carry so many implications that it is difficult to do so briefly. I will, therefore, attempt here only to highlight the most significant segments of this exciting book. At the outset, there is little doubt that when the body of Jesus was placed in the tomb after his crucifixion, the hopes of Jesus' followers also lay dead with his body.

What breathed powerful new life into that hopelessness, however, was the reality of the resurrection. On the other hand, it is quite clear that this resurrection of Jesus was a hard pill for his enemies to swallow. So almost immediately the reality of his resurrection was disputed, as is evidenced in Matthew's report in which the Jewish authorities claimed that the followers of Jesus had stolen the body (Matt 28:13). Such a claim was only the first in a long series of attempts to discredit Jesus and the resurrection. Many other theories have been proposed, as I have discussed in my book *Jesus of Nazareth*.[4] Indeed, some scholars like Rudolph Bultmann have argued that the factual event of the resurrection is "utterly inconceivable."[5] Yet a genuine physical resurrection is precisely what the book of Acts proclaims.

Moreover, what remains important to remember in any discussion concerning the resurrection is that it is difficult to discount the witnesses when their testimonies have been accompanied by the reality of their incredible transformations and fearlessness in proclaiming the risen Jesus. Those witnesses did not suffer from corporate hallucinations or fraudulently constructed reports. As a former lawyer, I can testify that their reports may not have all been identical, but that only makes the case stronger because it removes the question concerning a constructed collusion. Those witnesses had been terrified followers who fled the scene of Jesus' arrest to avoid being associated with Jesus. But almost overnight they became bold communicators of his resurrection. And they were willing to die for the new reality of the Living Jesus.

Moreover, harsh threats to silence them by the very people who earlier had terrified them and from whom they had fled were completely ineffective. Discounting their testimonies is a hard hurdle to overcome because it means that the discounters are duty bound to provide a more logical explanation than that such a miracle happened. But the miraculous did happen! Jesus is now alive and the book of Acts is a testimony to the reality of the miraculous Jesus.

The book opens in an intriguing manner by asserting that Jesus clearly "proved himself alive"[6] among them for many days[7] and taught them about the kingdom of God (Acts 1:3). But like so many of us, the focus of the disciples is still on themselves as they query, "Lord, will you now restore the kingdom to Israel?" (1:6). They have a great deal yet to learn about God's "kingdom," God's "timing," and God's "vocation" for them (1:7-8). But they will soon be learning about how God moves in the world. So, while they wait for God to act, they clear up some of the matters that need to be done like replacing Judas in order that their number will be restored to "twelve"—which represents God's people (1:20-26).

Then it happens! Pentecost arrives and with it the shocking empowerment of the disciples by the Holy Spirit (Acts 2:1-12). And as the prophet Joel had predicted, those who are empowered begin to share (cf. Joel 2:28-32) the good news that the Messianic Age has dawned. At that point, their communication is strangely "unhindered"[8] even by language barriers, which Luke must have recognized as the reversal of the curse at the tower of Babel (cf. Gen 11:1-9). How and what happened at that point is somewhat of a mystery, but Peter's message that follows is no mystery because he outlines the arrival of the new era. In this new era, God has begun the building of a new community that is summoned to proclaim God's message to all humanity (Acts 2:14-36). When Peter issues the call to repent and be baptized in the "name" of Jesus, the response is an amazing three thousand (2:37-41).

It has often been noted that at that point the Christian church was born. But perhaps equally significant to the church's birth is the fact that Luke identifies four crucial elements that should be evidenced in a true, functioning Christian community—namely, (a) authentic apostolic teaching, (b) community fellowship (*koinonia*), (c) community worship (symbolized in the breaking of bread), and (d) prayer (2:42).

As I have often told my students, sadly what has happened over the centuries of church history is that because of misconceptions and inadequate focusing, faith communities have tended to identify with merely one or two of these major elements and have then minimized the others. Such patterns that are the result of reactions and protests have led to the truncation of adequate Christian community life patterns. Moreover, for many churches the element that is most neglected, practiced superficially, or assigned to specialists is usually prayer. But prayer must not be a "tack-on" to the church's life. It is at the heart of worship and a mark of authenticity.

With such an auspicious beginning as Pentecost, the enemies of Jesus are alerted to the fact that his disciples might now be an even bigger problem for them than the single figure of Jesus, whom they assumed had been eliminated. But to the great distress of Jesus' opponents, these nondescript disciples begin performing acts of healing like Jesus had done—e.g., the lame man at the gate of the temple. And they do it (a) openly in public, (b) without the expectation of reward, and (c) in the name of Jesus (3:6)! Further, in their speeches they lay the blame for the "murder" of Jesus at the very doorstep of Judaism with the Jewish hierarchy. What is more telling, they assert that God has intervened and rectified the Jewish wrongdoing by raising Jesus from the dead! Then they add to the embarrassment by calling on the Jews to repent so that they will not to be judged by God (3:11-26). With such an appeal, the number of Christians continues to mushroom (4:4) and the establishment becomes more frustrated.

If you had been a member of the Sanhedrin, what would you have done? It is not difficult to guess. You would have brought these renegades before the high court and told them in no uncertain terms to cease and desist their preaching and teaching, especially in *that* name! And that is exactly what the Sanhedrin does. But when Peter and John are interrogated, they do not back down. Instead, they use the name of Jesus and they respond to the Sanhedrin's threats with the retort that they must obey God and cannot stop their witnessing (4:19-21). The gauntlet is thus thrown down.

As the disciples leave the court, they know that they are in great danger. But rather than retreating, they meet with the community of faith and pray for the continuing empowerment of the Holy Spirit and for boldness to proclaim the word of God.

Some contemporary readers may shake their heads at such audacity and think that these early Christians are simply foolish. Such a response, however, is not Luke's view because he informs us that the entire place where these early Christians are praying is shaken as God affirms their decision by further empowering them with the Holy Spirit (4:23-31).

True to our surmise, the high priest and his compromising colleagues among the Sadducees who have cuddled up to Rome are not finished with these renegade Jews. Accordingly, the high priest sends the temple guards to seize the apostles—particularly Peter and John—and put them in prison (5:17-18). But God responds and miraculously sets them free—giving them instructions to go to back to the temple and proclaim the gospel (5:19-20). When, therefore, the council meets to deal with the case, the prison guards are unable to find the renegades until someone reports that those same apostles are then preaching in the temple (5:21-25).

The council is shocked, but the disciples are again seized and brought summarily before the court. The obvious question leveled at the renegades is, "Why are you speaking in that name[9] and filling Jerusalem with your teaching?" The problem for the council is that the apostles are bringing a serious charge against their captors—namely, the blood of Jesus is upon the heads of the council members (5:28). Peter's short but bold response is that they must obey God rather than men (5:29).

Such audacity! The hostile reaction of the Sanhedrin is not unexpected. They are ready to kill these rebels and quash their activity. But then Luke adds that their senior Pharisaic statesman, the well-known Gamaliel, addresses the council and warns them to be careful lest they might be fighting God. Moreover, this revered teacher reminds them that if they are opposing the Almighty, they will not be able to stop the new movement (5:33-39). I pause here to remind us that Luke understood that God can work among the church's enemies. I wonder, do we have the same perspective? The council responds by beating the apostles, warning them again not to preach in the name of Jesus, and then setting them free.

The reaction on the part of the Christians is not one of fear but one of joy, and they regard their persecution as a blessing to suffer for the name of Jesus. They continue to proclaim Jesus as the Messiah (5:40-42). This pattern of willingness to suffer for the name of Jesus is a major theme in the book of Acts and is repeated several times. Christians are persecuted; they can even die! But the death of Christians does not wipe out Christianity. Stephen becomes the first martyr (7:54-60). He is followed by James, the brother of John (12:2). But even their deaths do not stop other Christians from proclaiming Jesus.

Saul (whose Hellenistic name is Paul) here enters the picture. He is designated as a special envoy of the high priest and serves him as a fierce persecutor of the followers of the "Way" (of Jesus). He is not only the official representative overseeing the death of Stephen (8:1) but is also given special orders from the high priest and dispatched to seize the Christians in Damascus. Then something strange and miraculous happens. The Living Jesus steps into the situation and confronts Saul on his journey. The result is the transformation of the persecutor into one of Christianity's most fearless and honored proclaimers. So, instead of seizing the Christians, Saul quickly astounds those in the Syrian capital with his arguments for the legitimacy of Jesus. His advocacy of the Christian way makes him a marked man and in turn leads to the beginning of his persecution (9:1-22).

Elsewhere, Peter is busy proclaiming Jesus and healing people who are Jewish (9:32-42). But Peter is also in for a surprise. The Lord has other plans and is determined to take Peter out of his comfort zone. As this disciple is taking an afternoon siesta on the roof of a house in Joppa, he suddenly has what might be called a "daymare" (rather than a "nightmare") in which a sheet comes down from heaven that contains what looks like a zoo, and he hears a voice saying, "Rise, Peter, kill and eat." Being a practicing Jew, however, he responds that he does not eat non-kosher food. Whereupon the voice replies, "What God has made pure, do not call unclean!" When that vision happens three times, it is clear that God is trying to speak to him (10:9-17). As he is rousing himself, three messengers from Cornelius arrive, telling him that God instructed Cornelius to send for him. The picture starts to become clearer.

Fast forward—after Peter travels with the Gentiles to the military head-quarters of Caesarea Maritima and proclaims the good news of Jesus to the Gentiles, the unexpected and miraculous takes place. The Gentiles are blessed with the coming of the Holy Spirit, clear evidence that a major barrier has been crossed. Then Peter is left with a question: What should he do with these Gentiles? His decision is to baptize them into the Christian community (10:24-48). But that act is contrary to all the earlier thinking of the Jewish Christian leadership in Jerusalem. They were certain that Gentiles had to become Jews in order to become Christians (11:2-3). Yet when Peter tells his story to the people back in Jerusalem, they realize that God must be doing something very new in their midst (11:16-18). Luke understands that it is generally hard for humans to accept change, but God is not an absentee deity with respect to this world. We as non-Jews should, therefore, be grateful that some of these early Jewish Christians were responsive to God's Spirit of change.

As you might have guessed by now, crossing barriers is another major theme in the book of Acts. It is inherent in the strategic blessing that takes place at Pentecost (2:1-12), and it is reasserted in this Cornelius story. There are other crossing points as well. When the Greek-speaking widows complain that they are experiencing discrimination in the daily distribution of support, the church quickly moves to correct any sense of prejudice by appointing seven wise men *with Greek names* to rectify any possible sense of unfairness (6:1-6). Then one of these wise stewards (deacons) named Philip is involved in carrying the gospel to the Samaritans, whom the Jews rejected as "half-breeds."[10] His evangelistic work is confirmed by the visit of Peter and John with the subsequent gift of the Spirit to these people (8:4-17).

The highpoint involving Philip in Acts, however, is his meeting with the African (Ethiopian) eunuch (a man who has been castrated in order to serve in the palace chambers with women) and the baptism of that eunuch into the Christian faith (8:26-38). In reflecting on this story, it is important to remember that in Deuteronomy 23:1, it was decreed that a eunuch "would not be able to enter the assembly of the LORD." Yet in Isaiah 56:4-6 the Lord promised that a new era would come for eunuchs who honor God. In the arrival of this new era, the eunuch would no longer need to say, "I am a dry tree" because God promised, "I will give in my house and within my walls a monument and a name better than sons and daughters." Indeed, the promise continues, "I will give them an everlasting name which will not be cut off." Luke undoubtedly views the story of Philip and the eunuch as providing a powerful signal that the promised new eschatological era has begun.

But Christian egalitarianism and the perspective that all people should be treated equally in the church, as they are by God,[11] has been slow in being actualized. Even in the book of Acts, Luke indicates that after Paul returns from his first missionary journey that involves Gentiles, it takes a council meeting of Christians in Jerusalem to hammer out the recognition that the Gentiles do not need to become Jews in order to be accepted as Christians (Acts 15:19-20, 27-29). The battle over abandoning both (a) the keeping of the law as the standard for judging the authenticity of a relationship with God and (b) circumcision as the symbol of acceptability within God's covenant among Christians is not easily won for Paul and Christianity. His letter to the Galatians (see below) bears witness to the fact that even some Gentiles thought that the law and circumcision could provide them with additional human symbols of their acceptability by God. But Christians can be forever grateful that Paul did not budge on the fact that salvation is by grace through faith and not by the outward symbols of Judaism.[12]

In returning to the unfolding of the story in Acts, however, it is quite apparent that the theme of Christians suffering for their faith continues throughout the central sections of this book. Herod Agrippa I not only gains great acceptance from the Jewish citizenry by killing James, John's brother (12:2), but is also emboldened by his experience with James to imprison Peter with the intention of satisfying the Jewish thirst for ridding the nation of these upstart Christians.

Nevertheless, while Peter is chained between two guards in prison, the church is praying fervently for his safety and release. In response, God sends an angel to deliver him. Then Peter does what is most natural. He goes to the house of John Mark's mother where the church is meeting and praying. But when he knocks on the door, the Christians inside do not believe he is there. Indeed, they tell the maid, Rhoda (Rose), that she is "mad." When he enters the house, however, they are all stunned (12:8-17). This story certainly reminds us of the weakness of Christian faith and the fact that we seldom expect God to do the miraculous.

Then, Luke adds a concluding detail to indicate that God effectively removes the persecutor from the scene by describing Agrippa's death as "eaten with worms"—a typical ancient designation for the justifiable suffering or death of someone who was regarded as evil and deserved a painful demise.[13]

With the conclusion of these stories of the early disciples in Israel, Luke shifts to narrate the fascinating episodes of what has become known as the first missionary journey. The journey begins with Barnabas and Saul/Paul, joined by John Mark, for their visit to Cyprus.

After ministering in Salamis, the team travels to Paphos, the Roman capital of Cyprus. Here they encounter the proconsul Sergius Paulus (a Roman senator) and his magician Elymus/Bar-Jesus who is undoubtedly bent on showing the proconsul his worth and on frustrating the testimonies of the missionaries. Paul recognizes his activity as inspired by the devil and confronts him directly as one who perverts the truth and is opposed to the work of the Lord. In this battle of wills, Elymus is no match for Paul, and God uses Paul to strike him with temporary blindness. The effect on the proconsul of what he witnesses is complete astonishment, and Luke suggests that his encounter leads the proconsul to believe the powerful teachings of the missionaries (13:4-12).

Shortly thereafter, the missionaries press on to Perga on the coast of Asia Minor where John Mark leaves them and returns home to Jerusalem. The reason for his departure is not clearly stated, but Paul's rehearsal of Israel's misunderstanding of God's purposes in the synagogue at Pisidian Antioch, coming soon after John's abandonment of the mission, together with Luke's reference to him by his Hebrew name "John" probably suggests that he may not yet have been prepared to cross boundaries in mission for the Living Jesus. He will learn to do so later—but probably not then. The proclamation of the missionaries in Antioch concerning forgiveness and freedom in Jesus, however, proves to be so attractive to the Jews and the proselytes that the Jewish leadership there becomes jealous. In their frustration and rage, these Jews promote unrest and persecution against the missionaries, forcing Barnabas and Paul to leave the area (13:38-50). As a sign of their treatment by those Jews, the missionaries shake the dust from their feet—a sign that they are returning their rejection to the heads of their opponents—and they depart (13:51).

The story of rejection continues. Paul and Barnabas move on to Iconium. But the situation is not much better there, and they are threatened with stoning by the Jews who incite the townspeople against them. Accordingly, they again are forced to leave and move on to Lystra (14:1-6). When they enter Lystra, Paul heals a cripple who has never walked and the people respond excitedly by hailing Barnabas as Zeus and Paul as Hermes—gods who have come down in human form. When the people try to offer thankful sacrifices to them, the missionaries immediately try to convince the people of their humanity (14:8-15). Unfortunately, the situation is soon interrupted by the arrival of Jews from both Antioch and Iconium. The accolades promptly cease as the Jews convince the people of Lystra that the missionaries are troublemakers. Thus, the same people who at first attempted to worship them as gods turn on them, stone Paul, and drag him out of the city, leaving him for dead. But when the believers later encircle him, he is rejuvenated and the next day he and Barnabas travel to Derbe where they complete their mission with little hindrance. After many become followers of Jesus there, the missionaries return to their home base in Syria via the same cities where they had been persecuted and rejected (14:19-22).

The Christian situation in Palestine, however, is not completely peaceful. When they are back in Judea, a major controversy comes to a head. Some Christians continue to dispute with Paul and Barnabas that the Gentile converts need to be circumcised and subject to the Jewish law. The missionaries are insistent that such a view is not the gospel, and so the Jerusalem Council (mentioned above) is called. At that meeting, Peter reminds the gathering of his earlier experience in Caesarea where he learned that the Holy Spirit makes no distinctions. Those in attendance also receive the stirring report concerning the recent mission.

Then James, the half-brother of Jesus and the chair of the meeting, declares on behalf of the assembly that the Gentiles will not need to become Jews in order to become Christians. But he adds that they should at least observe the Noachian rules/ethics,[14] namely that the Gentiles should avoid idolatry and immorality and eschew drinking blood and eating meat that has been strangled and that still contains the blood in it (15:20). To ensure that the message will be correctly understood, the council provides a written report of the decision, but (since it is an oral culture) they also send two representatives from the meeting to confirm the decision face to face with the recipients (15:27-28). Following the council's favorable deci-sion—which in fact supports Paul's earlier arguments in Galatians (see my discussion below)—and with the accompaniment of Justus and Silas (the council's envoys), Paul and Barnabas leave for Syrian Antioch, the place from which the first missionary journey had begun (15:30-35; see also 13:1-3).

The second missionary journey[15] begins with the intention to revisit the places on the first journey, but a sharp dispute arises between Paul and Barnabas over John Mark. Because of John's earlier abandonment of the mission, Paul refuses to have him on this subsequent journey. So they split. Barnabas takes his deviant nephew Mark and heads back to Cyprus (15:39) with the result that there is no further mention of Barnabas in the rest of Luke's account. But I pause here to note that Luke changes and uses instead of John's Hebrew name his Hellenistic name, Mark, knowing that the caring Barnabas is responsible for rescuing Mark (cf. Acts 15:37, 39). Moreover, Paul later writes that Mark was useful to him (cf. 2 Tim 4:11) and served as part of his company (cf. Col 4:10 and Phlm 24). Also, as I have already noted, Mark became a companion to Peter (see my comments in chapter 2 above; cf. 1 Pet 5:13). Disputes in the church can be difficult, but we need to thank God for caring rescuers like Barnabas. If disputes occur in our current Christian communities, we should also pray that they might end with positive results.

While Barnabas returns to minister in his home country of Cyprus with Mark, Paul heads back to his home territory of Asia Minor with Silas (Acts 15:41). Then in revisiting the Roman province of Galatia, Paul discovers the young man Timothy and invites him to join the mission (16:1-3). On this journey, Paul is led by a vision of God not to enter Bithynia (in Northern Turkey today) but to cross over into Macedonia. Thus, for Luke a new bridge is crossed as Paul carries the gospel to mainland Europe. The encounters that follow in this new phase of Paul's ministry are truly fascinating.

The important colonial city of Philippi is first on his agenda.[16] There Paul meets Lydia/the Lydian woman at the riverside and initiates the first Christian community in that area. But there also pagan divination meets the power of the Living Jesus when a possessed woman who serves her masters in a profitable business of prediction troubles Paul. In that face-off, Paul casts out the spirit from her in the name of Jesus. But that act means that the prediction business comes to a screeching halt. In response, Paul is seized, beaten with rods, and thrown into prison by the magistrates for practicing a new religion. The story of praying and singing in prison and the earthquake that follows, opening the doors of the prison and loosening his chains, has been told and retold countless times in churches across the globe as a reminder of Christ's presence with his people. When Paul and

Silas do not try to escape but stay in the prison, the jailer is so impressed that he takes the missionaries to his home, washes their wounds, and becomes a Christian.

But Paul, who is a Roman citizen, has been beaten summarily without a trial—a violation of Roman law. So Paul forces the magistrates to come to the prison and apologize (Acts 16:35-39). People have often asked me why Paul did this. Was he simply being petty? That answer is hardly correct. Instead, one should remember that the legal charge was practicing a new religion in a Roman colony. As a Roman citizen and a Christian, he had not violated Roman law. Paul knew that the charge would not stand up in the court, and he was obviously concerned to ensure that the future proclamation of the gospel there would be unhindered (cf. Acts 28:31).

It is important for readers to recognize that one of the important themes in Luke's writings is that Christians are not guilty of breaking the law. That is the reason why in the Gospel story of the crucifixion Luke emphasizes a different aspect of that story—namely, the centurion at the cross does *not* say that Jesus is the son of God (as in Mark and Matthew) but instead says, "Clearly this man was innocent!" (Luke 23:47). Similarly, the thief on the cross echoes a comparable thought when he says, "This man has done nothing wrong!" (23:41).

The next major point on Paul's agenda in Acts is the colonial city of Thessalonica, the Macedonian capital. Here again the missionaries run into hostility but this time it is incited by jealous Jews who are incensed that people are turning to the Christian Way. So, according to Luke, they stir up the city and then report that the uproar is due to the arrival of the Christians whom they credit with turning "the world upside down" (Acts 17:6). While such a charge could be regarded as a violation of the *pax Romana*, it is hardly caused by the missionaries. Instead, it is a Jewish ploy, and in times of unrest officials may not always look for the actual causes. Thus, when they cannot find the missionaries, they seize local Christians and charge them with sheltering people who claim to serve a king other than Caesar. That forces Paul to move on to Beroea (17:1-10). There the Jews seem more open-minded, but the situation does not remain stable for long because the Thessalonian Jews arrive and again stir up trouble. As a result, Paul is escorted out of the city for Athens (14:10-15).

In Athens, according to his pattern, Paul speaks about Jesus in the local synagogue but also addresses people in the agora/forum. Since freedom of dialogue especially in the market is a custom in Athens, Paul debates with the Stoic and Epicurean philosophers who frequent the porches (*stoa*) there. When these scholars hear him talking about "Jesus and the resurrection," they assume that he is introducing some new foreign deities[17] into the city, which demands investigation! So Paul is taken to the Areopagus (the meeting place of the council that in Roman times was also designated as Mars Hill). As articulated in Acts, Paul's address to the council is an exceedingly astute presentation because it avoids the pitfall that led to the earlier condemnation of Socrates, who was charged with atheism.

Instead of attacking their gods, Paul simply affirms their worship of an "unknown god" and then proclaims to them that Jesus is that unknown God (17:22-23). Then, undoubtedly looking up at the magnificent buildings on the acropolis, he pushes them to think beyond man-made temples and consider that God is indeed God of the whole earth and reflect on the fact that all humans are bound together and answerable to the risen Lord (17:24-31). The mention of the resurrection, however, is a hard pill for them to swallow because of the Greek belief in the immortality of the soul. They adjourn the session in some frustration, but it is clear by that time that Paul has already convinced at least one of the council members—a man named Dionysius—of his logic (17:32-34).[18]

But the small, academic city of Athens is not Paul's primary goal. His goal is the magnificent new city of Corinth, the capital of Achaia, which Julius Caesar ordered should be rebuilt in 44 BC after it had been devastated a hundred years earlier by Lucius Mummius because its people dared to rebel against Rome. In Corinth Paul meets fellow tentmakers Aquila and Priscilla, who had arrived from Rome because of the decree of Emperor Claudius that all Jews were required to leave since they were disturbing the tranquility of the city (18:1-2).[19] The three quickly become colleagues not only in tent-making but also in mission (cf. Rom 16:3). Among the early converts here is Crispus, the ruler of the synagogue. But most of the Jews refuse to entertain Paul's preaching and teaching, and when they throw insults at him, he shakes the dust from his clothes and ceases talking with them (18:6-8).

But having received directions from God to continue proclaiming in Corinth that Jesus is the answer to human rebellion, Paul and the missionaries obtain a place next to the synagogue where he speaks about Jesus for an additional eighteen months (18:9-11). Frustrated by the nearby presence and preaching of the Christians, the Jews and their new ruler of the synagogue, Sosthenes, bring charges before the proconsul Gallio against Paul and his colleagues. Their charges are basically that the missionaries are perverting worship in a Roman colony contrary to the law. But Gallio knows Roman law, and he interprets their complaint as merely a matter of personal preference. So, rather than hearing these charges, Gallio turns his back on the Jews and Sosthenes, who are then beaten before his *bema* (tribunal).[20]

With this visit to Corinth, Luke's fascinating account of the second missionary journey reaches its final stage and is quickly concluded by the return of the missionaries to Caesarea. Then they head to Jerusalem (the meaning of the expression "went up"[21]) and thereafter to Syrian Antioch (18:18-22).

The beginning of the third missionary journey is outlined briefly until Paul reaches Ephesus—the focal segment of this journey (19:1-40). Here, Luke informs us concerning the important catechizing of the Alexandrian preacher Apollos that took place under the tutelage of Priscilla and Aquila (18:24-28).[22] But Paul also takes on the task with about a dozen others who, like Apollos, know only the baptism of John (the Baptist) and have not heard about the Holy Spirit. When they are baptized in the name of Jesus, Paul lays his hands on them and they too receive the Holy Spirit and are empowered to proclaim Jesus (19:1-7).

The report that follows in Ephesus is, to say the least, both captivating and electric. As Paul spends three months dialoguing boldly with the Jews concerning Jesus, they stubbornly seek to counter everything he says. So again, he leaves the synagogue, moves to the hall of Tyrannus, and continues preaching and teaching for the next two years (19:8-10). His work is marked by many signs of miraculous healings and exorcisms. Some local exorcists, including the sons of Sceva, a priest, seek to use Paul's pattern of exorcism as a form of magical incantation and quickly learn that it is a huge mistake because the evil spirits seize them and send them running naked and traumatized. The result is that a sense of awe and fear settles on the city, so much so that former practitioners of the magical arts have a public burning of their items of incantation—valued at about fifty thousand pieces of silver.[23]

But another extraordinary episode here is seared into our Christian memories. It involves Demetrius and the silversmiths. Paul's preaching is so impressive that the silversmiths are convinced that it threatens their business of making silver images for the worship of the goddess Artemis/Diana. Fearing the economic impact of Paul's mission on their business and the sanctity of the temple (one of the Seven Ancient Wonders of the World), the silversmiths stir up the population of the city so that the people rush into the huge theater. Then they begin shouting, "Great is Artemis of the Ephesians" (19:28-29). The uproar lasts for several hours and naturally draws the attention of the Asiarchs (the town councilmen), who are concerned that the Romans headquartered in Pergamum at the time will not view their uprising positively.[24] The magistrate seeks to placate the crowd by asserting that the sacred stone that fell from heaven (undoubtedly a small meteorite used to form the head of the statue of the ancient Magna Mater—the mother goddess) is their security to the legitimacy of their goddess and the future of her temple.[25] Finally, he reminds them that the Christians are not guilty of breaking Roman peace, but he warns them that they will be held responsible and that such actions will not sit well with the proconsul (19:30-41).

With the conclusion of this event, the missionaries take leave of Ephesus and head for the Greek peninsula where Paul stays for about three months before intending to leave again for Syria by sea from Cenchrea (the seaport of Corinth). But since a plot by the Jews is discovered, he goes north through Macedonia and arrives at Troas from Philippi (20:1-6). In Troas Luke recounts another fascinating story involving a young man named Eutychus who is sitting in the window and goes soundly to sleep while Paul preaches for hours. The man falls three stories to his death but is miraculously revived by Paul, who then continues to talk until the time comes for his departure at dawn (20:7-12).

Then, for an unexplained reason, rather than joining his companions on the ship Paul travels across the peninsula on foot and meets his companions at the southern port of Assos. Why he did so remains a mystery, but it may relate to a personal desire for time to contemplate his forthcoming bondage. Or did he also reflect on the significance of that fabled region where ancient Troy was located? Was he thinking of the birthplace of Cleanthes, the renowned Stoic thinker, and the retreat center used by philosophers including Aristotle? Whatever may have been the reason, when he reaches Assos, Paul is ready to board the ship bound for Miletus and his historic farewell address to the Ephesian elders.

In that address Paul reviews the fact that he has been faithful in proclaiming Jesus and the gospel to them and that he is now bound by the Holy Spirit to return to Jerusalem, where he will suffer and be imprisoned. As he informs them that it will be the last time they will see him, he staunchly warns them that enemies of Jesus will try to weasel their way into the faith community and seek to destroy their fellowship (20:18-32). He also reminds them that he never sought to profit financially from them but paid for his own living because he wished to follow the model of Jesus that

"It is more blessed to give than to receive" (20:33-35). This address is one that every preacher, teacher, and witness of Christ should read and reread as he or she seeks to represent the living pattern of Jesus to others in this era of growing biblically illiteracy.

With these concluding words, Paul prays with them and, in the midst of tears, he boards the ship and departs for Syria. At Tyre and Caesarea, he is warned repeatedly that going to Jerusalem will mean imprisonment. But such information is not news to Paul, and he begs the messengers to desist from their warnings. Finally, they agree and respond, "The will of the Lord be done!" (21:1-14).

In Jerusalem Paul reports to James and the elders the incidents concerning his mission. They praise God for the report and they likewise respond with the news that thousands of Jews have also accepted Christ and become Christians. But they are greatly concerned because reports are circulating that Paul has been telling the Gentiles that they do not have to follow the law of Moses or circumcise their children (21:17-21).

In an effort to forestall trouble, the leadership proposes a strategy to convince the Jews of Paul's personal loyalty to the precepts of Israel. Paul honors their wishes by taking a vow, paying for the expenses of the purification for himself and several others who accompany him, but that plan is destined to fail (21:23-26). The reason is that Jews from Asia who had observed Paul in the temple raise a protest, seize him, and charge him with preaching against the law and the temple (21:28; cf. the charges against Stephen at 6:13) and with violating stone boundary in the temple, which warned any Gentile of death by crossing into the Court of the Jews. Although those Jews have seen Paul in the city with Trophimus, an Ephesian, Paul has not violated the decree as they suppose.

But in times of mob action, people seldom stop to inquire concerning the legitimacy of charges. Fortunately for Paul, the tribune who is in the tower of Antonio next door arrives on the scene immediately and rescues Paul from the bloodthirsty mob bent on killing him. The tribune immediately arrests and chains Paul, and then his guards start to carry Paul away (21:27-35). At that point Paul asks (in Greek) for permission to speak to the mob. After determining who Paul is and that he is not a rebel or an assassin, the Tribune grants him permission (21:36-40).

Paul's temple address (like Stephen's earlier address) is an example of how mobs listen to speeches for particular expressions or words that will electrify them. As Paul addresses them in Hebrew, the mob is silent until he reports that God has sent him to the Gentiles (22:21). From that point on, the crowd calls for his elimination. So the tribune brings him to the tower, where Paul is ordered to be examined by beating (a common practice among the Romans for prisoners other than Romans). At that point Paul raises the issue of his Roman citizenship, which completely changes the approach to Paul by the authorities (22:22-29). The next day Paul is brought by the Romans before the Sanhedrin in an effort to determine the reason for the Jewish hostility toward him (22:30),

Paul's address before the council once again must have been fascinating as he asserted his personal integrity. Ananias, the high priest and Sadducee, commands one of his assistants to strike Paul, which is met by Paul's sharp retort of calling Ananias a "white-washed wall" who acts outside the law. Those nearby respond by asking if that is the way Paul addresses the high priest, to which Paul replies that he did not recognize Ananias as such. That reply is intriguing and not necessarily an apology because Ananias is a "godfather figure" and not politically the high priest (he operates through his sons and in-laws and hardly lives like an authentic religious leader). He is known for both his luxuriousness and his ruthlessness.[26] The subsequent statement of Paul that "You shall not speak evil of your rulers," however, is a clear indication that Paul intends to live within the intentions of the law (23:1-5; cf. the mock trial of Jesus before the council at Luke 22:64).

Then, since Paul is well acquainted with the composition of the Sanhedrin, he uses the religious and philosophical differences between the Pharisees and Sadducees to claim his Pharisaic heritage concerning the resurrection, angels, and spiritual experiences. With this approach, he sets the council members to arguing among themselves. The Pharisees declare that he is innocent, a view the Sadducees would have vehemently opposed. Realizing that the argument could degenerate and has the potential for violence, the tribune removes Paul to the safety of the Antonio tower.

The situation continues to deteriorate, especially after the tribune learns of a plot to kill Paul in an ambush (23:12-22). He then does what for him is most logical. He assembles a huge force of two hundred soldiers, a similar number of spearmen, and seventy cavalrymen along with two centurions. Then, in the middle of the night with a letter of explanation, he dispatches them on a forced march to Antipatris beyond the mountains. From there the cavalry carries Paul to Caesarea and the governor (praefect/procurator), Felix (23:23-33).

Five days after Paul's arrival, Felix assembles the court and Ananias appears with his Roman judicial expert, Tertullus, who charges Paul with being a sectarian troublemaker and a desecrator of the temple (24:1-9).

Paul responds by indicating to Felix that he has been in Jerusalem for less than two weeks and he knows that Felix understands Jewish patterns of protest as well as the people called "Followers of the Way"—Jesus followers or Christians (whom the Jews regard as a cult or even a heretical sect). Moreover, Paul argues that Christians really worship the historic God of their forebears and that he certainly did not cause a riot. Felix adjourns the hearing, awaiting the presence and further report of the tribune from Jerusalem before deciding, but he gives Paul freedom to have visitors (24:10-22).

To make another point, Luke inserts a brief detail that Felix summons Paul to appear before him and his second wife, a Jew who is the sister of Herod Agrippa II, expecting to learn more about Jesus and his followers. But to the surprise of the governor, Paul focuses not merely on his case but also on justice and ethics—matters that clearly pertain to the personal life of the governor. Not ready to be critiqued about his morals, Felix dismisses Paul but seeks a bribe from him. When he receives none, Paul languishes in prison for two more years until Felix is replaced by the more respected Porcius Festus (24:24-25:1).

Soon after his arrival, Festus visits Jerusalem and quickly learns that the Jews seek to interrogate Paul back in Jerusalem. So Festus schedules a preliminary hearing in Caesarea in which Luke indicates that the Jews cannot substantiate any of their charges. Nevertheless, in an effort to placate the Jews, Festus proposes to try Paul's case in Jerusalem. But Paul knows that Festus realizes he is innocent and that the proposal is a Jewish ploy to eliminate him. As a Roman citizen, he appeals to Caesar, and since the appeal is legitimate, Festus responds, "To Caesar you will go!" (25:1-12).

At that point, Festus receives a state visit from King Agrippa II (a friend of Caesar) and Bernice, at which time Festus outlines the case including the fact that he does not have adequate charges concerning Paul except some superstition about Jesus, who is dead but is claimed to be alive. Agrippa's response is that he would like to hear the case. Festus is more than pleased to comply because he needs more information for the emperor (25:13-27).

At the assembly, Paul's response is in the form of a personal testimony concerning his transformation (26:2-23). Festus breaks into the speech, thinking Paul has become crazy. But Paul says that he has not lost his mind and addresses Agrippa as one who would believe his account. The reply of Agrippa is a classic one that has been repeated by many but unfortunately has often been poorly translated as "Almost you persuade me to be a Christian." Instead, it should be rendered as a question: "In a short time, do you think you can persuade me to be a Christian?" (26:28). The response of Paul is also a classic answer to such a dismissal: "I pray that not only you but everyone . . . might become [Christian] like me" (26:29). The verdict of Agrippa could be rendered as "not guilty" to the charges. But the appeal has been made; so to Caesar Paul will have to be sent (26:32).

The final journey in Luke's narrative of Acts is bursting with energy as the prisoner, Paul, virtually becomes the director of the episode. The commander of the entourage is a centurion named Julius, a member of the elite Augustan Regiment. The ship, which in today's terms was registered in the province of Asia, travels north from Caesarea to Sidon and then hugs the southern coast of modern Turkey because of the winter winds. When they arrive at Myra in Lycia, the centurion then engages an Egyptian ship that is headed for Italy (27:1-6). After weighing anchor, they pass Rhodes and enter the open sea. With great difficulty, they are able to sail to the south of Crete, finally stopping at the small port of Fair Havens.

Paul warns everyone that great danger lies ahead for the ship if they continue. But the centurion and the ship's captain pay little heed to Paul because they want to reach the larger port of Phoenix before stopping for the winter (27:9-12). So they set sail when the crew senses they have an acceptable breeze, but almost immediately a fierce northern wind—the ancients called it "*Eurakulo*"—strikes with devastating force and drives the ship in a southwesterly direction that could easily send them to the graveyard of ancient shipping on the deserted coast of North Africa. The crew does everything possible to secure and lighten the ship. Then, for many days during a storm-blackened sky, the ship is tossed and battered so that all hope seems lost (27:13-20). It is then that Paul reminds them of his warning. But he also seeks to calm their fears by informing them that an angel of the God "whom [he] served" has informed him that he will reach Rome and his scheduled trial before Caesar. Moreover, his God will graciously spare all who are traveling with him, although the ship will be lost on an island (27:21-26).

The rest of the story is almost incredible as the ship enters shallower waters and the sailors seek to escape in the lifeboats under the pretense of making the ship more secure. But Paul warns the centurion of their plans to escape, and the soldiers cut the ropes on the little boats. Then Paul advises everyone to take food lest they become too weak to survive. Moreover, demonstrating for these pagan sailors, soldiers, and his captors his confidence in God, he takes bread after the model of Jesus, thanks God for it, breaks it, and eats it.[27] So everyone gains confidence and eats. Then the crew lightens the ship and prepares to beach it, but it strikes a shoal, becomes wedged in the rocks, and begins to break apart. Reacting to the possibility that the prisoners could escape, the soldiers are ready to kill all of them. But the centurion intent on saving Paul prevents the slaughter so that everyone is able to reach shore either by swimming or clinging to parts of the ship (27:27-44).

The island where they land is Malta, and since the survivors are wet and cold, they build fires to warm themselves. In the process of gathering wood, a venomous viper bites Paul. As he shakes it off, the people of the island watch the event and assume that he will die. Since he escaped the wreck, they think that "the fates" must be proving Paul to be an exceedingly evil murderer. But when he does not die as they expect, they change their minds and judge him to be some kind of god. Then, as the islanders consider his incredible power, they bring their sick to Paul for healing. When the winds change, the islanders provide gifts and supplies to the company as they board another Egyptian ship and depart via Syracuse for Puteoli, the harbor near Naples. There they are met by Christians who welcome them, and, after a week's reprieve, Paul and his company take the Appian Way north for Rome, where he stays at his own expense but under guard (28:1-16).

In Rome he invites the local Jewish leaders to a meeting and explains his situation to them. Since they have no correspondence from Jerusalem concerning him, they agree to assemble and hear his report. Their response to his extended presentation concerning Jesus is at best mixed, and as they depart Paul evaluates their visit using the judgments of Isaiah that their eyes and ears are unable to understand the working of God in their midst (28:25-27). With those prophetic words as a foundation, Luke sums up Paul's story in Acts with his declaration that "the salvation of God would be sent to the Gentiles and they would accept it!" (28:28).

Luke concludes this exciting book with the fact that Paul continued to live in Rome for two years preaching and teaching about Jesus to those whom we might today designate as the biblically illiterate. But even though Paul was a prisoner and in chains, the final words in the book of Acts can accurately be rendered that his preaching and teaching concerning Jesus was "unhindered"—or "not chained."

Of course, many questions have since been asked about why such an exciting book ended in this way. Was Paul still alive when the book was written? Probably not. But Paul's living is not the point of the book. Why then did Luke leave the story unfinished? What was he trying to say by ending his fascinating book in this manner?

Here is the issue: an unfinished book needs to be finished. But who will finish it? The answer is you and I. We must live and write our sequel to Acts. We are called to witness, to teach, to heal, and to care for others in the power and Spirit of the Living Jesus! Will we do it? That is the question we must ask in our era of increasing biblical illiteracy. Humans may be weak and restricted in their opportunities to share the message and care for others in the name of Christ, but do not think for a moment that the Living Jesus Christ is bound or restricted! Jesus is alive and wants to use his followers to unchain the world.

How would I encapsulate this fascinating book? It is intended as a message for Christians to realize that effective communicating of Jesus does not depend on human ingenuity or power. It depends on Jesus Christ, who is alive and is *not* dead. This Living Jesus can continue to do the miraculous through us today. The question is, are we ready to be his transforming agents of renewal?

Questions for Reflection

- What stories in the book of Acts are the most gripping for you? Why? What about them gives you a sense of empowerment?
- Do you ever feel helpless in this era of increasing biblical illiteracy? When? Why? How can the dynamic of the Living Jesus be rekindled in our day? Is such a dynamic possible today? If so, what is the source? Would we recognize it? Would we try to turn it into some kind of church program?
- How does reading the book of Acts challenge you as a communicator of the gospel?
- How can you help others in your faith community discover the power of the Living Jesus today?

Notes

1. While we are not certain why Luke chose to address both his works (cf. Luke 1:3 and Acts 1:1) to Theophilus, it was a common practice in the Hellenistic world for authors to show their gratitude in this manner, much as we dedicate books today. It is also intriguing to speculate on how Theophilus received his name, which roughly means "lover of God" or "one loved by God." Was it a Christian name? The idea proposed by some that it was a designation for all the readers of these books is highly unlikely, although it may appeal to some as a way of communicating with readers.

2. The book of Acts and Christian tradition are clear that the author Luke intended for Luke-Acts to be treated as a united story about how Jesus both began and continued to work out divine purposes in the world (cf. Acts 1:1-4). Luke, the writer of both books, was a Gentile and companion of Paul. If the "we" sections of Acts (16:10-17; 20:5-17; 21:1-18; 27:1–28:16) reflect personal reminiscences of Luke and are not merely a stylistic pattern of describing sea voyages, as some have suggested, then Acts provides a testimony to their close relationship, a fact that is confirmed by the comments that Luke was a physician and a "beloved" companion of Paul (Col 4:14; Phlm 24; 2 Tim 4:11). While the setting for the writing of these works could have been in Syria or Achaia and dated prior to 70, I am of the opinion that they were probably written after the fall of Jerusalem. I find no reason to assume that Paul was still alive at the time of the writing of Acts simply because Paul is still alive in the story. But the issue remains unsettled.

3. For some helpful resources on Luke see Fred Craddock, *Luke* (Louisville: John Knox, 1990); R. Alan Culpepper, "The Gospel of Luke," *The New Interpreter's Bible*, vol. 9 (Nashville: Abingdon, 1995); David E. Garland and Clinton E Arnold, *Luke*, Zondervan Exegetical Commentary on the New Testament (Grand Rapids: Zondervan, 2011); Mikeal Parsons, *Luke: Storyteller, Interpreter, Evangelist* (Peabody MA: Hendrickson, 2007). See also Darrell L. Block, *Luke*, New International Version Application Commentary (Grand Rapids: Zondervan, 1996); Francis Bovon, *Luke the Theologian*, 2nd ed. (Waco TX: Baylor, 2006); Hans Conzelmann, *The Theology of St. Luke* (New York: Harper & Brothers, 1990); Joseph A. Fitzmyer, *The Gospel According to Luke I-IX and X-XXIV*, Anchor Bible (Garden City NY: Doubleday, 1981, 1985); Joel B. Green, *The Gospel of Luke*, The New International Commentary on the New Testament (Grand Rapids: Eerdmans, 1997); I. Howard Marshall, *The Gospel of Luke: A Commentary on the Greek Text* (Grand Rapids: Eerdmans, 1979).

4. The Year of Jubilee was to be announced and celebrated every fifty years (immediately after the seven times seven number of years) when debts were to be forgiven. It was to be a time of genuine redemption or emancipation of God's people (cf. Lev 23:39-55) and the opportunity for a new start (cf. 25:8-24). Whether a total Jubilee was ever really celebrated is a question because the rich and powerful were not generally prepared to return land and property they had obtained in transactions. As a result, Jubilee was spiritualized by most Jews and became more of an eschatological hope and a futuristic dream.

5. For some helpful resources on Acts see Joseph A. Fitzmyer, *The Acts of the Apostles*, Anchor Bible (Garden City NY: Doubleday, 1998); David W. Gill and Conrad Gempf, *The Book of Acts in Its First Century Setting: Greco-Roman Setting* (Grand Rapids: Eerdmans, 1994); Colin Hemer, *The Book of Acts in the Setting of Hellenistic History* (Tuebinen: Mohr/ Siebeck, 1989); Luke Timothy Johnson, *The Acts of the Apostles*, Sacra Pagina (Collegeville MN: Liturgical Press, 1992); Jerome H. Neyrey, ed., *The Social World of Luke-Acts: Models of Interpretation* (Peabody MA: Hendrickson, 1991); John B. Polhill, *Acts*, New American Commentary (Nashville: Broadman, 1991); Robert W. Wall, "The Acts of the Apostles," *New Interpreter's Bible*, vol. 10 (Nashville: Abingdon, 2002) 1–368; William H. Willimon, *Acts*, Interpretation (Louisville: John Knox, 1988); and C. H. Dodd, *The Apostolic Preaching and Its Development* (London: Hodder & Stoughton, 1936).

2. The summaries are at 1:11; 2:42 (with an expansion at 43-47); 5:41-42; then a preliminary summation at 6:7 followed by the next summation at 9:31; 12:24-25; 15:30-35; 16:5; 18:22-23 (with a transition at 24-28); 21:13-14; 23:11; 26:32; 28:28; and the concluding summary at 28:30-31.

3. My designation for each of these speeches is as follows: Peter's Pentecostal sermon (ch. 2), Peter's explanation after the healing of the lame man (ch. 3), Stephen's address (ch. 7), Peter's message to Cornelius (ch. 10), Paul's sermon at Antioch (ch. 13), Paul's Areopagus address in Athens (ch. 17), Paul's farewell address to the Ephesian elders at Miletus (ch. 20), Paul's temple address in Jerusalem (ch. 22), Paul's address before Agrippa II (ch. 26), and Paul's speech to the Jews in Rome (ch. 28).

4. See Gerald L. Borchert, *Jesus of Nazareth: Background, Witnesses, and Significance* (Macon GA: Mercer University, 2011) 233–35, 237–39.

5. By means of his distinction between *historisch* and *geschichlich* (fact and meaning), Rudolph Bultmann attempted to differentiate between an actual event and its theological significance. He did not deny that the disciples believed that Jesus rose from the dead but felt that such belief was merely the faith of the disciples. Therefore, he argued that the church's faith is based not on the reality of the resurrection but simply on the belief of those who believed in the resurrection. See his important essay "New Testament and Mythology," *Kerygma and Myth*, ed. Hans Werner Bartsch (New York: Harper & Brothers, 1961), especially at 37, 39, 41–42. He was followed to some extent by Norman Perrin, *The Resurrection According to Matthew, Mark, and Luke* (Philadelphia: Fortress, 1977) and by Reginald H. Fuller, *The Formation of the Resurrection Narratives* (Philadelphia: Fortress, 1980) who sought to begin the discussion by examining Paul's experience of the risen Jesus and then using that analysis to evaluate the Gospels and the non-canonical texts. The problem with that methodology is that Paul made no claim that his experience of the risen Jesus was identical to those of the earlier witnesses. Indeed, he even admitted that his experience was to be differentiated in terms of time and what such a difference would mean. For my further discussion on the subject see Gerald Borchert, "The Resurrection: 1 Corinthians 15," *Review and Expositor* 80 (Summer 1983): 401–15. For further information see also the discussion in Grant R. Osborne, *The Resurrection Narratives: A Redactional Study* (Grand Rapids: Baker, 1984).

6. The Greek word *parestesen* at Acts 1:3 can be translated as "presented," but it carries the idea of a clear reality or proof.

7. The number "forty" is a familiar biblical expression that basically means "many" although for Western mindsets it is pointless to argue that it is not an exact number.

8. I use the concept of "unhindered" here because the book of Acts ends with that concept. God loosens chains and restricting bonds so that the gospel can be communicated freely in the world.

9. Notice that while the Jews had ceased using the name of YHWH because of their fear of God's judgment, they may have refused to dignify the cause of Jesus by ceasing to use his name. But the reality is that the disciples were bringing a serious charge on the Sanhedrin that was tantamount to a condemnation.

10. For a helpful introduction to the Samaritans, please see, for example, R. T. Anderson, "Samaritans," in *The International Bible Encyclopedia*, rev. ed. (Grand Rapids MI: Eerdmans, 1988) IV:303–308.

11. Paul is clear on the issue that there is no distinction with God between the Jew and the Gentile. See for example his arguments in Romans 1:16-17; 2:9-11; 3:9, 21-24, 27-31; and 4:16-17.

12. I pause here briefly to note that there are a number of different views of baptism as the symbol and sign of membership in the Christian community. While some Christians speak of baptism as a means of grace, it is crucial to remember that grace and faith are not to be treated as things that can be exchanged but are intricately woven together in the relationship between God and humans. As humans walk with God (the Hebrew *halak* is significant here), God provides them with a living sense of their acceptability and their access to the divine presence. In this way, mere humans are blessed with the assuring sense that they are living within the loving and saving oversight of God.

13. Josephus Flavius, *Antiquities*, XVII.5 details the horrible physical condition of Agrippa's grandfather, Herod the Great, the murderer of many of his family members and anyone whom he suspected of treachery. Josephus indicated that among the long list of diseased problems that Herod suffered, he lay in his bed in pain and smelly liquid collected at his feet, his genitals were "putrefied," and he was infected with "worms." Furthermore, Josephus concluded that Herod's condition was "God's judgment upon him for his sins."

14. The Jewish concept of Noachian ethics/laws within their legal logic argued that people from all nations of the earth should at least know and obey God's fundamental moral precepts because all people are descended from Noah. Those fundamental precepts decreed that immorality and idolatry were both a violation of God's will. The concept of not ingesting blood grows out of the strict commandments from Moses in the Torah. Because life is in the blood and life belongs to God, anyone who eats blood is viewed as being cut off from the company of faith (Lev 17:10-14; cf. also Lev 1:17; 7:26-27; Deut 12:16). Gentiles often drank the blood of animals because of the beliefs that the strength of these animals was passed on to them. The condemnation of both immorality and idolatry is a repeated refrain in the New Testament (see for example Paul's instructions to "flee" them in 1 Cor 6:18 and 10:14 as well as the condemnations in Rev 2:14 and 2:20). For a helpful discussion on the Noachian commandments, see W. D. Davies, *Paul and Rabbinic Judaism* (London: S. P. C. K., 1948 and other editions) 114–19.

15. For further information on the cities of Greece and Western Anatolia (Turkey), please see my work, Gerald L. Borchert, *In the Footsteps of Paul and John*, vol. 2 of The Lands of the Bible (Cleveland TN: Mossy Creek/Parson's Porch, 2012). See also Clyde E. Fant and Mitchell G. Reddish, *A Guide to Biblical Sites in Greece and Turkey* (Oxford: Oxford University Press, 2003).

16. For my article on this important site see G. L. Borchert, "Philippi," in *The International Standard Bible Encyclopedia*, rev. ed. (Grand Rapids MI: Eerdmans, 1986) III.834–36.

17. Note that the names in Greek for "Jesus" and "resurrection" are masculine and feminine, and the Greeks often deified ideas as well people.

18. I would pause here to take issue with the well-known critique of Philipp Vielhauer—"On the 'Paulinism' of Acts," trans. Wm. C. Robinson, Jr., and Victor P. Furnish in Wayne A. Meeks, *The Writings of St. Paul* (New York: W. W. Norton, 1972) 166–75; first printed in *Evangelische Theologie* 10 (1950–51): 1–15—in which he sees a totally different theology in this speech and the theology of Paul's letters because his basic sources of Paul's theology are too restrictive.

19. See Seutonius, *Divius Claudius* 24.4.

20. For some added insights into Crispus and Sosthenes, see my further discussion on 1 Corinthians 1:1, 14 (below).

21. The expression "went up" in the minds of the Jews would refer to Jerusalem, the city of God. While it is true that Jerusalem is in a mountainous region and regarded as geographically "up," it was also for them a spiritual designation. See for example Psalm 122.

22. Because Apollos is here (Acts 18:24) identified as both an eloquent preacher and an Alexandrian Jew, some scholars have argued that he was probably the writer of the book of Hebrews, a book that is not written in the typical Koine Greek of the rest of the New Testament. It is written instead in a neo-classical Greek, known in Alexandria. The argument is plausible, but as I have indicated in my discussion on Hebrews (above), the idea is still speculative. If we knew more about Apollos and if he was from a priestly clan (which I think may be suggested by the content of Hebrews), then we might be able to make a firmer decision. What we do sense is that in the minds of some Corinthians, Apollos may have been a more captivating speaker than Paul—a fact that may have caused them to compare him to Paul in their divisiveness (cf. 1 Cor 1:12 and 3:5). This party spirit among the Corinthians may have been one reason for the hesitation of Apollos in not wanting to return to Corinth (cf. 1 Cor 16:12).

23. While we are not sure of what kind of coins or their rate of exchange in today's market, the value would have been an impressive fortune.

24. Ephesus was a great independent colonial city in the Roman province of Asia. Some scholars argue that by the time of Paul, the Romans had moved the capital of the province of Asia from Pergamum to Ephesus, but that transition took place later so that by the time John wrote the book of Revelation, the transfer had occurred. For more on Ephesus please see my encyclopedia article, G. L. Borchert, "Ephesus," in *The International Standard Bible Encyclopedia*, rev. ed. (Grand Rapids MI: Eerdmans, 1982) II.115–17.

25. It is evident that the Temple of Artemis did not retain its important role as the most sacrosanct worship center and banking institution in western Anatolia. Only one pillar stands today as a stark reminder of where one of the wonders of the ancient world once stood. The stones of the grand temple were scavenged by many people, but they were primarily used in the building of the Basilica of St. John in Ephesus and in the Hagia Sophia Cathedral in Constantinople/Istanbul built by Constantius, the son of Constantine, in AD 360, then replaced by Theodosius II and finally completely reconstructed to become the most impressive structure of its time by Justinian in AD 537.

26. For some further information on this misanthropic priest see Josephus Flavius, *Antiquities* XX.213–14 and *Jewish War* II.440–442.

27. Of course, Luke would hardly have missed the important worship implications of Paul's actions at the meal as he was marking the celebration of the Lord's Supper and the presence of Christ in his own life.

Chapter 5

The Portraits of Jesus the Christ in the Epistles of Paul

FAITH at the beginning is a fearful thing

If Protestants had a patron saint, it would undoubtedly have to be the Apostle Paul.[1] There is no question that Paul was an amazing person. Indeed, I have frequently told my students that when I was doing my doctoral work at Princeton, Ashley Montague, a well-known agnostic, was invited to dialogue with the members of our New Testament seminar. In that class Montague asserted forthrightly that even though he was not committed to all of Paul's perspectives, he was convinced that Paul was as great a thinker as Plato or Aristotle. There is no doubt in my mind that this agnostic was correct on Paul's brilliance, but it is not my goal here to discuss Montague's views. My goal is to help you sense why I believe that Paul's vision of Jesus made such an indelible impact on his thinking and his work as a model follower of the Lord.

I believe it is crucial for Christians today to appreciate the fact that almost at the beginning of Christian history, God foresaw the need to call into the service of Christ a focused and gifted person like Paul. This Paul was well versed in cross-cultural patterns of thinking that greatly helped the church formulate the strategic implications in the coming of the unique person we call Jesus Christ.

Many Christians know that Paul's Epistle to Romans is a major theological treatise, and some may be aware of the so-called "Roman Road"— a summary of selected verses that outline some aspects concerning the doctrine of salvation in Romans. And even if they have not heard of that summary, they may be familiar with a few verses like Romans 3:23 and 6:23. These verses point to the universality of sin (humanity "falling short" of God's will) and the fact that "eternal life" is a free gift of God that has been made available through Jesus. These verses are indeed an important introduction to reflecting on Pauline thinking. But Paul's understanding of what Christ has done for humanity goes much deeper.

In addition, if Christians have attended church or Sunday school for some time, they probably are aware that Paul was radically transformed from a zealous Jewish persecutor of Christians ("followers of the Way") into a fervent missionary of the same Jesus these Christians had been proclaiming. Indeed, many contemporary Christians may tell you that after meeting Jesus on the road to Damascus, the transformation was so radical that Paul's name was changed from Saul to Paul. They unfortunately do not realize that most Hellenistic Jews of economic standing at the time gave their children both a Jewish (Hebrew) name like Saul and a Hellenistic (Greek or Latin) name like Paul so that they could function well in their cross-cultural environment.[2]

Moreover, whether Christians realize it or not, in his "first" book—Galatians—this zealous Paul indicates that he is more than willing to take on anyone including the earliest followers of Jesus (Gal 2:9) in order that the gospel of Jesus will not be adulterated. Paul's clear goal is both to safeguard the meaning of the crucifixion and resurrection of Jesus and to articulate with integrity the core significance of what Jesus, the Christ, did for humanity in a world-class, logical manner (cf. Gal 2:1-21). Galatians is so crucial to the correct understanding of Christianity that when the editors of the Cornerstone Commentary (developed for the New Living Translation) asked me what commentary I would like to write, I hesitated not one minute and answered "Galatians!" You may better understand my reasoning as you follow my discussion below.

In the context of Paul's commitment to Jesus and in response to the powerful saving impact the death and resurrection of Christ made on his own life, we discover the internal strength of this man called Paul. He was able to endure an almost incredible barrage of sufferings, the list of which almost baffles the mind (see 2 Cor 11:23-33).

With these thoughts in mind we must ask, for Paul, who was this Jesus? The answer is multi-dimensional. Jesus is the unquestioned "Son" of God according to Galatians (cf. Gal 1:16 and 4:6). He is likewise, according to Romans, the promised "Messiah" from the royal line of David (cf. Rom

1:3) and God's new model for humanity—the second Adam (cf. 5:12-21 and 1 Cor 15:20-25). But he is much more because he is also the image of the invisible God and the firstborn of all creation according to Colossians 1:15. And thankfully, according to Philippians 2:5-11, he—as the divine servant—is the one who humbled himself and died on the gruesome cross for humanity. As a result, every person in all of creation will ultimately bow and acknowledge that this "titan" Jesus is the "Lord" (*kyrios*) to the glory of God! To follow the heroic Paul and witness with him to the reconciling Christ (2 Cor 5:19) whom he proclaimed as Lord (2 Cor 4:5) is both an immense task and a rewarding duty for any person called to communicate God's word to people today, especially to those who may be unfamiliar with the Bible.

Paul's First[3] Letter: His Bombshell to the Galatians[4]

The gospel was at stake! Christian freedom was at stake! And even though Paul had not written anything that survived before this bombastic document, Galatians is one of the most crucial writings in the history of Christianity.[5] Of all the books in the Bible, Martin Luther knew the importance of Galatians, and he called this book his "Katerina" after his wife, Katerina von Bora. If Paul had not written any other book, the Christian church would still stand in his debt for this God-inspired work.

Galatians is a bold confrontation with slippery thinking and confused living concerning the coming of Jesus. Moreover, this letter is obviously intended to dismantle any attempt at adding human effort or status as a basic ingredient to the divine gift of salvation in Jesus Christ. I repeat, the gospel concerning salvation in Jesus is nothing less than God's free gift to a sinful and rebellious world. Therefore, Paul will challenge anyone (even an angelic visitor from heaven) who dares to alter such a perspective. Indeed, he declares a twofold indelible curse (*anathema*) on anyone who advocates an adulteration of the gospel (Gal 1:7-8).

Furthermore, Paul is fierce in his claim that his understanding of the good news in Jesus did not originate with mere human logic or tradition but came directly by revelation from God (1:11-21). Because of this firm conviction with respect to his divine appointment and his understanding of the meaning of the gospel, the Greek text pictures him as standing nose to nose in confrontation with Peter's misunderstanding (2:11). Paul is adamant in opposing human patterns for gaining access and acceptability with God apart from the grace of God in Christ Jesus. He is ready to take a stand against anyone—including the entire so-called hierarchy of the

Jerusalem church—if they dare to deviate from the universal understanding of sin and the universal invitation to salvation that comes from the cruci-fied-risen Christ (2:8-10, 12-21).

With this clear conviction of his authentic message articulated in the first two chapters, Paul turns his keen academic mind to demolish the spurious views of his Galatian opponents in chapter 3. He first categorizes as utterly stupid the Gentile attempt to add law and its outward sign of circumcision to the free gift of salvation, which was given by Jesus. Then he takes on their whole understanding of the law and clarifies at least four important issues: (a) the giving of the law was a temporary solution to the problem of sin; (b) the law came much later than God's great intention to redeem the world; (c) the law is now basically passé; and (d) the law is powerless to provide the salvation that the Galatians are seeking (3:1-14).

But it is crucial to recognize that Paul is not opposed to the law, nor does he consider it to be negative (cf. Rom 7:7-12). He is opposed to using law (or any human effort by sinful humans) as a means of gaining a saving status with God. Instead, the function of the law serves to indicate God's expectations for humanity, and failure in even one part of the law means failure of the whole law (3:11). Throughout both Galatians and Romans, Paul stresses that obedience to the law or rules does not mean that a person can thereby gain acceptance with God. Acceptance comes only through divine graciousness in Christ. It is true that law is an aspect of God's graciousness, but in God's great story of bringing wholeness to humanity, the law is God's way of helping humans recognize that God has standards for living (3:21-22; cf. Rom 3:19-20, 28-31). It is, therefore, imperative for humans to understand the difference between God's standards and God's acceptance.

The law then is a pattern of living that God has mapped out for humans to help them understand the nature and universality of human disobe-dience. What God wanted was for humans to walk (*halak*) with him in obedience like Enoch and Abraham. God wanted humans to be obedient companions. But as I have repeatedly argued and noted in chapter 1 of this book, humans turned the response of walking (*halak*) with God into a set of prescriptive rules (*halakah*). Indeed, the rabbis identified what they considered to be 613 such prescriptions in the Torah (the Law/Pentateuch) and then debated their meanings and their relative levels of significance.[6] These prescriptions and the way they were interpreted greatly disturbed Jesus (see for example Matt 12:9-12; 15:1-15; 23:16-26). Humans consis-tently substitute a relationship with God for a set of rules—and then they weigh the level of seriousness of each rule. It is a common pattern of mortals who attempt to control their "god" and their "destiny" through such religious thinking.

When Paul was confronted by the living Jesus on the way to Damascus (1:15-17; cf. Acts 9:1-19), however, his entire life was transformed and he came to recognize the exciting reality of truly walking (*halak*) with God! Therefore, as you read the epistles of Paul pay particular attention to how often he uses the holistic idea of "walking," that is, "living" or "conducting" one's life with God and the Spirit. In Galatians, Paul reaches his major exhortation by challenging his readers to "Walk by the Spirit" and reject the way of the flesh—the way of making the self the center of one's life (Gal 5:16).

Notice then what the role of the law was meant to be. The law was to be understood as kind of a substitute companion-custodian-instructor (*paidagogos*) to help humans understand their need for the Savior who was to come (3:23-24). But now that Christ has come, there is no longer a need for this old companion because people have a new companion if they truly belong to Christ. It is pointless to think about adding law and circumcision to life with God when one is baptized into Christ (3:27). It is also pointless to make such human distinctions as race, economic status, or differences between males and females because everyone is equal in Christ Jesus (3:28). Moreover, Christians are now, through Christ, legitimate heirs to God's promised inheritance through Abraham (3:29). What is more, in Christ we have been given access through prayer to God as our heavenly "Father" (4:6). Then, to make sure humans understand that this access to God as Father is without distinction for all Christians, Paul uses both the Aramaic and Greek words for "Father" (*abba, ho pater*). When one is interpreting Galatians, reaching clarity on this issue is crucial. Paul means that *in Christ* there should no longer be such human distinctions.

Have most people in the world and even in the church grasped the immense significance of Paul's message? Probably not! I would reiterate what I tell my students: humans will have either *rules* or *the Ruler!* Which will it be for us who seek to live in this era when people know less and less about the Bible? Will we choose to fall back into the slavery of rules and distinctions, or will we help others discover the freedom—the universal liberty—that is in Christ Jesus?

Paul thunders his own answer to these questions when he writes, "For freedom Christ has set us free" (Gal 5:1)! Then, to make sure the Galatians understand his point, he warns them severely that returning to the slavery of law and rules is falling from grace (5:4). And, like a skillful rhetorician, he closes the noose on his opponents by adding that those advocates who seek to reintroduce the law and circumcision should castrate themselves (5:12). His words may seem harsh to us, but Paul is not playing games with the gospel or with their salvation.

To make sure, however, that they understood that his goal is *not* to harm or minimize their experience with Jesus, he reasserts his call to freedom and authentic living. Yet he carefully admonishes them not to use their freedom as an opportunity for self-serving purposes. Their mission in life is to love other people and accept their vocations as servants of Christ (5:13-15). In order to accomplish this divinely ordained mission, they will need to "walk" with Christ/the Spirit (5:16). Doing so will take the place of rules and prevent them from following the disobedient patterns of humanity (the flesh; 5:19-21). Moreover, walking with the Spirit will produce in them fruitful lives that will reflect the attributes and ways of God without the need for the bondage of rules or law (5:22-24).

Having begun this message in a bombastic manner, Paul does not close his letter in the same tone. Instead, he exhorts the Galatians to live and walk by the Spirit of God (5:25) and to care for the "household of faith" (6:10). Following this pattern is for him clear evidence that the new creation is already becoming present in them and that the "God-given pattern" intended for Israel and for followers of Christ is being achieved (6:15-16).

Understanding and sharing this message with others is a remarkable invitation to enter the sanctuary or heart of Pauline thought. In this letter, one can touch a fervency of commitment to Jesus and the gospel that is lacking in much of contemporary lukewarm Christianity. For those who are among the growing number of the biblically illiterate, this message will supply an exciting sense of what authentic belief in Jesus means. For the Christian reading this book, welcome to the reality of the Living Jesus and to a powerful taste of the gospel—the most vibrant message in the world!

Questions for Reflection

• How well do Christians understand the portrait of Jesus Paul was painting? What was Paul saying to the Galatians? In what ways are we communicating this powerful message to others? How might we be charged with promoting rules and laws rather than freedom?

• How does "walking" with Jesus Christ and the Spirit make a difference in your life? How are you communicating that difference?

• How have we been promoting or eliminating distinctions among people? If you have been following the pattern Paul has advocated, how have others responded? If you have focused too much on distinctions, what can you do to change your pattern of living and communicating?

Baptism and the Pinnacle of Pauline Christology: Paul's Letter to the Colossians[7]

How would you like to send a letter of Christian advice to a church you have never visited? What would you say to strangers about Jesus and faith? Where would you start and what would you emphasize? This situation confronted Paul[8] as he began to think about writing to the Colossians (and by the way to the Romans as well). The style Paul uses in addressing the Colossian church has resulted in a profound document that is masterfully developed. It unites a brief but thorough articulation of the significance of who Jesus is with a critique of several religious and philosophical approaches to gaining meaning in life. These analyses are framed in a rather unique sermonic form on the significance and implications of Christian baptism. There is little doubt that the writer was simply brilliant in the construction of this epistle.

Before I turn to discuss the content of Colossians, however, several matters need to be understood concerning the nature of Paul's writings because they impact the way we read and communicate the messages of the New Testament. Understanding these matters is important for interpretation.

To state that Paul had not visited the churches in the tri-cities of the beautiful Lycus Valley—namely, Laodicea, Hierapolis, and Colossae—does not mean he had no knowledge of the Christians there. Obviously he must have known Epaphras, the apparent founder of the church in Colossae (4:12; cf. Phlm 23), and perhaps he had met Nympha in whose house the Colossian church was meeting (Col 4:15). But the crucial fact is that Onesimus, the runaway slave whom Paul led to Christ, came from that area. Following his conversion, the slave (whose name means "useful") had won his way into Paul's heart and become useful to Paul during his imprisonment (Phlm 11). In talking about his past lack of faithfulness to his owner, Onesimus must have shared a good deal concerning his homeland so that through these contacts Paul would have sensed that he understood their situation fairly well. In addition, even though Paul would have wished to retain the assistance of Onesimus (v. 13), he recognized his duty was to return the slave to his master. In doing so, however, he instructed Philemon to treat Onesimus no longer like a slave but as a "brother" in the Lord (v. 16).

Some people in recent years have wondered why Paul did not protest more vehemently against the institution of slavery (e.g., 1 Cor 7:21-24). But such a stand is a contemporary way of thinking. It would have brought Paul into political conflict with the Romans. Paul was too wise a thinker to take such a political stand at that time. Yet Paul's call to treat a slave like a brother (cf. Phlm 16) meant that as a Christian, he envisaged the end of slavery. This statement reflects the same major theological commitment that is present in Galatians 3:28 (his earlier work) to the effect that Christians are "all one in Christ Jesus." So students of the New Testament should recognize that it is imperative to read beyond the mere words of a text and understand the historical and social contexts in which such a text was written.

The next matter concerns the nature of the letter-writing process in the ancient world. I would remind readers that penning missives like our New Testament books was a special skill in the time of Paul. Therefore, since letter writing was so highly valued, these documents were often circulated to others besides the recipients—for their instruction as well. Such is the case with Colossians (cf. Col 4:16). Paul's skill was with words, not the actual writing/penning of his letters, so he used amanuenses (secretaries) to prepare his manuscripts (cf. the note on Tertius in Rom 16:22). But in order to protect the integrity of his letters, Paul often added his identifying mark or greeting in his own larger handwriting, as he does in Colossians 4:18 (cf. Gal 6:11; 2 Thess 3:17).

Protecting the integrity of his messages (cf. 2 Thess 2:2) was crucial because Paul regarded his letters to be much more than mere friendly correspondence. He understood them to be extremely important messages—namely, instructions on behalf of God in Christ that were to be communicated to Christians and observed by them. While Paul may not have fully recognized at the time the ultimate significance these letters would play in the history of Christianity—as inspired canonical documents (the measure or standard of Christian faith and life)—he did believe that he was writing in the spirit of the risen Christ. Accordingly, he was serious that they were to be followed (cf., for example, his discussion at 1 Cor 7:8, 10, 12).

Remember that Paul was educated as a Jewish rabbi and understood the nature of treating biblical texts with the greatest of care so as not to make any changes. Indeed, because the communication pattern of his time was primarily oral, rabbinic teachers expected their students to memorize the texts of what we today call the Old Testament. And they were instructed to pass on orally to others both the biblical text and the teacher's interpretations *unaltered!* Such is the significance of the rabbinic combination of terms like "received" (*parelabon*) and "delivered" (*paredoka*) that is found at several places in Paul (see my comments below at 1 Cor 11:23; 15:3).

What is remarkable for our era is the fact that, although we have smartphones and Internet connections that offer vast amounts of knowledge, there are still an astounding number of people in our time who are unaware of the basic stories of the Bible. The early Christians realized they had a God-given duty to communicate the message of who Jesus is, what he did for humanity, and the incredible implications of his future coming or return. We are also called to this task. Without further delay, let me turn to Paul's letter addressed to the believers in Colossae.

As you are probably aware, Paul used a salvation-oriented, brief schematic triad of faith, hope, and love (found in 1 Cor 13:13; cf. Rom 5:1, 2, 5) to discuss various aspects of the Christian life. But did you know that the final word in that triad usually indicates the focus of the discussion? Thus, when the final word is "love," the emphasis of that book falls on living the authentic life. But readers should understand that at times the triad was used by Paul in a different way, following the more normal temporal order of faith, love, and hope. Such is the order found in 1 Thessalonians 1:4-5, and it reflects the usual order of the three stages of salvation—namely justification, sanctification, and glorification. As Paul indicates in the Thessalonian context, the normal order would be an initial "turning" away from patterns hostile to God (faith), then living for and "serving" God (love), and finally "waiting" expectantly for the return of Christ and our future destiny (hope; cf. 1 Thess 1:9-10).

In the Colossian letter Paul also uses the more normal order of faith, love, and hope (Col 1:4-5) because he wants his readers to sense the greatness of Jesus Christ as the eschatological reality of life. The Christian's hope of a future inheritance with the beloved Son of God in his kingdom is of crucial importance to him here (1:11-14). This statement thus provides Paul with the basis for introducing his most elevated confession concerning Jesus. The description of Jesus in Colossians 1:15-20 is one of the highest christological assertions in the New Testament—at least on a par with the prologue of John (1:1-5, 9-18) and the introduction to the sermon called Hebrews (1:1-4).

This christological hymn of Colossians is a magnificent portrait of Christ Jesus who is portrayed as being in the very image (*eikon*) of God, even though God is invisible (Col 1:15). Moreover, as the later creeds affirm, this early hymn already proclaims that Jesus is to be understood as the firstborn (*prototokos*) in all the created order, and by implication he was neither created nor made.[9] Instead of being created, Christ himself was personally involved in the creation of everything—which included not merely inanimate stuff but all mortals as well as all spiritual authorities and powers (1:15-16; cf. John 1:1-2). Therefore, Paul firmly asserts that all of creation not only belongs to him but also finds its rationale for existence and continuation in him (1:17). Accordingly, this Jesus the Christ is the supreme head of the church and the ultimate Lord of everything. For Paul, this supreme ranking of Christ reflects the immense significance and power of the resurrection (1:18). Just think about this picture of Jesus the Christ. Does it not send shivers up your spine?

The way Paul develops this hymn, however, draws our attention not only to creation but also to his basic concern for Christ's mission and for the church. The people of God are the ones who recognize that Christ is supreme, the unquestioned head of the church body, and the initiator of the faith community through the power of the resurrection. In spite of Christ's incredible power and standing, his goal was not self-serving but was to bring reconciliation and peace to all humanity—indeed all creation—through his sacrificial death. This reconciliation will ultimately be possible because the fullness or completeness (*pleroma*) of God resides in him (1:18-20; cf. Phil 2:4-11).

The sheer magnitude of this hymn is so awe-inspiring that it should cause everyone to pause and give thanks to God for the gift of Christ Jesus. But the implications are even more stunning because Paul's readers are immediately reminded that they do not deserve to be related to Christ. They, like all people, have been enemies of Christ (Col 1:21). Yet the loving God has made divine reconciliation possible not only for them but for all humanity. There is, however, an important proviso inherent in this great promise—namely, that in joining Christ's body (the church), humans with the help of God are expected to stand firm in their commitment to Christ and to his purposes. Then, to punctuate his personal seriousness concerning humanity's need for steadfastness and faithfulness as it relates to God's graciousness, Paul notes the significance of his own vocation as a minister (1:23). He does not take his calling lightly!

In this respect, it is significant to remember that even as he wrote these words, Paul was *not* a free person. He was a prisoner (4:18), enduring suffering. Nevertheless, he is able to rejoice (1:24; cf. Phil 1:18; 4:4; etc.) in sharing with the Colossians his wisdom and understanding of the transforming work of Christ. Such joy in the face of trauma is the result of nothing less than a deep understanding of the marvelous mystery of Christ. Paul therefore expects his words to be taken seriously, and he warns them, much like the preacher of Hebrews did, that his desire for everyone who bears the name of Christ is that they become mature in life (Col 1:28; cf. Heb 5:11-6:3).

With the magnificence of Christ as a background and their need for maturity as his rationale, Paul turns in chapter 2 to address the problem of false or inadequate perspectives for life. He is aware of the fact that he has not personally been in the Lycus Valley and has not ministered to the people in Colossae or Laodicea (Col 2:1). So he charges them to hold fast to Christ and not be led astray by people using fancy arguments and brilliant rhetoric to deceive them. Clever words are never the test of authentic faith (2:1-6).

Paul is familiar with the dangers and weaknesses of Greek philosophical thinking concerning their gods and their speculations about the elemental powers or spiritual forces in the universe. So he reminds them that in Christ the "full power" (*pleroma*) of God is present (2:8-10). They do not need any other power because after the death and resurrection of Jesus, those so-called "powers" were rendered powerless for those who live in Christ (2:15)!

Moreover, Paul trusts that the recipients of this letter will recognize that he, as a former Jewish rabbi, is aware of the illogical Judaizing attempts to convince the Gentiles of their need to be circumcised in order to be fully saved. Adding requirements to the free gift of God's marvelous salvation is for Paul a total misunderstanding of the gospel. Today, such attempts continue to be a threat to the authentic communication of the good news and must be continually resisted.

Instead, Paul wants his readers to realize that Jewish circumcision has for many simply become an external mark on the body that means very little (cf. Rom 2:25-29; 1 Cor 7:19). If the Colossian Christians understand Christian baptism correctly, they would recognize that they have been circumcised internally by God and do not need such external tattoos or human markings. Paul believes that they should already have experienced the existential reality of both Christ's death and his powerful resurrection in their baptism (2:11-13). For them, legalism and mere forms have been abolished by the cross (2:14). And as I suggest below, Christians today need to understand the great significance of their baptism and should be forewarned of some parallel dangers in the way we often regard our church forms and practices.

For Paul, ritualism was demonstrated by the coming of Jesus to be merely a shadow of reality. Therefore, ritualistic rules concerning eating and drinking certain foods and observing certain feast days are insignificant in the light of Christ (2:16-19). These forms have a semblance of human wisdom but are merely human standards and practices or pseudo-philo-sophical disciplines. They have little power by themselves to relate humans to God and the divine will (2:20-23)

Having thus introduced the subject of baptism in chapter 2, Paul uses that introduction to summon Christians to live for Christ in the power of their risen Lord. Baptism for Paul implies the "set of one's mind" (3:2). It involves one's will (whether one has been baptized as an adult or has reaffirmed one's earlier baptism as a child). Accepting and living out one's baptism is a key component of being a Christian. Baptism for Paul is not a passive acceptance of a past event in one's life. For him, baptism must be an active and ongoing reality in life. Otherwise, it has no eschatological (futuristic) significance.

It is interesting at this point to note that the early church's instruction book known as the *Didache* directs in chapter 7 that baptisms should take place in living or running water, symbolic of a living reality.[10] And here in Colossians it is imperative to watch how Paul uses the baptismal language of "putting off" or "putting away" as well as "putting on" to discuss Christian life patterns. As the candidates for baptism take off or shed old clothes and put on new clothing, they thereby portray a determined goal of living the new life. It symbolizes for Paul a determined path on the part of Christians to follow Christ by putting off the ways of the old life and putting on Christ and his model of new life (Col 3:1-17).

I would warn contemporary Christians who read this section not merely to scan these seventeen verses quickly as though they are a mere list of Hellenistic virtues and vices. Paul intends for these items to be taken seriously as a model of what Christians—those who have turned to Christ and been baptized into him—are to be like. Accordingly, they are instructed to eliminate from their lives everything that does not conform to life in Christ and to clothe themselves with characteristics that will make their lives resemble Christ.

Paul concludes these potent verses with the all-encompassing charge that in whatever words or actions one is engaged, everything should be done in the name or the nature of the Lord Jesus. When one recognizes that becoming Christ-like is the result of God at work in a person, one is duty-bound to give thanks to God through Christ for the amazing transformation of one's life (3:17).[11]

Paul moves to wrap up his instructions for the Lycus Valley followers of Jesus with a brief reflection concerning the Christian perspective on Hellenistic household codes—instructions that involve relationships between wives and husbands, children and fathers, slaves and masters (Col 3:18–4:1). It is crucial for contemporary Christians to recognize that all Christian relationships are to be understood as subject to the Lordship of Christ. Moreover, as indicated in 1 Peter, when one compares Christian codes with those common in the Hellenistic world of that time, one discovers that the Hellenistic codes were made by husbands, fathers, and slave-masters not for themselves but for their wives, children, and slaves. There were no codes or rules for the makers of the rules. But Christian codes are very different.

I suggest that every reader should peruse the more extended code in Ephesians 5:21–6:9. If one does, one should quickly discover the interesting feature in which the big stick falls on those who would normally make such codes. Note the following as examples: (1) Husbands must be willing to die for their wives (Eph 5:25). (2) Fathers are warned not to discourage their children and are responsible for their proper raising in the ways of the Lord (6:4). And (3) masters are forewarned not to threaten their slaves because they have a master in heaven who is impartial in evaluating the actions of people (6:9). One is also reminded of a similar code in 1 Peter (see above), where if Christian husbands do not treat their wives with honor, they will have problems in their prayers and therefore their lives with God will be greatly impaired (1 Pet 3:7). That text also reminds us of the fact that husbands and wives are joint heirs of Christ's grace—an echo of how Paul begins his extended code in Ephesians with a foundational collegial assertion that all Christians should be subject to one another out of reverence for Christ (Eph 5:22).

Paul concludes the brief but focused letter of Colossians in chapter 4 with a summons to pray not only for the people in their church and community but also for him. His concern is that he might continue to be faithful in declaring the mystery of Christ, even while he is in prison. He also calls them to be wise and gracious in their conduct so that their lives and witnessing might reflect a Christ-like authenticity. Then he closes this message with a personal commendation concerning Tychicus and Onesimus, who are delivering this letter, and he finishes with a few additional personal greetings and instructions.

The final words of Paul in this letter before his ending in "grace," however, should again draw our close attention because he asks them to "Remember my chains!" (4:18). We know he is in prison, but these words flash to us like a neon sign. The point is that this powerful letter was not written when Paul was free. He was a prisoner! At the time he was probably incarcerated in Rome, quite possibly in the time of the megalomaniac Nero.

Yet like the letter to the Philippians, there is not a shred of defeatism evident here. Paul has learned the strategic lesson that whatever might be the state of his mortal life, with Christ he can be content (cf. Phil 4:11). The reason is that Paul's mind and heart are focused on the greatness of Christ, and he uses his imprisonment as an opportunity to witness for his Lord. Thus, in this letter he instructs the Colossians to set their minds not on the things of this world (Col 3:2-4) but on the victorious Christ and to live in the power of the risen Lord.

What a model for Christians today! To study and teach this book can be a marvelous inspiration both for those who share its message and for those who receive its instructions.

Questions for Reflection
• How does the portrait of Christ in Colossians impact you as a Christian? What aspects do you find most powerful? What aspects do you think may speak most powerfully to those in our growing biblically illiterate generation? How did the portrait of Christ affect the way Paul directed his message to the Colossians?
• As you have reflected on the household codes in Colossians, Ephesians, and 1 Peter, how might understanding their origins make a difference in the perspectives of our faith communities?
• How is baptism viewed in your Christian fellowship? Could Paul's model of understanding have any implications among your family of faith? Explain.

With Paul's bell-weather words from Colossians in our minds, we turn now to review 1 Corinthians, Paul's most detailed set of instructions for dealing with concerns in that church—instructions that went on to affect many who were living the Christian life in his day and in ours.

A Dialogical and Extended Piece of Advice for Christian Living—Paul's First Letter to the Corinthians[12]

Have you ever wondered about how successful Paul was in his ministry and in writing his letters? Did people believe what he said or did he have problems convincing them to change their ways? If you are wondering, study the Corinthians correspondence a little more closely and you may have an answer. Perhaps you may be in for some surprises. One of those surprises may be finding that the problems of the Corinthians were not so different from those that are experienced in the twenty-first century, although they are certainly clothed in a different garb than they would be today.

Another of those surprises may be discovering how much contact Paul had with the Corinthians. Before I turn to this fascinating letter of 1 Corinthians and highlight how Paul sought to deal with the thorny issues of living an authentic Christian life, allow me to pause briefly and discuss his contacts with the Corinthians.[13]

As I have stated elsewhere, Paul probably began his evangelization of Corinth in AD 50 or 51when he also appeared before the *bema* (the judgment seat) of the Proconsul Gallio, a Roman Senator (cf. Acts 18:12-17).[14] Then, he wrote a letter (which has been lost) concerning immorality, idolatry, greed, and a few other matters (cf. 1 Cor 5:9-13). The Corinthians obviously also wrote to him about marriage and personal relations as discussed in chapter 7 of our 1 Corinthians (7:1).

Thereafter, Paul sent Timothy to them to outline his views more thoroughly (4:17), and he may even have dispatched our 1 Corinthians with his young colleague at that time. Paul also tried to get others like Apollos to visit them then but was unsuccessful (16:12). Sometime around AD 55 he made a painful visit to the Corinthians (2 Cor 2:1) and wrote a tearful letter that has also apparently been lost (2:4). Then, while traveling to Macedonia, he met Titus who had just been in Corinth and who brought him good news concerning that community of faith (2:12-13). In response, he penned at least chapters 1 to 9 of 2 Corinthians, which were full of joy and comfort. He apparently was also ready to dispatch Titus and a well-known preacher (Apollos?) with the letter so that the Christians would be reminded of their task of raising the money for the poor (8:16-24) (in Jerusalem?; cf. 1 Cor 16:1-4).

But for some unexplained reason, the tenor of 2 Corinthians changes in chapters 10 to 13, and Paul promises to come to them. But he also warns them that he will find out what is going on there (2 Cor 13:1-2). One wonders what happened. Did he receive bad news concerning their recent activities, or do these chapters belong to an earlier/later negative letter, as some scholars have suggested?[15] The answer remains foggy at best, but it is clear that Paul had his problems with the Corinthians. I have often said to my seminary students, "Pray that you do not get called to 'First Church of Corinth!' in whatever denomination you might be serving."

From the above brief description, one might naturally presume that 1 Corinthians would be filled with negative issues concerning Christian living and would be dialogical in nature. Yet after the usual type of Hellenistic epistolary introduction, Paul almost surprisingly gives thanks for them and their Christian pattern of life. His words suggest that they seem to be knowledgeable and endowed with spiritual giftedness (1 Cor 1:5-7). As such, one might also assume from this description that these recipients were mature Christians. But it becomes quickly evident that such is far from the truth, and the opposite is the reality because the reader is thrust almost immediately into a series of reports that have come to Paul concerning a web of frustrating relationships in Corinth. The Christians there seem to be like squabbling children who are filled with divisive attitudes and practices.

Indeed, members are claiming to follow various Christian leaders such as Paul, Apollos, and Peter, and some are even playing the one-upmanship game by claiming simply to follow Christ (1:12). One can sense exasperation in Paul when he asks, "Is Christ divided?" Do they not understand their unity with Christ in baptism? As one reads this chapter, one can sense that there seem to be obvious similarities between the Corinthian factionalism and some church squabbles and divisiveness in the twenty-first century. Church squabbles are not a recent phenomenon because people have not changed very much over the centuries.

Now, rather than detailing all the matters in this extended letter, let me attempt to highlight the important issues in this letter and comment briefly on Paul's view of Christ as a basis for relating our understanding of 1 Corinthians to our era of growing biblical illiteracy.

By opening 1 Corinthians with a discussion concerning divisiveness and the Corinthian self-centeredness, Paul reveals that they have a poor understanding of who Christ is and what the Lord has done for them. They may have been able to dialogue freely about some aspects of Christianity and consider themselves among the spiritually elite, but at heart they are self-oriented. Rather than discussing doctrinal issues (which they may think they understand) as he did in the letters to the Romans and Galatians, Paul focuses on his own lack of eloquence (which is frankly not the case). Then he settles on explaining the seeming foolishness of the Christian gospel. But into this discussion on foolishness he strategically inserts the crucial issue of power (1:17-18). In all their divisiveness they are settling for a human pseudo-idea of power and are missing the true source of personal power for living. Need I say anything more about how people miss the crucial issues of life—even today?

The Corinthians may think they understand Christ and the importance of his death and resurrection, but as you read this extended letter notice how many times Paul says something like, "I would not have you to be ignorant" or "Do you not know?" Paul, the genius, is being rather kind to them, yet at the same time his message has the bite of brilliant sarcasm. He knows how to challenge their inflated egos. But his goal is to help them recognize that the way of Jesus is very different from the way of the world.

Like many Greeks at the time who were syncretistic in thinking, the Corinthians attempted to unite Christ with the wide range of ideas in their egocentric, cross-cultural world. Paul understood their pattern and knew it would not work. So in his letter he reminds them that the Greeks seek wisdom and the Jews want powerful revelations from God like the plagues of Egypt. Thus, the message concerning Jesus seems to be "foolishness" (*moria*) to the Greeks, and a crucified savior seems to be a powerless death perspective to the sign-seeking Jews. The message of Jesus does not seem to make either logical or demonstrable sense (1:22-23). But the reason is because God will not fit into the teacups of human minds. Nor can God be accessed by computer chips of today. Human wisdom, knowledge, and skills are incapable of defining or encapsulating God's Son or his ways.

Accordingly, Paul is perfectly ready to admit that Christians are neither wise nor powerful by worldly standards. Yet such a reality should not bother them (unless of course they are self-centered). But he declares to them that God is able to use both the weak and the foolish to accomplish his purposes so that boasting by humans is effectively silenced (1:26-29). Because Paul clearly understands the reality of God, he does not try to promote his own brilliance in his presentation of the gospel. Instead, he wants his Corinthian children to recognize that the fantastic power of God has entered the world in Jesus (2:1-5). Paul, however, does not despise wisdom but understands that God's mysterious wisdom is beyond the capacity of the world to grasp. If humans recognized God's wisdom, they would never have crucified Christ (2:8).[16]

In order to help them recognize their problem, Paul turns to the issue of differences among people. He outlines that some are "spiritually" oriented (*pneumatikoi*), others are unspiritual (*pseuchikoi*), and still others are just carnal (*sarkinoi*). It is doubtful that Paul means for these categories to be eternally determinative, but he wants his Corinthian children to realize that some people are "unspiritual" and obviously not interested in the ways of God.[17] On the other hand, he recognizes that others are clearly sensitive to the leading of the Spirit. But there are still others like the Corinthians who seemingly want to be spiritual and yet are so caught up in the ways of the world (the flesh) that he categorizes them as carnal. The unspiritual of course need to be evangelized, but they are not his focus in this context. His concern is with the carnal ones—like the Corinthians—who are tied up with themselves, even though they claim to be Christians. They are not living in the Spirit, and that is the reason he reintroduces the issue of their divisions. Although he regards them as Christians, they are still "of the flesh" and do not have the mind of Christ (2:16; 3:3). In other words, they have not grown in their faith but are like babies still drinking the milk of the Christian message, not ingesting the solid food of the gospel (3:1-4).

For Paul, their divisiveness reveals that they do not understand the great story of God's dealings with humanity. They are focused on matters such as power, prestige, and wealth as well as the people they know and where they stand in society. It reminds me of real estate people who chant, "Location, location, location!" But Paul would have said, "No, no, no," and instead responded, "Foundation, foundation, foundation!"

Indeed, their foundation is exactly what he addresses next. He identifies himself like the architect (Gk., *architechton*) who is engaged in building them—his children in the faith—into a temple. He is convinced that he has laid the correct foundation, which is Christ. Others who come after him need to be conscious about the structure and the building materials they are using because what is built on the foundation will be tested by fire (3:10-17). Accordingly, he is troubled about their construction materials— evidenced in their boasting because it means that they understand neither God nor Christ (3:21-23). They are simply acting like big windbags (4:6).

Instead of such boasting, Paul pictures his role and those of the true apostles as "under-rowers" (*hyperetes*), the bottom-level slaves in a Roman galley who hardly have enough wind/air to breath while they work (4:1). In addition, the Corinthians are here portrayed like rich people and even like reigning kings (4:8) while the apostles are being treated like the final spec-tacles in the arena games—those killed for entertainment by wild beasts (4:9). So he appeals to them to copy him (4:16) and recognize that Chris-tian life is measured not by boastful talk but by divine power in one's life. Furthermore, he warns them that they need to realize that he can exercise the power of God in judgment (4:20-21).

Having laid this proper foundation of Christ for life, Paul turns to focus on some of their many problems. He chooses as his starting point what for him is virtually an intolerable situation—namely, a man is "shacking up" with his stepmother. In a permissive generation like today, some may not regard that situation to be the worst example of moral laxity, but in Paul's time it was abhorrent, even for the pagans (5:1). His response to their permissiveness is to castigate the church for their laxity and to commission them to "deliver the man to Satan" (excommunicate him).[18] Paul's goal is not mere punishment; his hope is that the man will realize the significance of his exclusion from the powerful presence of God surrounding him in the community and be led to repentance (5:3-5).

The force of this text can only mean that Paul must believe that God's amazing power resides through Christ in the community of faith! If there is a lack of such power in the church today, perhaps the reason is that the church does not take the powerful "presence" of Christ seriously. And maybe, like the Corinthian church, it is time to recognize that there may be too much "leaven" (*zume*) or compromising of the standards of God in the church (5:6-8). What do you think? Does the church live out of God's presence and exhibit the power of the Spirit in this generation? Is it focused on the wind of talk or on the dynamic of the divine Spirit?

The next issue Paul addresses involves the Corinthians' possessions and wealth and how they are using the law courts to assist them in obtaining rights and possessions. Great care must be exercised because a hasty reading of this pericope (passage) can lead contemporary Christians to reach a misunderstanding concerning law and the use of the courts. As a former lawyer, I have watched people cheat others out of their businesses and their inheritances by using the offices of the courts and other means. The focus here should not be put on the law courts *per se* but on why those agencies are being employed. Law can be used legitimately or illegitimately. The concern is this: are the courts being used today as a means for assisting people to accumulate wealth and possessions in unconscionable ways, or are the goals and means both responsible and Christ-like?

The stress of this Pauline text should be placed on the motives for using any human institution or authority. Paul does not want the Corinthians to make the accumulation of possessions and ownership rights their goal in life. Therefore, he advises them "Why not be ready to suffer injustice? Why not be willing to be cheated?" What he has discovered in Corinth must make him cringe because he finds Christians using the court system to cheat other Christians (6:7-8). It is clear to him that they have hardly understood the coming of the self-giving Christ. Do you see then how important Paul's living portrait of Christ is for his thinking?

Before going on, I must pause here for the sake of my readers to reflect briefly on Paul's tangential comment—namely, that Christians will judge the angels (6:3). This comment is clearly not the main focus of the text and should not be used for arguing about matters concerning the *eschaton* (the end of times). The reference here is a kind of rabbinic proof-text for illustrating Paul's perception that righteousness on earth has eternal ramifications—particularly in judgment. For Paul, Christians who have genuinely lived the model of Christ in the world are in fact the living bearers of God's standards. While they never become perfect on earth, their lives already serve as one of God's means for executing judgment now. Reflect on what that pattern suggests for the future.

Turning to 6:9-11, we come to a significant summary text (similar to Romans 1:29-32). In our contemporary world, this text has been the subject of considerable debate and controversy. Here Paul lists a number of activities from which he believes the Corinthians are delivered by Christ and he uses several transformational words—"washed," "sanctified," and "justified"—to emphasize this point (6:11). He also notes in this context that people who continue in those activities will be condemned and will be unable to "inherit the kingdom of God" (6:9)! When we scan the list of activities, it becomes immediately apparent why this text is a major problem for today's society.

Paul here both gives thanks for their deliverance and warns his Corinthian children not to engage in such practices because of the eternal consequences. The rejected activities include immorality and idolatry, which are often singled out in the New Testament as condemned (see 1 Cor 6:9, 18; 10:14; other examples are Acts 15:19-20 and Rev 2:14, 20). Then Paul adds stealing, drunkenness, and even greediness. We may be uncomfortable with his categories, but the discomfort reaches a hostile stage for some in our permissive generation when Paul also adds the activities of the two partners in a homosexual relationship (6:9). It is at this point that serious debates often ensue in our churches, leading to heated arguments, condemnations, and even church splits.

This issue will not be handled easily today because people often do not even desire to discuss it in a congenial manner or attempt to arrive at peaceful understandings. Undoubtedly like you, I have associates who are convinced that Paul and the ancients did not understand much about homosexuality—especially in light of modern research on the subject. It is hardly my goal in this brief statement to argue for or against the legitimacy or illegitimacy of Paul's view on homosexual intimacy. But I do want to point out that, as he writes, Paul obviously knows people who are involved in many of the practices in this list, including greed, and he indicates that they are able to overcome them through the power of the Lord Jesus and the work of the Spirit of God (6:11). What is important for all Christians to understand is that Paul believes that the power of God can deal with difficult issues in life.

I do not know what problems and concerns face you and your friends, but please remember that God is not helpless. Do not give up on God's power to transform and bring resolutions to difficult issues or to help Christians learn how to love one another. The early church was able to reach a resolution on the difficult issue of circumcision in Acts 15 (see above), although not all early Christians followed that agreement. The church has done so—at least in part—on other issues such as racial differences. Christians may be able to do so on the issue of homosexuality if we are willing to seek the wisdom of God and listen to honest research on transgender issues, but most of all if we can truly love those with whom we radically disagree. There are lessons we can still learn about the nature of humanity and the nature of the genetic ladder. The Living Jesus can walk with us through the fog of our mortality if we do not pretend to have all the answers neatly packaged in legalistic formulas.

I must add that over the years I have become more careful about judging others who have patterns in life that are different from mine. As children of God, we should be people who are concerned about those who need God's power by sharing with them both the forgiveness of God and the amazing grace of Christ without necessarily accepting their weaknesses or foibles. The creator is able to re-create—even me! Our task in the church is to model the gracious spirit of the one who called us to wholeness when we were helpless. May God help all of us never to forget that, except for the grace of God, we also would stand condemned.

Paul believes firmly in the grace of God, but he is quick to add that some Christians' actions and behaviors completely violate the graciousness of God. He turns next to one such situation. Instead of admitting the necessity of true morality in conduct, the Corinthians sought to excuse their actions by arguing that "all things are lawful." Paul challenges their logic by saying that such an argument does *not* make those things "appropriate," nor does it keep people from being enslaved when practicing them (6:12). Not to be silenced, however, the Corinthians apparently counter that "food was made for the stomach." But Paul knows where they are going with that line of argument—namely, changing stomachs to sexual organs (and food to sexual activity)—and his response is a blistering retort that God can destroy both the food and the body that is used inappropriately (6:13).

At this time, Corinth is undoubtedly one of the most permissive cities in the Roman Empire, but Paul is not about to promote either prostitution or reverence of Aphrodite and Dionysus with the free lifestyle patterns of their devotees. So he responds to their argument with the assertion that the body is meant to be the temple of the Holy Spirit, and linking it to a prostitute is a categorical sin from which one must "flee" (*pheugete*, 6:18; cf. 10:14). For Paul, as a Jewish rabbi, such activity is a violation of the basic precepts of the Noachim ethics. Therefore, since from his Jewish perspective everyone goes back to Noah, those ethical precepts apply to all people, including the Gentiles (6:14-19). To glorify God with one's body, therefore, is the responsibility of the Corinthian Christians (6:20). Paul's focus is clearly on living for Christ.

Having dealt with immorality, Paul turns in chapter 7 to answer a number of questions the Corinthians posed to him in their letter concerning husband/wife relations and issues about marriage. The details in this section are far too involved to handle in a brief overview of understanding and communicating Paul's portrait of Jesus to others. But permit me to outline some important perspectives from the masterful apostle.

The first issue may have arisen because a married partner returned from a spiritual experience where one spouse (let us say a husband) became convinced that it would be spiritually advantageous to forgo sexual relations with the other (7:1). Paul faces that idea head-on because he understands the inherent danger in that kind of spirituality. He reminds both parties that they do not own exclusive rights to their own bodies but that sexual relations are a legitimate part of marriage. Any exception to such a relationship should be made by mutual agreement and should be temporary because Paul recognizes that the devil can cause great problems in a celibate marriage (7:2-5). Do you see how Paul's portrait of the self-giving Jesus helps formulate his thinking here?

Paul does, however, express the wish that because of the pressures of life for Christians and his view that the end of time and the *parousia* (the presence or return of Jesus) is coming soon, people will no longer need relationships like marriage (7:7, 26-29 and 31-35). Yet he realizes that everyone has his or her own special gift (*charisma*) concerning marriage, as well as other matters (7:7). Paul understands that he is not God—the one who has gifted people in different ways. Even though he has his own opinions, he seeks to find the middle ground on this issue. He certainly does not decry marriage as inappropriate for Christians as some have done on the basis of this text.

The next matter concerns divorce and remarriage. Paul has drunk deeply of the loving spirit of the Old Testament and of Jesus and thus recognizes that marriage is intended to be for life and divorce is a tragedy. But he understands that some couples reach the place where marriage has failed and divorce takes place, so he does not make divorce into an unpardonable sin (as some later church committees may have done). Instead, he understands that men in Old Testament times ruled their homes in such a way that they simply could put their wives out of the house if they no longer found them acceptable. Wives were then forced to fend for themselves, which often drove them into desperate conditions such as prostitution merely to make a living. As a result, Moses made these men provide their former wives with a divorce document so that each man agreed he no longer had any rights to the woman. Accordingly, she was no longer "bound"; she was free—free to marry again! Paul uses the expression of "not bound" in this text when he says God has called us to peace (7:15).

Paul's goal is for Christians to marry only other Christians and to live in harmony. But he knows that even Christians are fallible and often do not follow the pattern God desires. (I have written more elsewhere about the issue of divorce and remarriage. If you are concerned about this topic, I would ask you to consult my statement on the church's historic misunderstanding of divorce and remarriage.[19])

Of course, other areas could be discussed here, and Christians should carefully consider them when it comes to the matter of marriage. For example, Christians who live in North America (where there are many churches) may be able to find other Christians to marry. But what about places where there are few churches and where young Christian women may outnumber young Christian men by 8 to 1 or more (as I have found

in some settings when teaching in Japan)? Such a situation is truly difficult, and theological answers may be easier to provide than real-life answers
that work. In this chapter Paul also comments on relationships where one
partner becomes a Christian and the other partner remains a pagan. His
advice is to remain married unless the non-Christian wants to be free of the
marriage. In that case, the person is "not bound" (7:10ff).

Life is often too complex for easy theological answers. But the general
rule in Paul is that one should seek to follow the God-given patterns for
life unless such is impossible, and then one should strive to live at peace
in the spirit of Christ. Many people want easy "either/or solutions" to life.
The master teacher, Paul, does not choose that route. For example, consider
Paul's advice in regard to the situation of circumcision and uncircumcision.
He argues that since circumcision is not a primary matter with Christ, if
possible one should stay the way one was when one became a Christian
(7:18-19). Likewise, Paul advises a slave to remember that slavery is not his
or her primary reality in life, even though it might seem so. But if the slave
can receive freedom, then he or she should do so (7:21). With these brief
remarks, I leave this extended discussion. Overall, Paul's perspective seems
irenic, and I believe it provides an excellent model for us today.

As we turn to chapter 8, Paul introduces his second encompassing
concern—idolatry. The Christians he addresses are faced with this problem
because in most parts of the Hellenistic world even the food they eat is often
offered to idols. Is such food contaminated so that Christians should not
eat it? Paul's answer is, "No, the food is not changed." But the Corinthians
use this argument to satisfy their desire to participate in activities dedicated
to idols. Watch how Paul leads his Corinthian children through the maze
of their societal relations. His argument is as follows: Of course knowledge
concerning idols is important, but love is more important. Of course there
is only one God, but not everyone understands that fact. Of course food
is just food and it will not really make a difference with God, but our
actions may still be destructive to others. Therefore, if eating certain food
leads to destructive consequences for others, then in accord with our vision
of Christ we should be models of caring for others and avoid destructive
modeling by not eating it (8:1-13). That argument provides a wholesome
perspective for evaluating most of our activities.

Paul then uses this argument to evaluate his own ministry in chapter 9.
He obviously recalls that the Corinthians debated about his leadership and
argued about who was the best source of divine authority: namely, people
like Peter, Apollos, or Paul (cf. 1:12-13). He reminds them through a series

of diatribe-like questions that he is their apostle from the Lord and that the Corinthians are the confirmation of his apostleship (9:1-2). Accordingly, there is no reason for him to defend himself and his right to be supported by them as their apostle. As in the case of any of the other apostles, their support of him is a biblical mandate (9:3-12). But he makes sure they realize he has not made use of his rights to financial support in proclaiming the gospel to them (9:12-14). Instead, he reaffirms his integrity in matters of personal finance and asserts the privilege to boast concerning not using these rights.

But having spoken of supporting himself, he even rejects his self-affirmation because he realizes that he is indebted to God in Christ. He has been given a divine commission to preach the gospel. Indeed, he is bound like a slave to win people to Christ (9:15-23). And he asserts that his calling is to witness to *all people* by using familiar language he also uses in Romans (cf. Rom 1:16; 2:9-11 and 3:29-30)—that God is not partial and makes no distinction between Jews and Greeks (Gentiles). In meeting his goal of winning all people (1 Cor 9:19-23), Paul is willing to do what is sometimes today called "crossing the bridges that separate people." His goal of evangelism determines the means Paul uses. But the means will never be unjust[20] or divorced from the style or pattern of Jesus. That is the reason he adds here an athletic illustration; he is unwilling to be disqualified in his God-given race of life and service (9:24-27).

Paul's mention of disqualification reminds him that his major concern here is idolatry, and that idea vividly brings to mind the failure of the Israelites in the desert. Using the theme of baptism, he recalls for his Corinthian children that the Israelites experienced a miraculous release from bondage and passed through the sea just like Christians experience new life in baptism. Moreover, the Israelites were fed by God's manna—just as Christians experience the blessing of the Lord's Supper—but they nevertheless died in the wilderness (10:1-5). Then Paul forcefully reminds them that Israel's idolatry in the wilderness (the golden calf, etc.) and the concurrent immorality along with the constant grumbling meant that most of those Israelites did *not* reach the promised land. And to make his point clear, Paul twice indicates to the Corinthians (10:6, 11) that this story provides warnings *not* to follow the ways of the Israelites and their failures. Paul clearly intends that the story of Israel's apostasy should serve as instruction for all Christians to understand the significance of such warnings and be prepared to meet God's standards (10:11).

But notice that along with this forceful warning, Paul also issues a word of great assurance to the effect that no temptation will come to a Christian without God providing a way to handle its power and escape its consequences (10:13). As I have indicated elsewhere, this Pauline example of both the warnings and the promises (or assuring texts) provides insight into the magnificent balance or tension that is present in the New Testament. Paul's message of the gospel is not one-sided! As Westerners, however, we find such a tension to be difficult to integrate into our thought processes. We like clear alternatives, but the Bible is more holistic and life-oriented than most of our thinking and theologizing.[21]

The above warnings serve as the basis for Paul's further advice to the Corinthians, whom he addresses "as sensible [or reasonable] people." His concern is that they should not miss the implications of what he has to say concerning their situation. So he issues his second firm call for them to "flee" (*pheugete*, 10:14) idolatry (cf. 6:18 for immorality). The issue involves their continual pattern of mixing the unmixable. It is unconscionable for them to think that they can attempt to eat such meat in an idolatrous sanctuary and then participate in the Lord's Supper. Such an action is trying to play with both demons and God, but God will not tolerate these patterns of behavior (10:15-22).

Yet Paul does not want them to think that such meat is somehow contaminated as a food product. It is permissible to eat such meat in the homes of their pagan neighbors. His concern is the meaning of eating such meat for their neighbors. If a neighbor regards the meat as a sacred "offering," then the issue becomes not the meat as food but the neighbor's conscience. In such a case, the Christian is advised not to eat the meat so that the neighbor will not gain the impression that the Christian is a syncretistic person who can worship more than one "god." Christians worship God in Christ! They should never willingly join together such disparate worship practices (10:23-30).[22] Their goal should be to exhibit in their actions the vision of Christ and bring glory to God. In doing so, they will be instruments of Christ by assisting other people, including their neighbors, in gaining salvation (10:31-32).

In concluding this section of the letter, Paul offers himself as a model for them to copy (11:1). Imitation (*mimites*) was a major theme among the philosophers of his day, and Paul was prepared to give himself as a model because his model was in fact Christ!

The next section on church order follows naturally because Paul commends the Corinthians for paying attention to the important instructions (traditions) he "delivered" to them (11:2).[23] In the first part, Paul wants them to follow decent order in their church meetings. The question here often focuses on the role of women in public worship. But great care must be used not to misread the text. The passage should not be used to forbid women from praying or preaching/prophesying in public. Such practices are patently assumed for both women and men! The issue is one of following acceptable dress codes for both men and women. Paul wants the church services of the Corinthians to be acceptable to the Greeks, who tend to be fussy. As I have often indicated in my teaching, the Greeks tended to be fussy when it came to dress codes as can be witnessed from their tombstones. The grieving family would be pictured as standing while the deceased would be sitting. If it was a woman, she would be portrayed with a veil. The Romans were not quite so particular as we have discovered when archaeologists found portrayals even of Caesar wearing a veil while worshiping in the temple of the Vestal Virgins.[24]

Paul is generally quite precise in his thinking, yet coming from the rabbinic background in which he was educated, he sometimes uses rabbinic theories that we find rather strange today. Such a theory undoubtedly provides the background to the reason he gives for why women should wear veils—namely in order to protect themselves from angels (11:10). This theory probably arose from an interpretation of Genesis 6:1-4, where the strange *Nephilim* (often translated as "giants") are regarded as the offspring of the sons of "God" (a general expression for superhuman beings) who apparently pounced on women and forced them to have sexual relations. You may not accept Paul's rationale here, but remember that his argument was fairly common rabbinic logic and his goal was to maintain acceptable order in the church (11:13-16).[25]

The second part of this section concerns order in the celebration of the Lord's Supper. The Corinthians are using "the Supper" to highlight their differences by not waiting for each other and by getting drunk during the meal (11:21-22). Such actions hardly bring the blessing of Paul because they violate his portrait of Christ. Instead, he chides these Corinthians and reminds them that he has "delivered" the unadulterated tradition concerning the celebration of Christ in establishing the Supper. They need to understand that they are to follow his instructions about "giving thanks" (*eucharistesas*) for Christ's body (*soma*), which is the focus of the Supper, not their gluttony. They are also instructed to (a) "practice/do" (*poiete*) the Supper (b) in "remembrance" (*anamnesin*) of him (c) "until he comes" (*achri hou elthe*). These instructions provide a three-dimensional perspective—and involve the present, the past, and the future (11:24-26). It is important to realize that the Super does not merely look back as though we are attending a funeral or wake. Of course, the Supper recalls the horrific, sacrificial death of Jesus (past). But as we celebrate it (present), we also praise God as we look forward to Christ's glorious return (future)! Moreover, the church must not fail to discern the great significance of the Lord's Supper in terms of its powerful proclamation of the saving purposes of God for humanity and the unity of all believers in Christ. Failing to perceive its significance is a recipe for weakness in the church and condemnation upon its members (11:29-34).

The third and crucial part of this section for the Corinthians is the rather extended segment concerning the exercising of spiritual gifts. Again, in this brief treatment concerning Paul's portrait of Christ, it is impossible to detail the entire message here, but important aspects of Paul's instructions must be noted. The first aspect is how this dialogue begins. You can guess that Paul has significant things to say when he begins by telling them that he does not want them to remain "ignorant." Then he reminds the Corinthians, who love to speak in tongues, that they were once pagans and were strung along by dumb or "speechless" idols (12:1-2). The reason for this harsh introduction is undoubtedly because Paul regards the Corinthians as big windbags (cf. 4:6) who need to remember from whence they came and who they were. They were pagans, and their background is paganism; they are experienced in making human distinctions. They now need to realize that people who curse Jesus and people who confess him as Lord belong to radically different camps. Confessing "Jesus as Lord" is the work of the Holy Spirit (12:3). And the Spirit is the one who distributes the spiritual gifts—*not* according to human wishes but according to the divine will (12:4-11).

This idea of the superintendence of the Spirit is crucial for Paul because it removes from discussion the right of a person to boast before God. The Corinthians need to realize that they are now part of a faith community where they belong to one another in Christ. Like the various parts of the body belong together, so baptism unites Christians in one Spirit (12:12-13). Since all parts of the body are joined to one another, if one member suffers, all suffer. If one member is honored, all should rejoice (12:14-20).

This perspective is radically different from the thinking of most people in the world; humans are self-oriented and basically narcissistic. In contrast, the gifts of the Spirit should be viewed as constructive for the whole church—Christ's body—and not seen as divisive self-oriented characteristics (cf. Eph 4:11-12). Because his concern is for unity and interdependence among Christians, Paul inserts the famous hymn on love (chapter 13) into this section that is focused on dealing with the great divisiveness being experienced in the church.

While Paul ends chapter 12 advising the Corinthians to seek the higher gifts, he does not mean that love is necessarily to be listed in a ladder of gifts. Rather love—which represents the Spirit of the self-giving Christ—is to be understood as the foundation for all the gifts. The reason is that using any gift without love is fundamentally meaningless and accomplishes very little or, as Paul would say, "nothing!" (cf. 13:1-3). And since love should never run out (13:8), it will remain as a preeminent quality because, as John proclaimed, "God is love" (1 John 4:8). Moreover, God gave his Son, Jesus, so that all who believe in him might have life (John 3:16). And Paul would have responded, "Make love your goal" (1 Cor 14:1).

By emphasizing love, however, Paul does not mean to sideline his discussion on gifts. The Corinthians obviously find excitement and a sense of being among the spiritually elite by speaking in tongues, and that is undoubtedly the reason Paul begins his love hymn with speaking in tongues (13:1). Then he opens chapter 14 by advising them to pursue especially the gift of prophesy or proclamation (14:1). But notice that he does not condemn speaking in tongues (14:18); he merely recognizes that this gift as an experience is one in which a person's mind goes into neutral (14:14). But he clearly recommends to the charismatic Corinthians, for the sake of the gospel and of unbelievers coming to Christ, that they should focus their lives on proclamation rather than the more self-serving gift of speaking in tongues.

This issue, as we are painfully aware, was divisive in Paul's day and it continues to be divisive today. In the current debates on tongues speaking, charismatic proponents often cite the fact that Paul claimed that he spoke in tongues more than any of the Corinthians (14:18). Non-charismatic advocates counter that Paul rated speaking in tongues at the mere ratio of 5 to 10,000 against proclamation (14:19). But I must call attention to the fact that both ideas come together through these interlocking verses in the text. Please understand that my purpose here is not to debate the legitimacy of tongues or any spiritual giftedness but to focus our discussion on Paul's goal in Christ for winning the world to salvation. Arguments and making distinctions are the ways the devil sidetracks evangelism, not the ways of Christ. It is time for believers in the community of Jesus Christ to act as family. Speaking in tongues is not the key to whether one has the Spirit of Christ, and conversely it is not a key to whether or not a person is divisive. Love is the clue to the faithful and authentic use of any God-given spiritual gift. And it is imperative to remember how Paul summarizes his advice to the spiritually divisive Corinthians: he remarks that "the spirit of the prophet is under the control of the prophet" (14:32). He is saying that we are responsible for how we act within the community of faith and in the outside world as well.

Paul understands responsible actions, and he wants order not chaos in the church of Corinth. He does not want outsiders thinking Christians are like the women in the Dionysiac frenzied cults that mouth their senseless anthems or the Pythian priestesses who gorge themselves on a living animal while chanting their senseless intoxicated songs.[26] Remember that this letter was written to a place known for orgiastic worship practices and where madness was somehow thought to be a sign that a person had been seized by a god. Read again chapter 14 from this perspective and maybe it will make a little more sense. And note that Plutarch in his *Lives* indicated that as far back as Solon and Epimenides, there were laws in Greece that had been promulgated to curb ecstatic excesses of women and their orgiastic nocturnal activities with men. Even the well-known Roman writer Cicero mentioned that Rome had laws that curbed the nocturnal activities of these frenzied devotees of Bacchus and Dionysus.[27]

Before I leave this entire matter, I must pause to deal with the so-called silence text that is often used to place women in marginal roles within the church (14:34-35). Many scholars have grave doubts about these verses being authentically Pauline, especially since the statements go against what is said in 1 Corinthians 11:5 concerning women praying and prophesying/proclaiming publicly. Indeed, even the well-known conservative scholar Gordon Fee has doubts about the historical legitimacy of this text, especially since there is textual evidence that it is missing in one family of Greek manuscripts.[28] For my part, if I were to leave the verses in the letter, I would still have doubts about them representing Paul. They sound to me more like another example of the dialogical statements that came from the argumentative Corinthians rather than Paul, especially since these verses rely on the law for their support (14:34) while Paul consistently relies for his support on Christ and his vision of the Lord. Moreover, there seems to be a direct challenge to that perspective in 14:36. But I will not enter further into this textual debate here; I will simply leave you with my great doubt that these two verses represent the same spirit of Paul that is evident in the remainder of the letter.

Before I conclude my brief overview of this majestic, extended letter of advice called 1 Corinthians, it is essential that I deal with the letter's climax in chapter 15. Once again, it is not possible to detail the entire chapter but to pause only at the salient points. (For those who may be interested, I have dealt with this chapter more at length elsewhere.[29])

Paul begins this climactic chapter by reminding the Corinthians about the gospel and their salvation. Moreover, he again references the technical rabbinic words of "receiving" and "delivering" as clues to the fact that the information herein will be strategic for Christians (15:1-2; cf. 11:23). With such a start, the signal is sent to the reader that this chapter will be significant. The crucial theological facts are first stated: namely, Christ died for our sins; he was obviously dead and was buried; he was raised on the third day; and these events were a fulfillment of Scripture (15:3-4). Then, to make sure the Corinthians will have sufficient evidence of the resurrection, Paul provides two lists of the appearances of the risen Jesus (15:5-11).

Why is Paul so deliberate with the introduction to this section? The reason is that he understands clearly that the resurrection of Jesus Christ is the hinge point of Christianity. In fact, he declares that if Christ was not raised, then his own preaching and their faith will be empty (*kenos*, 15:14). Without the resurrection there would be no Church, no Christianity, and this book I am writing would be meaningless. So it is critical to note that some people in Corinth were typical Greeks who thought there was no such thing as resurrection (15:12). They were like the Areopagites whom Paul encountered in Athens and who believed in the immortality of the soul. They viewed any thought of the resurrection of the body as foolish and illogical (cf. Acts 17:32-34). They regarded the body as a physical chamber that was a temporary tomb for the soul. Indeed, Plato's view was that the goal of the soul was to escape from its bodily tomb and take wings in order to fly up and join the eternal soul. Of course, for Plato the philosopher would obtain his wings before all others because of his innate wisdom.[30]

The Corinthians are typical Greeks, and Paul, who was educated as a Pharisee, understands that in no way can humans attain their destiny of joining God in heaven merely by dying and being released from the body in order to fly up to the realm of God (or the gods). Resurrection is a gifted act of God and thus not in the control of mere sinful humans. If Christ was not raised, then the Corinthians are still in their helpless state of sin, and

Christians who died trusting in Christ are now hopelessly lost and indeed are to be greatly pitied (15:17-19).

But Christ has been raised from the dead! He is our guarantee of hope. In the resurrection, Christ has reversed the continual tendency of humans to sin and rebel against God with its devastating implications. For Paul (here, as in Romans 5:12-21), Christ is portrayed as the new Adam who has made possible new life for those who trust in him, and he has provided them with hope in the kingdom of God (15:20-24).[31] In this context, Paul briefly outlines his eschatological perspective—namely that all who belong to Christ will be made alive in him. Furthermore, when the end comes, death itself, the last enemy of life, will be terminated and God will be supreme (15:24-29).

Having supplied his understanding of the resurrection and new life, Paul addresses several important issues that are obviously troubling. The first involves the Corinthian practice that some people are being baptized for dead friends or relatives. Since we do not have an actual record of their practice stated, we can only surmise that the Corinthians were trying to make sure their dead colleagues and friends would somehow be marked (even possibly tattooed) and thus protected by the symbolic baptism so as to guarantee their acceptance by Christ.

In no way does Paul indicate an approval of this practice. Because of his emphasis on personal commitment, he would doubtless reject such a practice as totally unwarranted. But he employs their own practice as a means of showing them the illogical nature of their views. Baptism is an acknowledgment of the death and resurrection of Jesus. Why are they practicing it if they do not believe in the resurrection? Such thinking is illogical. And for good measure, Paul continues, why would he himself suffer so many hardships for the sake of Christ and the resurrection if he did not believe that Christ had been raised from the dead? He closes that argument by telling them they have been running in bad company and should be ashamed of such thinking (15:29-34)!

The second issue is that Greeks eschewed the fact that bodies were connected to souls. The natural question was, what kind of body will one have in the resurrection? Paul knows they are thinking of physical, fleshly bodies, and his goal is to move them beyond the mundane/earthly realm. To illustrate the relationship between dying and rising, he uses the picture of a kernel of grain that dies and a new stock that grows. Then he reviews for them the fact that there are varieties of bodies, including all kinds of fleshly bodies and even celestial or stellar bodies, and he finally moves to distinguish between physical and spiritual bodies. His purpose is to make sure they will not think of a resurrected body merely in terms of a physical, fleshly body. Finally, he returns to Adam as the man of earth and Christ as the man of heaven, and, in no uncertain terms, he declares that regular flesh-and-blood bodies will not enter the kingdom of God (15:35-50). For Paul the conclusion should be obvious. The image of the resurrected Lord should be stamped on everyone who claims the name "Christian."

The third issue involves the mystery of God's timing. Whenever God decides that the end will come and time shall be no more, then those who are still living and belong to Christ will not die. Paul contends that they will be transformed in the smallest moment of time (*atomos*), and the dead will also be raised (15:51-52). Then humanity will realize the reality of eternity. Both sin and death will be no more because God's victory through Jesus Christ will finally be accomplished (15:53-56). Accordingly, Christians should give thanks to God and stand firm in their commitment, realizing that nothing they do for the Lord will be empty (*kenos*) or of no consequence (15:58). Wow! How do you like that summary as a climax to this fascinating book? To emphasize the point Paul adds that the time will ultimately arrive for the end of evil and the final resurrection when God has promised victory (*nikos*) through the Lord Jesus Christ (15:57)! This resurrection is the epitome or the *sine qua non* of human existence.

With such a climax in mind, Paul concludes his most detailed letter of advice with the enjoinder for the Corinthians to remember their responsibility in supporting the poor of Jerusalem (16:1-4). He also includes his hope that both he and his colleagues might soon be able to visit them—even though none are really anxious to do so, at least not immediately (16:5-12)! Then, after adding some final bits of advice and a short series of greetings along with his usual personal certification of the letter (16:13-21), Paul provides these "tongues loving" Corinthians with an intriguing thematic chant that summarizes his views: *anathema, maranatha* (16:22). This unusual combination of words both declares a severe curse (*anathema*) on those who refuse to love the Lord and also invokes an expectant Aramaic prayer (*maranatha*) for the soon coming of the Lord! He closes the letter in a parental declaration of grace and love (16:23-24).

In summarizing this strategic work of Paul, I must pause to give thanks that God has allowed us to have a dialogical letter like 1 Corinthians. This epistle provides a firsthand encounter with how one of Christianity's greatest thinkers was able to apply his portrait of Jesus to actual human concerns and problems in life. Paul does not shy away from difficult issues but faces them head-on with authenticity and genuine Christian candor. There seems little doubt that his advice was not always gratefully received. I suspect that is the reason we do not have all of his letters. The Corinthians probably did not want his censures to survive, and therefore those other letters conveniently disappeared.

Thankfully, however, 1 Corinthians did survive as a priceless model of honest confrontation with inadequate and non-Christ-like patterns of life. Since Paul was convinced that the model of Jesus was the pattern for Christians to emulate in their lives, the pieces of advice recorded in this letter can form a strong foundation for developing crucial patterns of Christian behavior today. But just as Paul rejected legalism as the format for behavior, we too must not use his statements of advice as rules or laws for Christian life. Moreover, while he may have judged severely the inadequate and non-Christ-like patterns of the Corinthian actions and attitudes, he did not regard himself as divine. His advice even when severe was wrapped in love for them, and his goal was always redemptive rather than vindictive. That attitude and goal should provide a model for contemporary Christians who seek to communicate the love and spirit of the Living Jesus in this world today, where many are becoming more biblically illiterate and need direction and hope for their lives.

When this letter is correctly interpreted and proclaimed, it has the potential to shake lethargic "churchgoers" to their roots. Do we today have the will and strength of personality to communicate forthrightly the implications of the coming of Jesus as Paul did? That question should haunt us as Christians because Paul's letters were not always welcomed.

In closing my review of Paul's portraits of Jesus in these three strategic letters, I sense that a question may be on the minds of some readers in the light of my comments in chapter 1 of this book. They may justly ask me, "Have you actually preached each of these epistles in a single sermon?" The answer is, "Absolutely, yes!" And I have done so even with this long book of 1 Corinthians. You may be surprised to know that I did it at a seminary commencement! But I would not recommend such a practice early in one's ministry. Naturally, I did not include all the information contained in 1 Corinthians.[32] Yet when we know the purpose and the development of a biblical book, its message can unfold like a flower! May God bless you, dear reader, as you seek to absorb the portraits of Christ in Paul's wonderful letters.

Questions for Reflection

- The Corinthians were convinced that they understood the implications of the gospel. But in what ways did Paul show them that they were biblically illiterate? How does his treatment of knowledge have any relevance for us today? What are the implications of Paul's advice for us today in terms of our generation's views of sexual morality?
- How do you think Paul would confront us on the matter of idolatry today?
- Where do you stand on the role of women in the church? What is the significance of baptism and the Lord's Supper for your faith community? How does your church treat the issue of speaking in tongues? How important is the role of the Holy Spirit for you? For your church? Is the resurrection of Jesus central in your life? Explain.
- Are you ready to challenge your faith community to take Jesus as the model for life? What implications may follow for them and for you?

Notes

1. For some helpful works on Paul see Joseph A. Fitzmyer, *Paul and His Theology: A Brief Sketch*, 2nd ed. (Englewood Cliffs NJ: Prentice Hall, 1989); Judith M. Gundry Volf, *Paul and Perseverance: Staying in and Falling Away* (Louisville: Westminster/John Knox, 1991); Richard Longenecker, *Paul: Apostle of Liberty* (New York: Harper & Row, 1964); John B. Polhill, *Paul and His Letters* (Nashville: Broadman & Holman, 1999); Heikki Raisanen, *Paul and the Law* (Philadelphia: Fortress, 1983); Herman Ridderbos, *Paul: An Outline of His Theology* (Grand Rapids: Eerdmans, 1975; E. P. Sanders, *Paul and Palestinian Judaism* (Philadelphia; Fortress, 1977); Krister Stendahl, *Paul Among Jews and Gentiles* (Philadelphia: Fortress, 1976); Anthony Thiselton, *The Living Paul: An Introduction to the Apostle's Life and Thought* (Downers Grove IL: InterVarsity, 2009). Please also see my article, Gerald L. Borchert, "Romans, Pastoral Counseling, and the Introspective Conscience of the West," *Review and Expositor* 83 (1986): 81–92.

2. Similarly, Luke and Paul made use of alternative names as, for example, when Luke shifts between John and Mark in Acts 13:12, 15; 13:13 as Mark causes trouble by leaving the missionary team. Paul also shifts between the nicknames of Peter and Cephas (meaning "Rocky") when he both affirms and criticizes Peter's actions in Galatians 2:7-14.

3. For my detailed arguments concerning the dating of Galatians and its relation to the book of Acts, please see Gerald L. Borchert, "Galatians," in Roger Mohlang and Gerald Borchert, *Romans and Galatians*, vol. 14 of Cornerstone Biblical Commentary (Carol Stream IL: Tyndale House, 2007) esp. 248–51. I am convinced that Galatians was written after Paul's second visit to Jerusalem and prior to the Jerusalem Council (AD 49–50). That council meeting incorporated the logic Paul had worked out in this epistle. Galatians

represents the vibrant, bombastic style of the early Paul, precedes his arguments in the Thessalonian correspondence, and is prior to the writing of Romans.

4. For additional sources on Galatians see James D. G. Dunn, *The Epistle to the Galatians*, Black's New Testament Commentary (Peabody MA: Hendrickson, 1993); Ronald Y. K. Fung, *The Epistle to the Galatians*, New International Commentary on the New Testament (Grand Rapids MI; Eerdmans, 1988); Richard Hays, "The Letter to the Galatians," *New Interpreter's Bible*, vol. 11 (Nashville: Abingdon, 2000) 181–348; Richard N. Longenecker, *Galatians*, Word Biblical Commentary (Dallas: Word, 1990). See also C. K. Barrett, *Freedom and Obligation: A Study of the Epistle to the Galatians* (London: SPCK, 1985); Hans D. Betz, *Galatians* in Hermeia (Philadelphia: Fortress, 1979); E. DeWitt Burton, *The Epistle to the Galatians*, International Critical Commentary (Edinburgh: T. & T. Clark, 1921); Timothy George, *Galatians*, New American Commentary (Nashville: Broadman & Holman,1994); J. Louis Martyn, *Galatians*, Anchor Bible (New York: Doubleday, 1997); Ben Witherington II, *Grace in Galatia: A Commentary on Paul's Letter to the Galatians* (Grand Rapids MI: Eerdmans, 1998).

5. As I have stated elsewhere, Galatians is the Magna Carta of Christian freedom. See Gerald L Borchert, "A Key to Pauline Thinking: Galatians 3:23-29," *Review and Expositor* 91 (1994): 145–51.

6. The rabbinic view was that God had delivered not only a written set of prescriptions but also oral traditions concerning their interpretations, and those interpretations were ultimately codified in what is called the *Mishnah*. For information concerning the codification of these interpretations see Herbert Danby, *The Mishnah: Translated from the Hebrew with Introduction and Explanatory Notes* (London: Oxford University Press, 1933).

7. For some helpful works on Colossians see David E. Garland, *Colossians and Philemon*, New International Version Application Commentary (Grand Rapids MI: Zondervan, 1998); Andrew T. Lincoln, "The Letter to the Colossians," *New Interpreter's Bible*, vol. 11 (Nashville: Abingdon, 2000) 551–669; Peter T. O'Brien, *Colossians, Philemon*, Word Biblical Commentary (Waco TX: Word, 1982). See also Markus Barth and Helmut Blanke, *Colossians*, Anchor Bible (New York: Doubleday, 1994); Ralph P. Martin, *Colossians, The Church's Lord and Christian Liberty* (Grand Rapids MI: Zondervan, 1972); Eduard Schweizer, *The Letter to the Colossians* (Minneapolis: Augsburg, 1982); Markus Barth and Helmut Blanke, *Colossians*, Anchor Bible (New York: Doubleday, 1994).

8. I am fully aware that there are scholars who think Paul did not write this letter and that it was written after Paul by one of his unidentified followers. If you are of such an opinion, then just substitute "Paulinist" where Paul's name appears. Too much debate has ensued on this issue, and more focus should have been given to the content of this marvelous letter. I personally do not find the arguments for non-Pauline authorship of Colossians to be convincing today, but focusing on authorship here is hardly my goal. I would add in passing, however, that the old Tubingen hypothesis, which limited Pauline authorship to four books (Romans, 1 and 2 Corinthians, and Galatians), is certainly no longer viable. While Paul was in prison when he wrote this letter, we are not certain where he was. The traditional opinion has been Rome, but some have argued for Ephesus and even Caesarea for the prison letters (Philippians, Colossians, and Philemon). This letter may have been sent about the same

time as the letter to the Philippians that mentions the Praetorian guard, a Roman branch of the military, but this reference does not assist us much because that unit was not limited to being in the capital city (Phil 1:13). If Paul wrote the letter from Rome, a date of about AD 60–61 would be likely.

9. See for example the Nicene Creed in Henry Bettenson, *Documents of the Christian Church* (London: Oxford University Press, 1943, etc.) 35.

10. When one visits ancient Jewish Mikveh sites (lustration or washing pools) today, one is impressed with the intense efforts even the Jews exerted to make sure the water would be flowing water in their homes.

11. I would pause here to remind readers of the more extended statement for becoming Christ-like in Ephesians 4:17–6:20. There you will also discover that Paul uses the same baptismal language of "putting off" (4:21) or "putting away" (4:25) the ways of the old life and "putting on" the new nature (4:24) by learning to "walk" as children of the light with the Lord (5:1, 8-9). These instructions, however, are not intended to be a new set of rules or laws for Christians. Instead, they are a kind of a measuring rod or canon to help Christians gauge whether they are living in Christ.

12. For some helpful works on 1 Corinthians see Gordon Fee, *The First Epistle to the Corinthians*, New International Commentary on the New Testament (Grand Rapids MI: Eerdmans, 1987, 1994); Wayne E. Meeks, *The First Urban Christians: The Social World of the Apostle Paul* (New Haven: Yale University Press, 1983); Jerome M. O'Connor, *St. Paul's Corinth: Text and Archaeology* (Wilmington: Michael Glazier, 1983). Also see Craig L. Blomberg, *1 Corinthians*, New International Version Application Commentary (Grand Rapids MI: Zondervan, 1994); Gerald Borchert, "Assurance and Warning in 1 Corinthians," *Assurance and Warning* (Nashville: Broadman, 1987) 19–85 (repr., Singapore: Word N Works, 2006); Raymond E. Collins, *First Corinthians*, Sacra Pagina (Collegeville MN: Liturgical Press, 1999); David E. Garland, *First Corinthians*, Baker Exegetical Commentary on the New Testament (Grand Rapids MI: Baker, 2003); Richard B. Hays, *First Corinthians* in Interpretation (Louisville: John Knox,1997); Walter Schmithals, *Gnosticism in Corinth* (Nashville: Abingdon, 1971); Robert W. Wall, "The First Letter to the Corinthians," *New Interpreter's Bible*, vol. 10 (Nashville: Abingdon, 2002) 771–1003; Ben Witherington III, *Commentary on 1 and 2 Corinthians* (Grand Rapids MI: Eerdmans, 1995).

13. See Gerald L. Borchert, "Introduction to 2 Corinthians," *Review and Expositor* 86/3 (Summer 1989): 313–24.

14. Gallio was appointed to serve as the Proconsul in Corinth during the sixth acclamation of Claudius (AD 52–53). See my discussion in G. Borchert, *Worship in the New Testament*, 101–102. For information on the Delphic Inscription see A. Brassac, "Une inscription de Delphes et la chronologie de Saint Paul," *Revue Biblique*, W.S.X. (1913): 36-53.207-17.

15. For my further discussion on this issue see Gerald Borchert, "2 Corinthians," 317–19.

16. C. S. Lewis in *The Lion, the Witch and the Wardrobe* captured this idea beautifully in the killing of Aslan (the lion) on the stone table by the white witch and her evil minions who did not understand the "deeper knowledge."

17. The Gnostics later used these designated divisions in Paul to categorize people in a much more deterministic manner. If they had the spark of the divine in them and understood the secret knowledge of heaven, they were the spiritual ones and could not loose their status. They regarded those who were earthly or carnal as having no possibility of entering into their *pleroma* or heaven. They regarded the group they designated as the *pseuchikoi* as in the middle class, able to achieve the *pleroma* if they diligently worked for it. This type of determinism has sometimes been seen in Christian communities and especially among those who espouse a strict doctrine of reprobation or what has been called double predestination. See my further comments in Gerald L. Borchert, "Insights into the Gnostic threat to Christianity as gained through the Gospel of Philip," *New Dimensions in New Testament Study*, ed. R. N. Longenecker and M. Tenney (Grand Rapids MI: Zondervan, 1974) 70–98.

18. Paul would have been familiar with various patterns of discipline from his experiences in Judaism. Among them were curses such as "May the Lord swallow you up like Korah" (cf. Jude 11; Numbers 16:31-32), beatings (cf. 2 Cor 11:25), and shunning (cf. the *Manual of Discipline*, the rules of the community from Qumran).

19. See particularly Gerald L. Borchert, "1 Corinthians 7:15 and the Church's Historic Misunderstanding of Divorce and Remarriage," *Review and Expositor* 96 (1999): 125–29.

20. One of the great criticisms of Marxism is that its proponents were willing to employ unjust means to achieve just ends. But it is clear that if you use unjust means, you will never achieve just ends. This same reality applies to Christian evangelism. If you use non-Christ-like means, you will not produce Christ-like followers of Jesus.

21. The reason I wrote my book *Assurance and Warning* was to provide readers with a sense of the marvelous balance that God has provided to Christians in the New Testament. We must take both sides of the gospel seriously as applying to each of us personally and not miss their implications. Dismissing either side will ultimately lead to a heretical tendency in the church and its teachings.

22. For an important insight into the eating and sharing of meals, see the work of Pliny the Younger in Betty Radice, *The Letters of Pliny the Younger* (Harmondsorth: Penguin, 1969) 63–64 and Meeks, *The First Unban Christians*, 67–69.

23. The term translated "delivered" (*paradiomi*) is used in several places in this section and signals Paul's thinking as a rabbi. Especially when it is linked with *paralambano* ("received"), it signals that Paul is passing on information or tradition that has not been in anyway altered in transmission. See for example 1 Cor 11:23 and 15:3.

24. I am indebted to Richard Oster for his writings on this subject and particularly for his excellent paper, "Cultural Background to 1 Corinthians 11:4," delivered at the 1986 meetings of *Studiorum Novi Testamenti Societas*, which helped me to rethink this entire section of 1 Corinthians.

25. Another rather forced idea probably involves his allegory in Gal 4:21-31 concerning Hagar and Sarah representing two covenants and two mountains.

26. See Plutarch, *Moralia* 671.c and Pausamius, *Description of Greece.* II.2. See also Livy, *History of Rome* XXXIX.15 and Strabo, *Georg.* X.3.7. For the Bacchic chants see Iamblichus, *On the Mysteries* III.4-6 and the important *Hymn of Lysistrata* from Aristophanes as well as his comments in *Frogs*, 357.

27. See Cicero, *Laws* II.15.

28. See Gordon Fee, *The First Epistle to the Corinthians*, New International Commentary on the New Testament (Grand Rapids MI: Eerdmans, 1987) 699–710.

29. Gerald L. Borchert, "The Resurrection: 1 Corinthians 15," *Review and Expositor* 80 (1983): 401–15.

30. See Plato, *Phaedrus* 245–57.

31. Important for Paul is his portrait of Christ as the new Adam who has reversed the tragedy of sin. That portrait is used here in reference to his eschatological views, and in Romans 5:12-21 it is central to his discussion of salvation as he moves from justification (becoming reconciled to God) to sanctification (living out the implications of the transformed life). It is also important to recognize that Luke picks up this portrait of Christ as the new Adam in his genealogical table (Luke 3:23-38).

32. If you are interested in preaching or teaching on the entire book of 1 Corinthians, try breaking it into five sections: chapters 1–4, 5–7, 8–11:1, 11:2–14, and 15—Christian perspectives on knowledge, morality, idolatry, and church order, based on the resurrection.

Chapter 6

The Portraits of Jesus in the Gospel of John and the Book of Revelation

We come finally to the magnificent Johannine writings, which are among the most varied and challenging works in the New Testament. Probably written in the closing decade of the first century of the birth of Jesus, these works provide vivid insights into how Christians envisioned and employed their portraits of Jesus in their struggles to survive during a period marked by the intense persecution of Jesus' followers.

The five-volume Johannine canon includes two brief letters (2 and 3 John) that likely accompanied the delivery of the theological essay we call 1 John as well as the Gospel of John and the book we call the Revelation or Apocalypse of John. For the purposes of providing insights into these Johannine portraits of Jesus, I have chosen here to discuss the latter two works because of their importance and great differences in structure and type. The Gospel is among the most beloved documents of the Christian church, and Revelation is among the most speculative and misunderstood texts for the Christian community. The Gospel contains undoubtedly the most quoted text of the New Testament (John 3:16), and Revelation contains perhaps its most fervently debated (Rev 20:1-8) passage in Scripture.

These differences in the Johannine works point to the great variance in the types of literature that exist in our Bibles. They have also led to passionate questioning by some concerning how such a variance could have

come from the pen of a single authorial source. While I do not intend to
debate the issue of authorship, I would suggest that we should refrain from
placing the biblical authors in strict boxes and limiting our concepts of
what kind of literature people are capable of writing.

In this regard, I should note that my wife and I read many of C. S.
Lewis's books to our boys around the dinner table and at bedtime as they
were growing from childhood into their teenage years, and we all enjoyed
the Aslan stories, the space trilogy (especially *Perelandra*), and *The Great
Divorce* with its bus ride to heaven. Then we eventually came to *The
Pilgrim's Regress*, and I had the task of explaining each of the houses visited
by Pilgrim and introducing our boys to the philosophical implications of
each setting. Lewis's imagination was still there, but the story involved much
more than The Chronicles of Narnia and other, earlier works. Sometimes
it was tough for our boys to grasp, but we helped them and they began
to see the differences in Lewis's ability to write from both the right- and
left-brain hemispheres, even though I did not at the time explain many of
the ramifications to our boys. What is imperative to understand is that the
same man who could write captivating dreams and visions was fully capable
of logical, philosophical left-brain thinking. And I make these comments
without considering Lewis's academic work as a seasoned professor.

I am sure that you recognize where I am going with this point. I try to
be careful about saying that the Gospel and the Revelation are so different
that the same person couldn't have written them. Perhaps my comments
about C. S. Lewis will help you understand why I have spent little time
on authorship questions. But I will mention some fascinating literary and
grammatical features of these Johannine works that should be part of any
such discussions. Some Western left-brain thinkers in the early church and
Patristic period certainly wrestled with the differences in these books, but
most were content with attributing them to the author "John." For those,
however, who would be interested in pursuing the development of traditions concerning John, I recommend consulting the intriguing work by my
former colleague Alan Culpepper.[1]

I would propose that we in the twenty-first century *not* swallow the
Sanhedrin's (Jewish High Council's) evaluation that the early disciples as
mere fishermen were low-class workers (*am haeretz*) who were "unschooled"
or "unlearned" in matters of religion (cf. Acts 4:13) and therefore incapable
of creative and sophisticated thinking, especially after decades of reflecting
on their powerful experiences with Jesus. If we do that, we just might have
the wrong impression of the people Jesus chose.

So before turning to the marvelous Johannine books, permit me to note a few of their fascinating features. Some writers have noted that the book of Revelation contains examples of poor Greek, and I would agree that even a first-year Greek student would tell you that *apo* is hardly used with the nominative case such as in the statement about God, namely "the one who is, who was, and who is to come" (Rev 1:4). I would immediately respond that it may be terrible Greek, but it is great theology! God is the unquestioned subject of John's thinking. But, to carry the matter further, the temporal order of this statement seems badly skewed because, for us, time is best understood as past, present, and future. But here and at 1:8 the present is emphasized. Yet isn't that idea what John in the Gospel empha-sizes when the Jews think Jesus is crazy in saying, "Before Abraham was, I am" (John 8:58)? Isn't Jesus picking up the strange statement of God about "I am" from Exodus 3:4 when he also says in John 6:20, "I am," as he is getting in the boat after walking on the water? And why does John repeatedly use the "I am" prefix to ideas such as "the bread of life," "the light of the world," "the door," "the good shepherd," and "the resurrection and the life," to name only a few (John 6:35; 8:12; 9:5; 10:7, 11; 11:25; etc.)? I would remind you that the Seer of Revelation is also fully aware of the usual temporal order because, in contrast to Revelation 1:4 and 8, he uses the order of past, present, and future at 4:8.

With these brief insights to whet your appetite for studying the marvelous portraits of the Johannine Jesus, I turn now to discuss the magnificent Gospel of John and then the dramatic book of Revelation.

The Magnificent Gospel of John[2]

This magnificent Gospel that Clement of Alexandria called "the Spiritual Gospel"[3] has been my companion since I was admitted to an isolation hospital when I was in sixth grade. At the time I was told that I could have no visitors and I would not be able to bring anything back from that experience since everything would be burned. Yet I did bring back some-thing: many verses from the King James Version of the Gospel of John that I dutifully memorized in response to the many letters and cards I received while I being stuck repeatedly with penicillin. But that experience seared in my mind the importance of this book for my life and future ministry. John's words have prodded me ever since, and I am convinced that the portrait of the Living Jesus in this book is one that can challenge people in our growing biblically illiterate era to find a relationship with God that can change the way they live and lead them to the portals of eternal life. It is therefore without excuse that I have detailed at some length the magnificent portrait of Jesus as provided by one who may have best reached into the sanctum of God's heart.

As John 21:25 indicates, much more could have been written about Jesus than is penned in this Gospel. Indeed, I readily admit that over the decades I have written much more about John's Jesus than he wrote. But I have hardly come close to approximating the depth of his work. Still, I pray that I have caught a little of the significance of his purpose statement (John 20:30-31), which makes it clear that the reason for his writing is that his readers might believe that Jesus is God's Son, the unquestioned Messianic messenger who was sent to bring *life* to all who believe and are committed to him. I would only add that this purpose statement could easily serve as an excellent rationale for the entire New Testament.

To help you understand the brilliance and complexity of this book, I must tell you that when I teach the Gospel of John, I have consistently assigned my students the task of writing their papers on one of the great themes of John. I have watched in delight as many have reported to me that, whatever theme they have chosen to examine, they have thought that their theme was probably the most important one. Those responses reveal just how interlaced and pervasive are the themes in this book and how gifted was the writer of this Gospel. So whether one focuses on "life" or "light" or "truth" or "believing and knowing" or "the dark side and evil" or "judgment" or the issue of the "I am" or a number of other themes, one is in for a wonderful journey of gaining new insights into John's Jesus and into the meaning of his coming.

But there are other intriguing aspects of this Gospel that can challenge readers and provide them with fascinating surprises. One such insight for Westerners who often focus on nouns is the crucial importance of some verbs in this testimony. John refuses throughout his Gospel to use the nouns for "knowledge" (*gnosis*) and "faith" (*pistis*). Instead, he uses only the verbs for "knowing" (*ginosko* and *oida*) and for "believing" (*pisteuo*). The reason undoubtedly is that John is making a correction to misunderstandings of Paul and others concerning "salvation" that were creeping into the church. It is not mere "knowledge" or mere "belief" that is the foundation of Christianity—a problem that still haunts the church today! Indeed, it is not "what you know" or "what you believe" that is strategic for Christianity. The focus should *not* be primarily on supplying information to people or making mere faith affirmations—a left-brain approach. It is "who you know" and "in whom you believe/put your trust" that is essential for Christian life.

The focus must be one of putting into practice a living relationship ("walking") with the one in whom you believe or the one you know. Yet to make it clear what I mean, I turn to Paul and remind you that as a former rabbi, he would hardly have fallen into the word-oriented trap that has caught not only many ancient Jews but also many contemporary Christians. John also knows the danger of shifting from the verb *halak* ("walk") to the noun *halakah* (which became a commitment to rules and creeds).

Like Paul, John is not oriented to mere ideas. Thus, as John seeks to paint his portrait of Jesus, he used the term *logos* ("Word") for this divine reality. But *logos* here is not merely a Greek philosophical personification as in Philo. The "Word" is John's way of referring to the divine *persona* that became embodied or truly incarnated as a human (John1:1 and 14) and whose name was "Jesus." This Jesus was fully human and at the same time was divine (in the "bosom of the Father"). This Jesus accordingly was able to reveal God's self to mortals (1:18). Moreover, John is fully aware that God is able to transform people so that they can follow their Lord and embody as humans some of the divinely given qualities of their living Lord. What then becomes clear in John is that just as Jesus abides in the Father (God) and is one with the Father, so Christians are expected to abide in Jesus (15:4-5)—even though they *never* become one with Jesus or the Father (namely, they never become divine).

For John, Jesus knows the mind of God and was sent to communicate God's will to humans. Moreover, just as God has life and is a life-giver, so the Son has life in himself (1:4) and can be identified with the earlier Jewish picture of the apocalyptic "Son of Man"—the divine Cloud-rider of Daniel 7:13, the one who is the judge of the world and the dispenser of both life and condemnation (see John 5:21-29). This portrait of Jesus that John paints is obviously a high Christology, and John's view of Jesus as the divine Son impacts everything he says about communicating the gospel to the world. Such a picture is not easy for narcissistic, self-oriented humans to take. But just as God wanted to "walk" with humans in the garden of creation (Gen 3:8), human affirmation of God's Son is not a requirement for the Savior of the World (4:42)! Yet such an affirmation of "believing" or trusting obedience (1:12) is the foundation for human acceptance by the divine-human Son. Getting the correct perspective on the relationship between Jesus and the Father and between Jesus and the believer is crucial for an adequate understanding of John.

John's starting point, like that of Genesis, is the creation of the phenomenal universe in which we live. The existence of both God and Jesus, this eternal Son (here designated as the "Word"), is presupposed, and both have been active from the beginning in all of creation (John 1:1-2 and Gen 1:1). But darkness and rebellion against God are also presupposed, even though humans cannot answer—and the Bible does not answer—the ultimate question concerning the problem or origin of evil. Although God's creation is "good," humans cannot blame God or Jesus for the existence of sin, rebellion, or evil in the world. What humans can do is turn "toward God" (*pros ton theon*);[4] as their model, Jesus—the Word—is constantly oriented to God (John 1:1). Here then is our prime example of how early Christians began to wrestle with the task of trying to explain the multiple facets or personae of what Christians, in their later confessions such as the Nicene Creed, have come to understand as the "Triune God."

I repeat that John does not leave his magnificent portrait of Jesus, the Son of God, in the ethereal realm. This "Word," persona or epitome of God, became truly human in order that God could "grace" humanity with his Son, Jesus the Christ (1:14-18). There is a problem in the application of this text, however, because a number of evangelists tend to use John 1:12 as a minimum statement about becoming a Christian since the King James Version translates this verse as "*even* to them that believe on his name." But the word "even" is not in the Greek text!

Believing in this Jesus can never simply be an idea or making a statement about Jesus. Believing in Jesus involves a commitment of one's life to him—namely, "walking" with Jesus as one's Lord. It is a life commitment, as though the name or the portrait of Jesus were emblazoned or tattooed on one's life (cf. Rev 22:4).

The stories that follow this Prologue in John (1:1-18) are aimed at picturing for readers how such a life commitment to Jesus might be understood in the midst of a world entangled in darkness. Our evangelist opens his series of testimonial narratives with the story of another man named John who comes baptizing people as a witness (1:6-7) and who calls them from the wilderness to "make the pathway for the Lord straight" (1:23). When the religious leaders who think they have the stages of the messianic era figured out try to determine the pigeon hole of potential messianic figures where they might fit this Baptizer (1:19-22), he responds that he is merely an unworthy voice announcing in the wilderness the coming of the expected one—whom they do not know (1:26-27)!

But this genuine messianic witness points his own disciples towards Jesus as the Son of God who will be God's sacrificial "Lamb" and "take away the sin of the world" (1:29, 36). In the remaining verses of this first chapter, the evangelist unfolds a series of confessional designations affirming that Jesus is indeed the Messiah (1:41), the anticipated King of Israel (1:49) who epitomizes in himself the new Bethel or house of God and encapsulates all the hopes of Israel dating back to the midnight dream of their forefather, the patriarch Jacob (1:47-51; cf. Gen 28:10-22).

In the next three chapters, which I have designated as the Cana Cycle,[5] the evangelist, John, begins to lay out crucial insights concerning Jesus and the fact that humans cannot put Jesus into a test tube or computer chip nor can they control his destiny. Moreover, in this text we learn that humans—including the disciples and even Jesus' Jewish mother—are not permitted to define the ministry of Jesus (John 2:3-5). Indeed, he is the one who recognizes the approaching of his strategic "hour" (2:4)—the haunting reminder throughout the Gospel of his coming sacrifice. But before that hour arrives we learn that his powerful acts ("signs" in John) are hardly intended for show but to lead his followers to understand who he is so they might entrust themselves to him (2:11).

As a literary genius, John next transfers the story of the cleansing of the temple from the end of Jesus' earthly ministry to almost the beginning (2:13-22). This shift has often created problems for Westerners who want a "Life of Jesus" to be written in chronological order. But this Gospel is hardly a pedantic newspaper or television report. It is a magnificent testimony! The shift should signal that Jesus was hardly going to be accepted by the religious establishment (cf. 1:11) because their commitments prevented them from accepting the truth. To their astonishment, God's presence was not confined to a man-made temple (*hieron*, 2:14). God presence was in Jesus, a living sanctuary (*naos*—2:19). And to make this shift of events for the careful reader patently clear, John adds a post-resurrection perspective at 2:21-22. Remember, this Gospel was written many years after the death and resurrection of Jesus, and it is a testimony to the power of the risen Jesus—one who is present today! Moreover, even though chronologically at this point in the Gospel Jesus has only done one sign, John concludes this story with a summarizing statement that although people have seen many signs and are said to believe, Jesus does not believe or accept their believing.[6] Jesus simply does not believe or accept all human believing. He knows who is authentic.

Friends, we have only completed chapter 2 and you already have an artistic sketch of John's portrait of Jesus. Fasten your seatbelts as we continue into the Cana Cycle. The picture expands as Nicodemus, a rabbinic teacher who seeks Jesus because he thinks he knows who Jesus is and dares to come to Jesus only at night (3:1). He quickly learns that Jesus, the Creator, is also in the rebirth or re-creation business. Jesus invites him into a rebirth experience through water and the Spirit of God (3:5-8). This rebirth is not merely a matter of joining the "Jesus club" by means of some ritualistic act like baptism. The Jews have their lustrations (water washings in their homes or in the desert with the Qumran sect[7]) and the pagans have their baptisms like the Mithraic Taurobolium (the bull blood bath),[8] but Jesus is dealing with a new experience that involves not merely ritual but also the touch of God's Spirit. Human action alone cannot accomplish such a rebirth. It is the marvelous act of God through Jesus that enables humans to encounter the wind (Spirit) of heaven.

As the most quoted verse in Scripture (John 3:16) indicates, God's gift of love in Jesus enables mere humans to believe and experience eternal life. And it was God's intention all along *not* to condemn humanity but to provide for their rescue from sin, rebellion, and its consequent condemnation (3:17). Yet the reality is that humans reject the light that has come into the world through Jesus and fail to accept God's way to new life and re-creation. Therefore, they stand condemned (3:18-21) and will unfortunately experience the judgment of God (3:36). It is hard for us as humans in this permissive generation to recognize that God was not playing games in sending Jesus into the world, and it is equally difficult for us as Christians to recognize that our calling and task is to proclaim this serious message to a generation that knows less and less about the Bible. John's portrait of Jesus provides a stern wake-up call for us. The question is, what will we do with it?

As we move forward through chapter 4, John's portrait of Jesus continues to expand in terms of Jesus' mission to include the Samaritans. While the disciples are astonished that Jesus would even talk to a "despicable half-breed" Samaritan woman (4:27), Jesus leads her step by step through the process of uncovering her sordid life pattern. His ability to peel through the layers of self-protection brings her to the point where she is able to abandon her water pot and the reason she came to the well. Then she hastens to the men of the town, whom she obviously knows, and asks whether she could have encountered the *Tahib* (the Samaritan messianic messenger from God) whom they were all expecting (4:28-29). When the

Samaritans meet and talk with Jesus, they are convinced, and they issue for John and for Christians today what is one of the most important confessions in the New Testament: namely, Jesus is indeed "The Savior of the world" (4:42)!

Then the portrait of Jesus is further stretched in the concluding pericope of the Cana Cycle as Jesus encounters a Galilean officer. Here Jesus heals the son of the officer (4:47), but he does so in an astonishing manner. When Jesus berates the official and consequently the people for failing to believe, the man simply pleads with Jesus to come and heal the boy. When Jesus tells him to go and his son will be well, the man believes and does exactly what Jesus has told him to do (4:50). He leaves and the miracle is completed! The power of Jesus is like the power of God—not limited by space or time. Placing limits on the scope of the Son of God or on the nature of believing in his power is a recipe for misunderstanding the nature of the good news in Jesus. Time and space are created phenomena and are not eternal. God's Son is not bound by either of them. Do you realize the implications of such an idea?

We turn now to the storm clouds of conflict in chapters 5 through 11 and what I have called the Festival Cycle[9] that runs from Passover to Passover but begins with the issue of Sabbath, the key to the Jewish Festivals (see Lev 23).[10]

During his time on earth, Jesus, as the Son of God and Son of Man, regarded himself as Lord of the Sabbath (cf. Mark 2:28), but he did not want to demean Sabbath. He wanted humans to understand that Sabbath was not to be treated as a rule (like many of the Jews were doing) but as a precious gift from God to be used for God's purposes. So he was willing to heal people on Sabbath, even when the recipient was a miserable complainer like the paralytic in John 5 who blames Jesus even for his healing. Of course, the healing, along with the fact that the man carries his bedroll on the Sabbath, violates the rules of the rabbis. These Jews refuse to concede that their perspectives are in error because they use Exodus 31:12-17 and Numbers 15:32-36 to support their position that Jesus deserves to die (John 5:18). So the gauntlet is thrown down and the face-off between the Jews and Jesus is set.

The rule-oriented Jews can hardly accept the God-oriented perspectives of Jesus because their entire rabbinic system will be threatened with crumbling by Jesus, who assumes the freedom to work on the Sabbath based on his unheard-of claim that he has a personal relationship with God as his Father (5:17-18). But Jesus goes far beyond such assertions and claims that as the Son of God he is the divine agent of life itself (5:25-26), the executor of judgment (5:27), and the one who will be in charge of calling people both to the resurrection of life and to the resurrection of judgment (5:28-29). Such claims must have been nothing less than breathtaking for the Jews. Yet for John they confirm in bold-faced lettering the broad brush-strokes of the portrait of Jesus he briefly outlines in the Prologue to his Gospel.

This Jesus in John, however, does not stop with making such incredible claims; he goes further and, like a skilled attorney in a legal case, presents his supporting data concerning the integrity of both his acts and his statements. These witnesses include (1) the authentic testimony of John (the Baptizer) whom the Jews have investigated, (2) Jesus' own powerful signs (miraculous works), and (3) the confirming testimony of God, the Father, who sent the Son and whom the people talk about but whom Jesus asserts they do not know (5:33-38). In case these witnesses will not convince his stubborn antagonists, Jesus carries the argument into their court as he cites another testimony concerning him, namely (4) their own Scriptures (which they refuse to accept), and finally (5) he turns to their patron hero, Moses, who wrote concerning him. Then Jesus announces that, because of their refusal to accept him, Moses will become their accusing prosecutor rather than their supporting defense attorney (4:39-46). Do you see how the sharpness of this portrait of Jesus builds? Here Jesus has emerged as the eschatological judge of all humanity.

As we move forward in the Festival Cycle to the sixth chapter and the concern with Passover, the portrait sharpens again. While the conflict softens slightly, the overall impact continues to intensify. The chapter opens with the only two signs (miracles) that appear in all four Gospels— Jesus' feeding of the five thousand and his walking on water. The linking of these two miraculous events with Passover was undoubtedly regarded by John and the early Christians as a symbolic reminder of the Jewish exodus when God saved the people as (a) the death angel passed over the homes of the Israelites and then delivered them from the Egyptians through the miraculous control of the sea, and (b) thereafter God saved the people from starvation in the wilderness through the miraculous supplying of manna.

People recognize the feeding of the multitude with a mere five loaves and two fish as so historic that they conclude Jesus must be the long-anticipated Prophet who will be like Moses (John 6:14; cf. Deut 18:15). With their stomachs full, it is not much of a jump in their conquered state under Rome to attempt to make Jesus their king (John 6:15). But that is hardly the goal of the Son of God, so he and the disciples leave the scene and the sea story begins. John does not waste words as he recounts that Jesus retreats into the hills while the disciples are in the boat crossing north to Capernaum, and suddenly a fierce storm arises on the Sea of Tiberias (the Roman name for the Sea of Galilee). As we might expect after reading the other Gospels, Jesus rescues the frightened disciples. We might not pause much more on this story except for one statement that John picked up from Mark 6:50 and that thereafter became a major Johannine theme. As Jesus approaches the frightened disciples, he identifies himself as "I am" (*ego eimi*; often poorly translated) in John 6:20 (cf. Mark 6:50)!

The theological implications of this *ego eimi* ("I am") statement in connection with the miraculous signs of feeding and the control of the sea in the context of Passover must have been almost overwhelming for John. For him, the combined picture of the God of Passover (Exod 11–12), the exodus (Exod 14–15), manna (Exod 16), and the burning bush of Moses (Exod 2:13-14) must have jumped out at him and seared his memory as he pondered the person of Jesus who had been in their midst. But those thoughts were only the first stage of writing his magnificent "bread of life" account in which John makes it clear that God, not Moses, was the giver of the manna from heaven (6:32). Moreover, God is now giving them not merely bread for their stomachs, which provides only temporary sustenance (6:26-27), but, in the Son, the true bread of life that is eternal in nature (6:27). Now all who come to him might find their life appetites filled by the one who said, "I am the bread of life" (6:35). Those who believe in him should realize that they will be raised by him and experience eternal life (6:40).

But just as the Israelites grumbled in the wilderness, the Jews in the Capernaum synagogue likewise grumble when Jesus declares, "I am the bread which came down from heaven" (6:41, 59). But if such a statement causes consternation, Jesus continues by indicating that unless humans eat of the flesh of the Son of man and drink his blood, they "would have no life in [them]" (6:53). As you might guess, such a statement caused a great deal of confusion among his synagogue listeners, and that confusion has not subsided even today. Some may ask, was Jesus or John proposing that we engage in a form of cannibalism? The answer to such a question is obviously no, but some pagans hearing about the Christian rite of the Lord's Supper have thought so. Was Jesus or John suggesting that the celebration of Lord's Supper involves magical liturgical implications? The proposals of some Christian thinkers might confirm such a conclusion. What does it mean that those who eat "will live forever" (6:58)? The interweaving of ideas is difficult to follow.

Since John does not include an account of the institution of the Supper while each of the other Gospels do, some scholars would argue strongly that this text is a substitute for that account (cf. Mark 14:22-25; Matt 26:26-29; Luke 22:19-24). Then they may (or may not) add that the flesh and blood in this text is another way of referring to the actual changing of bread and wine in the Eucharist into the body and blood of Jesus. Others would counter that the change is not actual but symbolic. Those in still other traditions where a high degree of symbolism is considered less acceptable will seek a more literal understanding of the text, but none of these approaches provides easy solutions in terms of meaning. In every option, there are some difficulties with reaching a non-magical or automatic understanding on the one hand and clarity of meaning on the other hand. It would be pointless for me to suggest an easy solution to this problem text in a few words when the issue has been debated in thousands of pages over the centuries.

Whatever position one takes on this passage, it should be clear to readers that these words of Jesus in John created a major problem for Jesus' listeners, many of whom were "his disciples." John even takes pains to indicate repeatedly that the statement of Jesus was a "hard saying" for "many of his disciples" who also "grumbled" like the earlier Jews (6:60-61). As a result, many leave him so that Jesus questions "the twelve," asking if they also want to depart (6:66-67). The reason I include this discussion at this point is to make sure we all recognize that following Jesus is not an easy task. We may not like the words or acts of Jesus in the portrait that we are called to emulate. It may cause us to grumble. We may ponder the possibility of leaving him—even denying him like both Peter and Judas. But hopefully we will be redeemable like Peter (6:68) and not like the devilish Judas who went too far (6:70-71). As I reflect on this pericope (including Jesus' followers leaving him), I cannot help wondering if John included it because he had a similar problem of departure with the early Christians in his community (cf. 1 John 2:18-25). Indeed, there he reminds his readers that "many antichrists" are around (2:18), and they should understand the temptations in the world. Do you see the portrait of Jesus that is emerging? Is it what you thought it would be?

It is time to leave this reflection on Passover and turn briefly to the Festival of Tabernacles in the next three chapters (John 7–9). This section opens with three crucial statements: (1) the Jews are ready to kill Jesus;

(2) it is time for the most popular festival of the Jewish year—Tabernacles—when people are ready for their vacations and their annual religious camping experience; and (3) Jesus' brothers try to push him into making a public show of his messianic intentions in the capital city of Jerusalem, although even they doubt his claims (7:1-5). But Jesus is hardly open to political maneuvering or in manipulating people by showmanship—remember the devil's temptations concerning showmanship in Jerusalem (cf. Matt 4:5-6; Luke 4:9-11).

In Jerusalem the people are looking for him, debating his legitimacy, and waiting like a television camera crew for a showdown with the authorities (7:10:13). Instead of making a public display, however, Jesus comes to the festival privately (7:10). But the people find him and the face-off continues over his actions on the Sabbath, his astounding teaching, his debatable views of the law, and their own theories concerning the Messiah's coming (7:15-31). Because they are so earthbound in their thinking, when Jesus tells them they cannot join him where he is going, they can only imagine that he must mean he is going to the Diaspora (where Jews live outside of Palestine). But using one of the major features of the Tabernacles celebration—the prayers for water after the hot summer—as a key, Jesus calls the thirsty people to come and drink of the living water of the Spirit (7:37-39).

Confusion concerning Jesus at this point hardly diminishes, however, as people continue to take sides. Although the chief priests (Annas and his family) want Jesus arrested, the officers are unable to do so and a debate about Jesus even ensues in the council (Sanhedrin), with Nicodemus calling for openness in their decision-making process. But most of the council members have prejudged the question because in their minds Jesus is from Galilee (7:50-52).

The scene then shifts to the temple treasury (8:20), where Jesus issues a stirring invitation: "I am the light of the world; the one who follows me will not walk in darkness but will have the light that results in life" (8:12). As you might guess, that statement brings a face-off concerning Jesus and his relationship to God as his Father (8:13-19). Then it intensifies as Jesus reasserts an *ego eimi* ("I am") saying concerning himself (8:24, 28) and that he is from "above" while they (the Jews) are merely from "below" or "of this world" (8:23). Then Jesus makes the shocking claim that if they would follow him, "they would know the truth and the truth would set them free" (8:32).[11] The reaction is fierce and immediate as the Jews claim their kinship with father Abraham and that they have never been slaves

(8:33). Of course, they are not speaking historically but psychologically. Jesus counters their defense with the charge that they are hardly Abraham's children because they are seeking to kill him and are instead children of the devil because they follow the lying pattern of the devil (8:39-44). Their sharp response is that Jesus is a despised, half-breed Samaritan.

When Jesus next asserts that those who are loyal to him "will never experience death," they think he is illogical because Abraham died, and how could Jesus be greater than father Abraham or the prophets (8:53)? The reply in John is a classic supra-temporal assertion and another *ego eimi* affirmation of Jesus' divinity—"Before Abraham was I am" (8:58). That statement is more than the Jews can accept, so they grab stones to kill him. But the text says that somehow he is hidden from them (8:59). The magnificent portrait continues to emerge. Is Jesus superior to their hero Moses? Clearly, yes (5:45-46; 6:32-33)! Is Jesus greater than father Abraham? Absolutely (8:58)!

John then moves to bring closure to the Tabernacles discussion with the fascinating story of the blind man in chapter 9. He links it to the previous chapters by Jesus' reassertion that he is the "light of the world" in the wilderness/darkness (8:12; 9:5) and by contrasting the miserable, accusatory paralytic's responses of chapter 5 with the grateful, searching blind man of chapter 9. This later story is instructive and opens with the disciples trying to assign blame for the man's blindness. The issue, however, is complex for them because the man was *born blind* (even the rabbis argued about such a case). Their question is related to the age-old issue of theodicy (the problem of evil), an issue that resists easy answers. Jesus refuses to answer their quest for blame but points to the fact that the presence of God can be revealed in difficult situations (9:1-3).

Then Jesus heals the man by applying "spittled" mud to his eyes (like God formed Adam from clay and breathed life into him). The Jews investigating the Sabbath breach are not interested in the amazing healing. They seek to determine who is to blame for the healing (9:13-14). They first question the healed man to learn who the healer is, but he is no help because even when they give him their desired theological parameters for assessing blame, the man merely says that the healer must be a prophet (9:15-17). In disgust they turn to his parents, who willingly testify that the man is their son and that he was born blind, but they refuse to become further involved in the investigation lest they will be blamed and excommunicated (*aposynogos genetai*) from the synagogue. So in exasperation the investigators once again approach the man seeking confirmation of blame for the Sabbath breach. When they also give him further instructions on how to answer their questions by telling him to praise God but to realize the healer is a sinner (9:24), the former blind man gets frustrated and asks, "Do you want to become his disciples?" Wrong question! Then the man gives them his homespun theological evaluation that the healer must be from God, because who ever heard of a man born blind yet being healed (9:32)? Excellent perspective but wrong approach to an investigating committee. As might be expected, he is thrown out of the synagogue.

Case closed? No! Jesus finds the man and blesses him not merely with sight but also because of his insight. To the seeing Jews who have condemned the blind man, however, Jesus the healer becomes their judge and renders a "guilty" verdict (9:39-41).

As John moves to chapter 10, he almost buries the notation that it is the Festival of Dedication (Hanukah; 10:22). So readers are tempted to read over the statement and the accompanying explanation that "it was winter" without paying much attention to its cold implications. Of course, the month of Kislev (roughly our December) is wintertime, but time and temperature designations in John also carry spiritual implications (cf. "night" at 3:2). The end of Jesus' ministry is clearly on the horizon, and John wants us to recognize this reality.

Chapter 10 contains one of John's two magnificent *mashals* (extended parables "The Good Shepherd," 10:1-18, and "The Vine and the Branches," 15:1-11). Both are rooted in *ego eimi* ("I am") sayings and both provide insights into Jesus. Here Jesus is compared to a good shepherd who cares for his sheep and would risk his life to save them (10:11) from robbers, killers, and predatory animals like wolves (10:1, 10, 12). Indeed, this shepherd cares and would never abandon the flock like a hired hand when the sheep are being attacked (10:12-13). At night when the sheep are in the sheepfold, he lies at the entrance or gate and becomes the guardian door that protects the sheep (10:7, 9), and in the morning he calls and by his voice leads the sheep and they follow him (10:4). The verbal images John paints in this *mashal* are authentic and magnificent. When I taught in Israel I observed shepherds leading their sheep through the busy streets of Jerusalem with their calming voices. They provide a moving picture of a close relationship between Jesus and his followers, hardly one of a Greek philosophical *deus absonditus* (a hidden God), or a transcendent being as known in both Second Temple Judaism and Islam who simply gives rules and is basically removed from people, while keeping a record of their lives.

The Johannine Jesus is a present companion of believers who leads them throughout life.

Are the Jews in John's time ready for such a Jesus? Some think he is crazy and has a demon, while others cannot rationalize how a healer could be demonic (10:19-21). But the confusion in the crowd gives the investigators the opening they want to interrogate Jesus further. So they demand that he make it clear whether or not he is the Messiah (the anointed one of God—10:24). Yet it is only a ploy and Jesus knows it (10:26)! So he repeats the assertions concerning his unique relationship with the Father (10:30) and his mission to provide eternal life to his followers and protect them from robbers (10:27-29). It is what they want to condemn him for blasphemy, and they take up stones to kill him (10:31-33), but the death of Jesus will have to wait.

As we turn to chapter 11, we return to Passover and reach the climax of the Festival Cycle. While in the Synoptic Gospels (Mark, Matthew, and Luke) the cleansing of the temple serves as the final stage in the conflict with the Jews, John has already used that event in chapter 2 to highlight early in his portrait the rejection of Jesus by the Jews. So he chooses the story of the raising of Lazarus to portray the final stage of that conflict and to emphasize Jesus' incredible power.

The story is once again a classic. Jesus and the disciples are up north in Galilee when they receive a "telegraphic" message intended to hasten Jesus' return south because his friend Lazarus is very ill (11:3). My students sometimes think that Jesus' delay and response to the effect that it would be for "the glory of God" may be fine theology, but it seems to them a little hard-hearted. What is your opinion? Well, instead of packing up and going immediately to assist his friend, Jesus delays his return for two days and then tells his disciples it is time to head south (11:5-7). The disciples are in no mood for returning into the jaws of deadly conflict in the south, and they respond that if Lazarus is merely ill, he will recover (11:8-12). When Jesus tells them that Lazarus is now dead, it is as though the earth falls in around them. Then Thomas, realizing that Jesus will hardly be dissuaded from the journey, utters for all of them their sense of complete hopelessness when he says, "Let's also go and die" (11:16)!

When Jesus reaches the south, the scene is no better because Martha cries: if only Jesus would have been there, her brother "would not have died." The situation seems hopeless (11:21) since her brother has been dead for four days and the time has passed for any resuscitation.[12] She really thinks it is too late! When Jesus says that her brother will rise, it only brings a good Jewish Pharisaic recitation from her. She knows that her brother will rise in the resurrection (11:24). When Jesus tells her "I am the resurrection" and asks her, "Do you believe?" her response is a wonderful "Yes"—she believes and she will confess that he is "Christ, the Son of God, the one who is coming into the world" (11:27). Readers could easily regard that confession as a marvelous conclusion to Martha's story. Indeed, I have even heard an internationally recognized New Testament scholar end his sermon on that note. My response to him was, "Friend, that confession is not the conclusion to the story!" Martha is not unlike many of us who can recite our Sunday school lessons and confessions, but it does not mean we have spiritually digested and integrated them into our lives.

After the interlude of the story of Mary with her painful repetition of "if only you had been here, my brother would not have died" and the mourners' hopeless question about why the miraculous Jesus could not keep Lazarus from dying (11:28-37), we return to the crucial conclusion of the Martha story. Later, as Jesus views the tomb, he finally commands the mourners to "Remove the stone!" Then Martha reveals her understanding of Jesus as she cries out that it has been four days and the smell of the body will be horrible (11:39). I do not intend here to diminish the traumatic experience of mourning. But I am concerned about how seriously we Christians take our confessions. Friends, this book is written with the hope that the portraits of Jesus will not be merely words in the Bible but will become for us vivid challenges to the way we follow Jesus.

When Jesus shouts, "Lazarus, come out!" (11:43), John knows that Jesus has crossed his Rubicon. The Jewish establishment who assert they are loyal to God cannot tolerate one who has the power and authority of God, so in the meeting of the Sanhedrin the high priest issues the equivalent of an *ex cathedra* statement when he says, "it is appropriate for one man to die for the people than that the entire nation should be perish" (11:50). While John would hardly agree with the means/ends argument of Caiaphas, he views the words as a divinely oriented prediction concerning the mission of Jesus (11:51-52). So the order is given in the council for the arrest of Jesus (11:57)! Thus ends the first half of the book.

We move now to reflect briefly on chapter 12, which serves as the introduction to the second half of the Gospel and the prelude to the third major section that I have elsewhere designated as the Farewell Cycle.[13] This cycle is then followed by two smaller sections that should be designated as the Death Story and the Resurrection Stories.

The second half of the Gospel and its introductory chapter 12 begins appropriately with the anointing of Jesus for his death. This event alerts the reader like a neon sign to the fact that we have entered the final stages of Jesus' earthly ministry. Mary, the sister of the resuscitated Lazarus, uses the essence of nard for this crucial moment. A vial of this nard was very costly (roughly worth a year's wages for a blue-class worker—an *am haeretz*). One might even consider the value to be an excellent dowry for a woman. Judas, the company treasurer and thief (cf. 12:6), views the act to be nothing less than a foolish waste of money, but Jesus cuts his critique short and recognizes the event as a strategic symbolic act in preparation for his death (12:7).

John purposely sets this anointing story immediately before the crucial entry into Jerusalem that our church calendars identify with Palm Sunday. As such, it should help readers to interpret the meaning of the event in light of the death of Jesus. Be sure you pay attention to the fact that Lazarus is reintroduced before the entry and that his presence causes more people to come to Jesus so that the Jewish leadership is contemplating killing Lazarus as well (12:9-11). While the entry into Jerusalem may be viewed as a time of celebration in Luke (19:38-40), it is to be understood very differently in John.

Watch the reactions of each group. (a) The people in general, who hardly know what is going on behind the scene with their institutional leadership, welcome Jesus as "King of Israel" (12:13-15). (b) The disciples, who know a little about Jesus, are confused, and that confusion does not cease until after the death and resurrection of Jesus—his glorification (12:16). (c) The Jewish leaders, like the Pharisees, are frustrated because they are losing control and cannot contain the enthusiasm of the crowd (12:19). (d) And then there are the Greeks—those on the sidelines—who want a piece of he action. They come to the disciples (especially to one like Philip who has a Greek name) to "see Jesus" (12:20-21). Do you get the picture?

But what is the reaction of Jesus? That is the crucial question. John tells us Jesus understands that "The hour has come for the Son of Man to be glorified!" (13:23). That means it is time for Jesus to die—just like grain when planted in the ground dies before it produces the harvest. So the mission of Jesus involves his death (12:24). If the portrait of the Johannine Jesus was not apparent when the Baptizer introduced Jesus in the first chapter as "the Lamb of God who takes away the sin of the world" (1:29), it should be clear at this point. The Messiah definitely has the power and authority of God when on earth, but this portrait is not merely one of a conquering hero who rides into the scene on the white horse as in Revelation 19:11. But note that even in Revelation his robe is dipped in blood and his name is "the Word of God" (19:13)! John's message is consistent.

To make the matter even more emphatic, John here emphasizes that the followers of this Messiah "must follow [him]" if they expect to join Jesus in "eternal life" (John 12:25-26). Is the course easy for Jesus? The answer is a resounding "no!" It is painful and troubling for him. But this path was confirmed when God sent his unique voice from heaven (12:27-30). The sacrificial death of Jesus is the means God uses to bring people out of the darkness to life and at the same time judge the world and God's enemy—the so-called ruler of the world (12:31-33).

Did most people in the world at that time understand this mystery? Do they today? The answer has always been hardly! Yet for those who are able to follow Jesus—to "walk" in the light—the answer should be apparent. Sadly, many people love the dark world and its affirmation too much (12:34-50). The mission of Jesus in coming to the world was and continues to be to bring eternal life to the world and not to judge it now. But judgment on the last day has already been defined by his mission (12:47-50; cf. 3:17, 36). So the message of Jesus through John is that all who believe or commit themselves to this Jesus will not continue in the darkness but will find eternal life.

With this perspective in mind, we turn now to the third major section of John's magnificent work—the Farewell Cycle. This cycle contains not only a series of farewell messages but also a model act in which Jesus washes the feet of his disciples and concludes with a magisterial prayer encasing petitions that exemplify the mission of Jesus and the meaning of his "glorification." The format of this cycle is a marvelous construct that can be understood to be in the shape of a bull's-eye (or a chiastic structure[14]), the outside ring of which is chapters 13 and 17. Inside that outer ring are two segments dealing with loneliness and anxiety (14:1-14 and 16:16-33), and inside that ring are two segments on the role of the Paraclete or the Holy Spirit (14:25-31 and 15:18-16:15). At the center is John's second *mashal* or extended parable on the vine and the branches (15:1-17).

The cycle begins with the haunting note that it is nearly Passover, when Jesus will demonstrate that his love for his followers extends "to the end" (*eis telos*)—a clear indication that his purpose involves the ultimate sacrifice (13:1). At this point the devil is in the heart of Judas, leading him to betray

Jesus shamefully and thus initiate the final stage of Jesus completing his mission and returning to the Father (13:2-3).

It is time for Jesus to provide for his disciples an unforgettable model, so he washes their feet. In realizing how astonishing this act is, we must remember that a rabbi could ask his students to do for him what most household servants should do—but the rabbi could not ask them to touch his feet. Do the disciples understand the magnitude of this act by Jesus? Perhaps in part! At least Peter senses its social inappropriateness (13:8), so he refuses Jesus at first. But typical of the well-meaning Peter, when he learns that Jesus' act of humility has consequences far beyond his understanding, Peter requests not merely a foot-washing but a complete shower or bath. One can imagine that in the seriousness of that moment, Jesus smiles or grimaces, shakes his head, and says something like, "Feet enough, Peter!" And then he obviously adds the serious conclusion that cleanliness goes much deeper than such symbolic washing and that not everyone there is clean (13:11). While the statement obviously refers to Judas, my students often ask me, "Did Jesus actually wash the feet of Judas?" What do you think? Whatever your answer may be, do not reduce your portrait of Jesus to human vindictiveness.

This night is a time of great meaning and symbolism, and Jesus uses the event to show his disciples that just as he, their teacher, has been a servant, they ought willingly "to wash each other's feet" (13:14). Now to pursue my students' concern further, let us remember that Judas participates in this historic Supper event and probably even reclines next to Jesus (at his back while the beloved disciple is positioned in front of him—"at his breast," 13:23) since Jesus is able to hand his betrayer a piece of soaked bread (13:26). The significance of this picture of Jesus with his disciples is almost overwhelming. Jesus knows his betrayer, and to realize that betrayer is allowed to be a part of this strategic meal as Satan is taking control of him is mind-boggling. What a portrait of a welcoming Jesus! When Judas takes the little piece of bread, however, things change radically. It is then and only then that Jesus commands Judas to leave and do his despicable deed (13:27). It is then and only then that John indicates that "it was night!" (13:30)—a designation that in John is not simply a time notation. It is a flashing literary sign of the dreaded event that will soon take place.

Then Jesus issues what has become known in Christian history as "the New Commandment"—"Love one another! Just as I have loved you, you are to love each other." It is through such love, Jesus indicates, that all others will recognize people are his disciples (13:34-35). Are they ready for this farewell message? Hardy! Instead, Peter voices the confusion of the disciples when he asks, "Where are you going?" And he quickly adds that he will surely join Jesus, even if it means his death. But Peter does not understand what he is saying. Indeed, instead of following Jesus, Peter is informed that before daybreak, he will deny Jesus three times (13:36-38). The critical moment has arrived! We have finished the first stage of the Farewell Cycle, and we move inward and forward to stage 2, which is inside the outer ring.

John 14:1-14 next takes us to the sense of "lostness" or feeling of abandonment among the disciples and their consequent anxiety. With the climactic death of Jesus looming on the horizon, the questions facing the disciples are, will Jesus actually leave them, and what will his supposed abandonment mean? The response of Jesus given in John has provided Christians, the church, and its ministry with a classic statement concerning comfort in times of grief. "Don't be troubled," Jesus says, because he is going away to be with the Father and is preparing a place for his followers in God's dimension. Moreover, he will surely return and ensure them that they will be with him (14:1-3).

Do they understand what he is talking about? The answer must be no. His words are confusing to them, and they misunderstand his forthcoming departure as a literal "journey." Thomas, the practical one, voices their common concern as he says he wants to know "where" Jesus is going and asks if Jesus will give them a road map (like our "trip-tick" or "GPS" guidance pattern) of the actual way because these statements are too difficult for them to comprehend (14:5). At that point John indicates that Jesus issues another of his distinctive *ego eimi* sayings in which he identifies himself as the "Way" to the Father.[15] But Jesus adds that he is also "the Truth" and "the Life"—genuine qualities possessed only by God (14:6)!

Do the disciples get the meaning then? The answer is hardly. In exasperation, Philip begs, "Just show us the Father and we will be satisfied." Does Philip realize what he is asking? Not likely! To see God would be to die (cf. Exod 33:20)! As you ponder this encounter, have you ever wondered how Jesus reacted to such responses by his disciples? How do you answer humans who just do not get it? The answer of Jesus was basically, "When you have seen me, you have seen the Father"—which means, "Boys, you have been looking at the image of God! And if you still do not understand, look at my works! Can mere humans do them?" (14:8-11).

Friends, is the portrait of Jesus getting clearer? Yet what comes next could be more astounding and confusing. Consider those works of Jesus:

are they not amazing? If you believe Jesus, he says that his followers will do those works—and they will even do greater works (14:12). Really? Wow! In considering this idea, we know it does *not* mean we will be greater than Jesus. Yet perhaps there is an important truth hidden here; if our actions are linked to our relationship with Jesus, then what we do will bear witness to the divine presence in us. Thus, our requests made in his "name" or nature will testify to the authenticity of that presence in us (14:14; cf. 15:7). So, if we are united with him in the Spirit, can we not personally experience the miraculous working though us and bringing glory to the Father through the Son (14:13)? Accordingly, whatever we accomplish in the Spirit of Jesus will provide for us a genuine sense of God working through us and a wonderful experience of divine consolation.

If you have followed my thinking watch how it can be illustrated in the Johannine target. As we move closer to the center of the bull's-eye (the crossing point in a chiastic structure), Christians get closer to Christ, and that is probably the reason the circle within the target next to the center deals with the Paraclete—the Holy Spirit. As we move inward to that next circle, remember that inside the circle comes the center, the *mashal* of the Vine and branches (15:1-17). Do you see John's organization?

In this next segment before the center then (14:25-31), we encounter the first two of the five Paraclete (Comforter, Counselor, Supporter, Holy Spirit) sayings in John. These sayings are crucial because they supply us with divine insight into how significant Jesus is to our understanding of the relationship between God and humans. In the context of the first saying we discover that there is a condition to obtaining the Holy Spirit. That condition is loving Jesus and keeping his instructions because Jesus was our first Paraclete with the Father (note: the "another" *parakletos* at 14:15). Since, therefore, the first Paraclete is Jesus, when he sent his replacement he could genuinely say, "*I* will not leave you abandoned, *I* will come to you" (14:18). Such an interlaced idea, of course, is difficult for us to comprehend because we cannot imagine in our time- and space-bound humanness how the Triune God is interrelated. All our theological models of God ultimately fail to encompass this mystery, just as we fail to understand how Jesus is related to God (the Father) and how they share our love and obedience (14:20-24).

The second Paraclete saying carries this idea a step further. Not only will the Father send the Spirit to Jesus' followers in the "name"/nature of Jesus but the Spirit will also remind Christians of all the instructions of Jesus. Jesus will in turn continue to give them his peace—*eirene* or *shalom*

(14:26-27). This divine, peaceful Presence is God's great gift though Jesus that provides his people with comfort in times of trouble and fear (14:27). So, even though Jesus has gone to the Father, he still is able to come to us (14:28)! Remember, therefore, that the great enemy of God—the devil—has no power over Jesus (14:30).

With this mystery in mind, we turn to the center of our bull's-eye and one of the most profound pictures in the Bible—the *mashal* of the Vine and the branches (15:1-17). It is crucial to understand the relationships in this extended parable correctly. Remember that the *mashal* is a picture, so focus on the main relational points. Jesus is the Vine—the "I" of the parable. Humans are the "you"—the branches. God is the farmer/gardener—the one who prunes or makes sure the authentic branches are healthy, properly pruned, and productive and that the non-productive branches are removed (15:1-2).

The purpose of God is to maintain healthy, productive human branches that are the result of Jesus' word/action (15:3) and that are properly attached to (abide in) the Vine (15:4) and therefore bear fruit (15:5). A problem, however, is created if a branch misunderstands its nature and assumes (like Adam and Eve; cf. Gen 3:5-7) that it can be fruitful and independent apart from the Vine. In such a case, it will become hopelessly unproductive and will have to be removed and burned (15:6). On the other hand, if a branch remains properly attached to the Vine and Jesus' nature remains the dynamic part of that branch, then the branch can make requests of the Vine. The result will be that (a) an answer will be given and (b) God will be glorified in his proven disciples (15:7-8).

In addition, it is crucial to recognize that at the core of this *mashal* is the love of God. The Father loved Jesus who in turn loved humans and expected humans to love him and be obedient to him just as he has always been obedient to the Father. This interrelationship of love and obedience between the Father, Jesus, and the disciples of Jesus is the key to this parable and indeed to the proper understanding of the entire Gospel (15:9-10)! The result is that disciples should experience the wonderful gift of God's *joy* (15:11).

This love of God in Jesus then provides the foundation for the reintroduction of the new commandment of love at 15:12 (cf. 13:34) and the rationale for why Jesus was willing to come and lay down his life for humanity (3:16), especially for his followers whom he called his "friends" (15:13). Of course, it would have been legitimate for God, the Creator of all things, to have made humans as robots and demanded that these creatures serve as his slaves. Instead, God chose to create mortals with freedom to choose to follow or to reject him and his instructions. He gave that choice in the beginning and reaffirmed that pattern in the coming of his only Son, Jesus, who modeled divine love for the world. This beloved Son of God called his followers to be his "friends," blessed them with promises, and provided them with instructions to be obeyed (15:13-17), just like God called Abraham and others to be his friends, blessed them with promises, and provided them with instructions (cf. for example Gen 12:1-3; 17:1-8; Isa 41:8; 2 Chr 20:7). Like the God of the Old Testament, the portrait of the Johannine Jesus is a stunning picture of divine graciousness, but not all is right with the world and the rejection of love brings harsh consequences!

Having thus concluded the center of the target, we now move outward and briefly focus on the mirror-image texts of the Farewell Cycle. Returning to the three remaining Paraclete (Counselor, Comforter, Supporter) sayings, it becomes apparent that the context is one of hostility and persecution for both Jesus and Christians. As the people hate Jesus, so they will hate Christians (15:18-25). In such a setting, Jesus promises in the third Paraclete saying to send the Spirit of Truth from the Father to keep Christians from becoming a scandal ("falling away,"15:26–16:1). Fourth, in sending the Paraclete, Jesus' strategy in the world will be threefold. The Spirit will use Christians to convince the world: (a) that people are sinners; (b) that God has a righteous standard; and (c) that they are under judgment because of their alignment with the devil (16:7-11). Fifth and finally, because such a context is difficult, Jesus promises that Christians will be given the Spirit to guide them and make evident the intentions of Jesus (16:14-15). The result is that Jesus will be glorified in the work of the Spirit (16:13-15). Do you see how important the role of the Spirit is to our portrait of Jesus?

With this understanding, John next returns to the issue of loneliness and abandonment. He gives voice to the disciples' deep fears and announces that in a "little while" they will not see him and then they will see him again (16:16-17), but that sounds like double talk to them. So Jesus tries again with the illustration of a woman in delivery pains before the child is born but who rejoices once the baby is delivered (16:20-22). Likewise the disciples will later understand and be able to pray to God with their requests in the Spirit of Jesus and experience the joy of answered prayer, recognizing that God (the Father) does love the Son and has re-welcomed him into his divine personal presence from whence he came (16:25-28).

When the disciples responded that they finally understand what he is saying and that they believe him, Jesus must shake his head at their lack of perception, and then he tells them that they are about to abandon him. But he firmly asserts the Father will never abandon him (16:29-32).[16] Yet they are in this hostile world and need the consoling peace and knowledge that he is the Victor and that he can handle such hostility (16:33). With these words of the powerful, supportive Jesus (the first Paraclete) as a portrait spinning in our minds, we turn to the majestic prayer of Jesus as the final segment in the Farewell Cycle.

While the Synoptic Gospels, especially Luke (22:39-46), focus on the Gethsemane Prayer as the last preparation of Jesus before his arrest, John instead highlights the magnificent prayer of John 17. What I note here briefly besides the picture of the praying Jesus is that there is a sevenfold structure to this prayer that reflects significant features in the Gospel.[17]

This prayer contains the repeated refrain of "Father," which generally signals a prayer/petition of Jesus in John (cf. 11:41).[18] Then linked to the first petition to the "Father" is the haunting announcement that the "hour" has finally arrived for the Son's glorification (17:1; cf. the first use of "hour" at 2:4). This telling "hour" means that "eternal life" will come to humans through Jesus' horrific death and glorious resurrection (17:3; cf. 3:16-18). It is followed immediately by a second petition that calls for the "Father" to return Jesus to his preexistent glory, reminding us of the Prologue and that, before creation, "In the beginning was the Word!" who became flesh (1:1, 14).

The third and fourth petitions are set in the context of the hostile and hateful world where the disciples will live and be harassed just as Jesus experiences in the events of the Festival Cycle. Therefore, he calls on the "Holy Father," third, to "keep" or "protect" them by the authority of the divine "name" (17:9-11). Jesus is protector of the disciples while he is on Earth. None is lost, except the anticipated traitor (17:12). But the caring Jesus is returning to God, and he is concerned. Yet he does not pray for their removal from the world (which will mean the end of his mission). Instead, he seeks their protection from the evil one—the devil (17:15). In the light of such hostility, Jesus' fourth petition is for the holiness of his followers, namely that they will copy his model in a genuine, consecrated life (17:17-19).

The remaining three petitions focus on Jesus' desire that his disciples will evidence authentic Christian lives as his representatives in the world. Modeled on the unity of the Godhead, Jesus prays, fifth, that his followers will be united as the basis for their mission to the world (17:20-21). Jesus knows that a divided church will be a poor representative of God's intentions in the world. But somehow Christians still have trouble understanding this point since they seem to be primarily concerned about building their particular brands of the kingdom, like the early Jewish disciples after the resurrection who still talked about the kingdom of Israel (cf. Acts 1:2, 6).

Then, in the sixth petition, Jesus prays that his disciples will catch a vision of his eternal glory (John 17:24). Naturally, gaining a full picture of Jesus' glory is a futuristic vision, but if we could see more of it, even as in darkened mirror (cf. 1 Cor 13:12), I believe it would change the church and provide thousands of living examples of integrity in our era.

Finally, in the seventh petition Jesus seems to cry out in prayer to his "Righteous Father" that his followers will understand and follow his heart's longing concerning his new commandment to love one another (cf. 13:34-35; 15:12) after the divine model of God' love (17:25-26). Do you wonder when Christians will hear the longing of Jesus, repent of their self-centered ways, and embrace the prayer of Jesus?

This moving Farewell Cycle is thus complete. The heart of the loving Jesus who washed the feet of his disciples (13:5-17) is brilliantly revealed in the majestic prayer (ch. 17). The Lord who sought to calm the anxiety of his fearful disciples (14:1-14) reminds them that even though they might abandon him, he will never be abandoned (16:25-33) and he will send the Paraclete—the Holy Spirit—to be with them in every situation of life (14:15-30 and 15:18–16:15). Their calling, however, is to remain/abide in him because he is their foundation for security and their true model for loving relationships and authentic service (15:1-17). Friends, don't you think that John has sketched a magnificent portrait of Jesus? But it is now time to complete the picture and briefly conclude this magisterial portrait of Jesus with his gruesome death and powerful resurrection.

The death story of Jesus opens in the garden, with Judas bringing a contingent of soldiers and temple officers to arrest Jesus. But the way John narrates the story provides a different feeling than is given in the Synoptic Gospels. There is no prayer in the garden here, since we have just had Jesus' majestic prayer, and there is no kiss from Judas, the traitor, because John presents Jesus as one who is totally in charge. Therefore, Jesus identifies himself by stepping forth and uttering the inspired, "I am" (*ego eimi*). When he does so, the armed band falls helplessly to the ground (18:5-6). Then Jesus instructs the arresters to free his disciples (18:8). When Peter tries to protect Jesus with his puny sword, however, Jesus has to remind him that he is messing in divine business that involves the "Father" (18:10-11).

What follows is a brilliantly designed literary narrative by John in which Peter and his denial (note the *ouk eimi*—"I am not" of 18:17, 25) is interwoven and contrasted with the high priest's inauthentic questioning of Jesus (18:12-14, 19-24). That segment is then followed by a similar interwoven segment contrasting the weakness of the Roman judge Pilate who has little understanding of "truth" (18:38) and the strength of the accused Jesus who emerges as an authentic king and is hardly guilty of any crime (18:36-38). When Pilate recognizes that the Jewish charges are a charade, he tries to pacify the Jews through offering a quick-release plan by making them choose between Jesus and a radical insurrectionist (*lestes*) named Barabbas. His attempt fails because the Jews choose Barabbas (18:39-40). Not to be deterred, Pilate has Jesus severely beaten and dressed like a humiliated king. But that trick does not work because the Jewish leaders have tasted blood and want more—they want crucifixion! Then they add that he should die because he has made himself the "Son of God" (19:1-7).

Wait a minute! Pilate, the Roman authority, has not counted on dealing with "god stuff." It is time to reconsider! But when they reenter Pilate's chambers and he begins reexamining the prisoner, Jesus refuses to speak until Pilate tries to threaten him. At that point Jesus tells Pilate that he has no power except by divine will. That is enough for Pilate, and he tries to free Jesus (19:8-12). But the Jews have a trump card. They warn Pilate that if he tries to release Jesus, he is no "friend of Caesar." That statement is critical for Pilate because it is a technical designation/title that is bestowed by the emperor on elite Romans for their loyalty to the purple robe.[19]

At that point, Pilate is faced with "god stuff" versus real politics, and "god stuff" is destined to lose. Pilate is a climber, but in the end he falls out of favor with Rome and is banished. The Jewish leaders win the face-off here but not before John indicates that they themselves have committed the ultimate hypocrisy by stating, "We have no king but Caesar!" (cf. Samuel's anger in 1 Sam 8:4-7, 19-22). Yet Pilate still wins part of the face-off when the Jews try to have the charge on the cross altered to something like "Jesus said he was the King of the Jews" from "Jesus of Nazareth, the King of the Jews" (19:19, 21).

Some intriguing insights can be gained in this story if we pause to reflect. It is almost as though Pilate, the so-called authority, had no backbone until the point of the written charge on the cross. Have you ever wondered why? I suspect that John knew who was in control of the story! After all, Jesus, "the Lamb of God," died on the "day of Preparation" at the time the Passover lambs were being sacrificed (19:14, 30-31; cf. 1:29, 36).

Moreover, John makes it patently clear that the charge on the cross is meant to be recognized as a universal statement of the Kingship of Jesus because it is written in the languages of government (Latin), commerce (Greek), and historic faith (Hebrew), and Pilate will not change it (19:20, 22)!

As the company marches to Skull Hill, John emphasizes that Jesus carries his own cross piece. There is no Simon of Cyrene to take the burden from Jesus here (19:17; cf. Mark 15:21). And there are no weeping women along the *Via Dolorosa* ("Way of Sorrows," cf. Luke 23:27-31). But at the foot of the cross are two important scenes. Although John employs many allusions to the Old Testament, there are few direct quotes from it. But when the soldiers are "gaming" for Jesus' clothing, John cannot resist mentioning that this event is a fulfillment of the poetic couplet from Psalm 22:18. And since Ephesus is the site where John is traditionally said to have taken Mary to live, I suspect he cannot resist indicating that in last moments of his death and as the eldest son, Jesus appoints John to be the caretaker of his mother (John 19:25-27).[20] I should also add that since there are many theories concerning Mary in Christian theology, it is crucial to note that John portrays Jesus as being in charge of his mother and not the other way around (cf. John 2:1-5 as well as the proleptic statement of Jesus to his parents in Luke 2:49-50).[21]

The death scene also contains two important statements of Jesus from the cross. The first, "I am thirsty," is John's way of reminding readers that Jesus' death on the cross was an excruciating experience (John 19:28). And the statement, "It is finished," reminds us that even in death Jesus was in control (19:30).[22] At the end, Jesus determines the moment he will die, and to the surprise of the authorities he is dead before they anticipate it. So the soldiers do not need to apply the *crucifragium* (the breaking of the legs to hasten death so that the person will no longer be able to gasp for breath; 19:32-33). Instead, a soldier sticks the side of Jesus with a spear to make sure he is dead, and blood and water issue from his side (19:34).

The implications of these events must have been overwhelming for the Johannine community because an authentication of their "truth" is attached as a basis for believing (19:35). Both the piercing of Jesus and the fact that his legs were not broken must have served for John as incredible signs that his Passover Lamb portrait of Jesus was authentic. Here again he cannot resist citing Old Testament texts as fulfilling the divine predictions concerning the death of Jesus (19:36-37; cf. Exod 12:46; Num 9:12 and Zech 12:10).

But the issuing of blood and water from the side of Jesus must have been a kind of symbolic capstone. Those who are primarily left-brain thinkers who eschew symbolism will probably continue trying to determine how both blood and water could issue from the side of a dying person. I have read their articles and I do not wish to argue with them. But for those who have right-brain tendencies, the symbolic connections and implications with baptism and the Lord's Supper will probably jump out at them. Could John have contemplated such a connection? I suggest that we ponder the matter. Do you not think that writing his Gospel during the nineties of the first century after decades of reflecting on the death of Jesus and its significance could lead to such a powerful conclusion? Be careful not to make this magnificent testimony and its portrait of Jesus into a mere newspaper article or television on-site report. It is far more than such a pedantic narrative.

Jesus was dead—*dead-dead!* That is what I tell my students. Why do I use this expression? I do so because most of them are imbued with Greek thinking concerning an eternal "soul" and the afterlife. Most of them have little understanding of the meaning of resurrection and of time. But the Apostle Paul gets it right in 1 Corinthians 15 when he speaks of the crucial nature of the resurrection, and in the Areopagus (Mars Hill) Address of Acts 17 when he confuses the Greeks who believe in immortality of the soul. God possesses life. Jesus as divine possesses life. Humans do not! God gives humans life in creation and in the resurrection. Here then is the great mystery of Jesus. He actually died. But God raised him from the dead. So when Joseph and Nicodemus dared to take the body and bury it, Jesus was dead! And they buried him like a king with enough spice to bury a number of ordinary people—and indeed he is a *king* (19:39)! That point is important for John.

And what about the disciples? Their hopes lie buried with their king. Mary's weeping at the tomb (20:11-12) expresses the pain and anxiety they all feel, even that evening on the first day of the week when they meet in the room behind locked doors after some of them went to the empty tomb. Fear of the authorities grips them (20:19).

But the seeming impossible happens. God raises Jesus from the dead! The tomb is empty, and the burial clothes are still there (20:6-9). The body does not need them! Then this Jesus comes to them through the locked doors and bestows on them his "peace"—shalom (*eirene,* 20:19)! He is definitely alive and he breathes on them his Spirit, like God breathed on Adam when man became a *nephesh hayah* (a "living being"; Gen 2:7). Then, as in all appearances of God (theophanies) in the Old Testament, Jesus not only blesses them but also gives them a task—a mission. That mission is the proclamation of the gospel—both forgiveness and judgment! But Thomas, the realist, is not at this meeting and he doubts the actual bodily presence of Jesus. So he makes his challenge to believing—namely, that unless he can touch the wounds of Jesus he will remain skeptical (20:24-25).

Then it happens again a week later (next Sunday[23]): Jesus appears to them and this time the realist Thomas is with them. Can you envision the scene? Jesus probably says something like, "Hello, Thomas. Interesting seeing you here! I heard that you doubted my meeting with your colleagues. You wanted to touch my wounds? Well, come here. Put your finger right here in the place of the nail wound, and put your hand in my side."

At that point it all changes for Thomas. The doubter makes perhaps the most important confession in the New Testament—"My Lord and my God!" (20:28). It is a strategic confession for John because it provides the model of commitment for the confessing church, especially those who have not seen the risen Jesus and are coming to believe (20:29).

Finally, the Johannine summation concerning gaining life through believing in Jesus, the Christ, the Son of God must have been the original ending of the book (20:30-31). Indeed, A. Loisy declares at that point, "*Le Livere est fini, tres bien fini!*"[24] But that statement is not all John has to say, and as he reflects, he must realize that something more needs to be added. An appendix is required, and as our textual traditions confirm, there is no evidence that the gospel ever circulated without chapter 21. What was missing? The restoration of Peter and the rejection of the growing legend that John would live until Jesus would returned.

These two issues are tied together in the beautiful fishing story that mirrors the early calling of the disciples in Luke 5:1-11. In that earlier story, the disciples are cleaning their nets after working all night but catching nothing, and Jesus tells them to try again. In recasting their net, they find it filled to the breaking point. That experience is so stunning for Peter that he realizes he has been in the presence of divine mystery (5:8-9).

The post-resurrection story in John 21 may be a reminder of the earlier narrative, but it is much more complex and significant. The contrast between Peter and John (the beloved disciple) is highlighted here as it is in other Johannine pericopes, such as the foot-washing scene where John relays information to Peter (John 13:23-26) and the race to the tomb where John outruns Peter and is the one who believes (20:3-9). In this fishing story, Jesus is not in the boat. The disciples, who have fished all night and caught nothing, are told by a stranger on the shore to throw their net into the sea on the other side of the boat. Of course, such a suggestion seems foolish, but when they do so, the net is filled with fish. Then the other disciple tells Peter that the figure on the shore must be Jesus, whereupon Peter jumps overboard in haste to get to the Lord. When Peter and the disciples reach land, they find a charcoal fire there, and a serious conversation ensues between Jesus and Peter.

Jesus asks Peter three times if Peter loves him. Each time the probe goes deeper into Peter's psyche, and each time as Peter answers in the affirmative, Jesus tells him to feed his flock. The last question concerning Peter's love strikes hard. Readers often get tangled in discussions over the Greek words for love without understanding that *agapao* and *phileo* are interchangeable in John.[25] The reason Peter is psychologically and spiritually broken is that Jesus asks him a *third* time (21:17), and it is around a *charcoal fire* (*anthrakia* is used only here at 21:9 and at 18:18 in the New Testament)! Do you sense what Peter is experiencing in this event? Jesus takes him back to his failure around the charcoal fire. That is precisely what God does with us in order to bring healing and restoration.

But Jesus does something more with Peter in this experience. He gives him insight into his future—that he will die/become a martyr for the Lord (21:18-19). Peter can probably handle the thought of martyrdom because he has boasted that he would be willing to die that way (13:37), but comparisons are part of life, so he wonders about John. The quick response of Jesus is, "If I want him to live until I return, that is none of your business" (21:22). It is easy to understand how such a statement could lead to the development of a legend about John, but the legend is based on a misunderstanding. Legends are not confined to the ancients. That is one reason I have written this work—because even today we are creating legends about who Jesus is.

Therefore, in this era of growing biblical illiteracy, it is critical for us to grasp and live more fully with the authentic biblical portraits of Jesus, especially the Johannine Son of God. Indeed, in this magnificent Gospel, the one that I believe forms the high climax to the portraits of Jesus in the New Testament, Thomas's resurrection statement, "My Lord and my God," represents the unequivocal confession of an authentic Christian community.

Questions for Reflection

1. Since there seem to be a number of delineations, sketches, or poses in the portrait of Jesus presented by John, which ones are the most encompassing? Which ones appeal to your mindset the most? Why?

2. How does the death and resurrection of Jesus fit into your primary sketches of Jesus? How does Jesus' relationship with the Father fit into these sketches? What about the Holy Spirit?

3. Why do you think John goes back to the creation event to portray Jesus for his readers?

4. What descriptors would you choose to describe the Christian's relationship with Jesus?

5. How does Dr. Borchert's organization of this Gospel with two introductions, three cycles, and two story lines (death and resurrection) affect your developing an overall portrait of Jesus?

6. Why do you think Borchert regards the Johannine Gospel as the climactic book in the New Testament? To what extent do you agree? Disagree?

We are finished with the Gospel of John, which for me provides the climactic portrait of Jesus in the New Testament. We turn next to the book of Revelation, which brilliantly concludes our Bible and my study on the portraits of Jesus.

The Dramatic Book of Revelation[26]

The book of Revelation is an intriguing document that has probably engendered more and varied reactions than any other part of the New Testament. Some preachers dwell on it, while others avoid it like the plague, except perhaps for the letters to the seven churches and the vision of heaven. But these reactions arise from the nature of the book itself. Some books appeal to the reason like Romans. Some books appeal to the emotional side of people like Psalms. But the book of Revelation appeals to the imagination, and without a sanctified imagination, reading it in a meaningful way will be difficult, especially for many Westerners who often try to put it into a logical time scheme.

When I was in high school, I disliked Revelation because my Sunday school teacher tried to enlighten us every year about Revelation (and Daniel) with his ghastly charts. I surmised then that I would never spend time on Revelation when I left home for university. But I thank God that this opinion changed in seminary when I discovered that there was a vast collection of ancient apocalyptic books somewhat similar to Revelation.

Since my reevaluation of the book, I have taught it in many parts of the world. I now believe that this book is a genuine gift of God to the church, and it provides a great portrait of Jesus for those who recognize the significance of its vivid images and dramatic presentations. So, with youthful imagination and mature commitment to discovering truth, I invite you into Revelation and its rapidly changing scenes.

The book opens with the crucial Greek word *apokalypsis*, which we translate as an "unveiling" or "revelation." It concerns Jesus Christ and was delivered by God's appointed messenger (angel) via dramatic visions to John for God's people, and it relates to the near or certain future (Rev 1:1-2). That may be a mouthful, but it is a terrific introduction to the book. Pay attention, then, because the statement is followed immediately by the first of seven Beatitudes[27] in the book. This one pronounces a blessing on those who read and accept Revelation's message into their lives (1:3).

Like the Gospel of John, the book of Revelation is well organized. While the beginning of this "unveiling" may be a little confusing, it has three introductions. The first one, which we have just read, is an apocalyptic introduction. The second one (1:4-8) is in the form of a typical Greek letter from John to the churches in the Roman province of Asia (modern Turkey). After the typical Christian literary greeting of "grace and peace" (always in that order), it is written under the authority of the Triune God—namely, (a) the Father who surpasses our time designations ("is, was, and is to come"), (b) the sevenfold Spirit, and (c) the Son who is the authentic witness that rose from the dead. He is the reigning ruler of his people (1:4-6) as well as the one who will return to judge the world (1:7). As you might sense, it would be hard to encapsulate the work of Jesus in a briefer, better summary than what John has crafted here. Jesus is indeed the all-encompassing one (the Alpha and Omega), the almighty (*pantokrator*, perhaps the most powerful word in Greek; 1:8).

The third introduction (1:9-12) gives one the feeling that it sets the stage for a historical account. John, a prisoner on the barren stronghold island of Patmos, is instructed to fulfill his divine commission by relaying his spirit-directed message to the seven representative churches of Asia.

Immediately following these introductions, the reader is confronted by an awesome, ghastly, meaningful, symbolic portrait of Jesus. Although the images may appear strange, they are not difficult to decipher. The "Son of Man" is standing among his churches, robed as the divine priest. Since his hair is snow white, he reminds us of the Ancient of Days, and his flaming eyes tell us he can see everything (1:12-14). His polished bronze feet indicate that he stands absolutely secure, the sound of his voice is so loud that no one can miss his message, and his tongue is like a two-edged Roman sword so that his words cut both ways (in grace and in judgment). But his faithful people should not worry because he holds them tightly in his accepting (right) hand. And he radiates the glory of God like the sun in its greatest brilliance (12:15-16).

Suddenly, John realizes that he has been in the presence of God in Christ. In a powerful christophany (a vision of the exalted Christ) and typical of theophanies (appearances of God) in the Old Testament, John like other humans goes through the trauma of a death experience. But Jesus, the master of death and the grave, lays that accepting hand on John and speaks the anticipated blessing: "Don't be afraid." Then he commissions John to send his divine message to the churches (1:17-20). Isn't this picture of Jesus spellbinding? Don't you have the feeling that you are in for a dramatic and decisive message?

But you will have to wait for the core of the dramatic presentation because chapters 2 and 3 serve as a kind of sevenfold overview in seven scenes of the Christian church with both its wonderful features and its defiling pockmarks. These seven churches follow a kind of mail route along three major ancient highways. Were there more churches in Asia than these seven at that time? Of course![28] But seven is the number of fullness or perfection, and there is no theological reason for John to go beyond seven churches because they represent the entire church.

The letters to these seven churches are organized in a definite pattern, with an opening statement concerning the angel who represents each church and a clear identifying symbol or image referring to an aspect of the previous portrait of Jesus that addresses each church's situation. Thus, Jesus is viewed as the head or evaluator of each church. A theological analysis is then made of the church's strengths and weaknesses, and some reference is added to an aspect or aspects of the ancient city where it is located—an indication that John must be quite familiar with these cities. Words of commendation and/or warning are also given along with a clear reminder that Jesus knows each of their works and is the one who is able to declare either judgment and/or blessing upon them. Therefore, those who have ears to hear should pay attention to the messages that are being delivered to the churches.

It is unnecessary to detail fully the message to each church. Instead, it is more fruitful to summarize the nature of each church so that we are able to have a more complete picture of the variety of churches John has in mind as he is addressing the whole church. The church at (1) *Ephesus* is like a traditional church, whose members have been consistently loyal to Christ and who have patiently endured hard times. They are even able to judge heretical tendencies. But like many traditionalists, they have lost their early enthusiasm and love for Jesus and desperately need a change of heart (2:1-7). (2) *Smyrna* is a poor, suffering church that has been bearing the brunt of persecution (even from the Synagogue),[29] and it will continue to do so. For such a church, Jesus has no condemnation but only encouragement and the promise of future blessings (2:8-11).

The next two churches evidence related problems. The church at (3) *Pergamum,* the ancient capital of Asia with many temples on its magnificent acropolis and the seat of Roman authority, is best identified as a compromising church. There one is expected to worship *Dea Roma* and bow to Caesar, and idolatry and immorality are common temptations as they were to the earlier people of Israel. The need for repentance in the church is an obvious requirement (2:12-17). (4) *Thyatira* has a similar yet slightly different nature because it is the home of many trade unions with their rowdy meetings as well as their festive meals and celebrations to the union gods. Syncretism is a way of life here, and devilish practices are common. The fierce judgment of the Lord is on the horizon for such mixed patterns of worship and life ((2:18-29).

The contrast between the next two churches is vivid. (5) *Sardis* represents a dying church that thinks it is alive and doing well, but it seems to be dead or in a state of suspended animation. Just like the city's fortress that seemed impregnable yet was conquered because of the failure of its watchmen, so this sleeping church is in trouble. If it fails to awaken quickly to its condition, it will soon find itself beyond recovery. Nevertheless, even in such a dying church Jesus reminds us that there are a few who remain faithful (3:1-6). The next church (6) *Philadelphia,* like the ancient border city where it is located and that is constantly being attacked, is pictured as a weak and struggling faith community but one that is open to sharing the gospel. Even though this church is repeatedly buffeted, it remains faithful and so Jesus promises that its strength is a sign that it will inherit the city of God (3:7-13).

Finally, we reach the wealthy, uncommitted church of (7) *Laodicea,* whose members are apparently focused on the things of this world. Naturally, the Lord is aware of their lifestyle and what is important to them. Accordingly, John pictures Jesus as using the attributes of their prosperous city (their black wool industry and ophthalmology clinic) as the basis for summoning them to repent and change their ways so that they still might be welcomed and accepted by him (3:14-22).

In reflecting on these descriptions of the seven churches, one should realize that the types of people characterized herein may be found in any of our churches today. Therefore, if we have ears to hear, let us hear "what the Spirit says" to us in this era of growing biblical illiteracy. Jesus knows who we are! I would also add that the practice among some Christians who have attempted to relate their analyses of the churches in these chapters to periods of time as a means of predicting the return of Jesus or other futuristic events is a non-productive hermeneutic, foreign to adequate biblical interpretation, and meaningless to the original recipients of Revelation.

With these comments in mind, we turn to the main message of Revelation and its dramatic presentation. Chapter 4 initiates the drama with what could easily be described as a divine stage setting in which God, who sits on a heavenly throne, is introduced in a magnificent show of color, including a brilliant royal emerald rainbow (4:1-3). Forming the backdrop to God's presence is the historical setting of God's people represented by the twenty-four elders (twelve from the old covenant and twelve from the new) dressed in white—the symbolic color of the victorious ones (4:4). They are pictured as serving God in the presence of the world—all of God's creatures that are represented by the four living beings, namely a lion, a bull or ox, a man, and an eagle (4:6b-7). Then, following the opening drum roll of lightning and thunder and the illuminating of the stage lights (torches), the great drama is ready to begin (4:5-6a) with the musical overture by the earthly creatures with their eternal threefold song of praise to the Holy God in the context of history and time (4:8).[30] Responding antiphonally to this holiness chorus, the elders representing God's people fall prostrate before God and chant their own fourfold praise, making clear that all things exist by the will of God (4:10-11).

But knowing and understanding the will of God is not an automatic matter. Knowledge of God's will and intentions comes by revelation from God, and similarly our divine drama could not proceed without the script from God. That perfectly sealed script in the form of a scroll is in the gracious (right) hand of God. The question, however, is "who is worthy" to accept the scroll, obtain its message from the Holy One, and then deliver it to humanity? The answer at first is that "no one" in all creation can unlock the divine will, which greatly perturbs John (5:1-4).

But as John is lamenting the lack of a mediating agent, he is advised by one of the elders, just as the Old Testament predicted, that the answer will come in the form of a King—"the Lion of the Tribe of Judah" (5:5; cf. Gen 49:8-10; Isa 11:1-10). Yet as he waits, surprisingly onto the stage of history comes a "Lamb." It is standing, but it looks as though it has earlier been slaughtered. This picture is obviously another stunning Johannine Portrait of King Jesus, who was crucified at Passover time but then raised from the dead (Rev 5:6; cf. John 1:29, 36; 19:14-15, 30-31; 20:19-23). The world expected a Lion but is given a Lamb! Yet this Lamb is not weak; this Lamb has seven horns and seven eyes (the symbols of complete power and complete knowledge). Only this Lamb is able to receive the scroll from the enthroned God (5:6-7).

At that point, the representatives of all creation fall before the Lamb. Then they sing a new song of praise and worthiness because of the Lamb's sacrificial death as the means of saving (ransoming) people around the world[31] and transforming them into a royal priesthood for God (5:8-10; cf. 1 Pet 2:9). In response to their song, the huge angelic host of heaven joins them in a magnificent sevenfold acclamation of the Lamb beyond anything that the Roman emperors would have experienced. Then, in an ultimate affirmation of both God and the Lamb, all heaven and earth unite their voices in a joint fourfold acclamation, lauding and praising these divine *personae* forever and ever. The scene closes with the elders prostrating themselves in worship.

Do you have the sense that John is drawing us into the divine sanctuary where his portrait of Jesus is unveiled, and that Jesus' redemptive work (salvation) is so united with God that in worship it is impossible to separate them (5:11-14; cf. John 5:30)? With this elevated understanding of God in Jesus, we leave the introductory stage setting and turn to the organization of the remainder of Revelation.

Just as John's Gospel can be divided into three major cycles, this dramatic presentation of Revelation 6 to 22 can also be divided into three major sections or cycles, which are usually designated as (1) the Seven Seals (6:1-8:1), (2) the Seven Trumpets (8:6–11:19), and (3) the Seven Bowls (16:1-21), with some accompanying interludes. Also, following the pattern of the Gospel and between the second and third sections or cycles, there is a second introduction in Revelation that involves God's superhuman enemies and the drawing of the battle lines (12:1–15:8). It serves as a prelude to the concluding judgments and destruction of God's enemies (17:1–20:15) before the vision of heaven is added (21:1–22:15). Hopefully you remember that in the Gospel, the second introduction (the Palm Sunday event) stands between the Festival and the Farewell Cycles and before the Death and Resurrection Stories. In interpreting this dramatic book of Revelation, it is also helpful to remember that the various segments within the cycles are to be viewed as a series of tableaus or a slide presentation of pictures rather than a running video or a movie.

Turning now to the Seven Seals, we find that the first four segments flashing on the projector screen involve four riders on colored horses. The white one with a bow likely represents war; the red one with a sword represents violence; the black one with the measuring scales indicates economic imbalance where the rich are getting richer and the poor are getting poorer; and finally the bilious yellow-green one represents death. Together these four horsemen/scenes summarize the fact that the efforts or goals of the world are futile and lead to hopelessness (6:1-8).

At that point, the fifth seal brings to focus the cry of the Christian martyrs throughout the ages. Their pleas have been, "How long" will the Lord delay in bringing judgment? Many in John's day believed that the martyrs had direct access to the Lord, but John is quick to indicate that even the martyrs were not given the answer to God's timing. Instead, they were given the white robe to indicate that they were blessed as victors, but even they would have to wait for God's answers (6:9-11). In discussions of God's timing, I always point to the fact that even Jesus while on earth did not know God's timing of the end (cf. Mark 13:32). Accordingly, I doubt that any contemporary earthly predictors (whether ministers or so-called prophets) have such information.

But with God's blessing bestowed on the martyrs, John collapses the rest of time in the sixth seal and moves us to the end, when the whole created order crumbles as the stars fall and the sky is rolled up. At that point he indicates that everyone, including the enemies of God, will seek to hide from "the wrath of the Lamb." But, as you know, such an attempt will be futile (6:12-17).

With the breaking of the sixth seal, creation as we know it comes to a dramatic end. But don't get confused. This work is not a pedantic history book. It is a dramatic presentation! And as John indicates, there is a pause in the "unveiling" of reality as a mighty figure representing God steps on the scene and gives John (and us) a couple of insider views of God's people and their destiny (7:1-3).

With the first glimpse, please do not get confused. The 144,000 do not represent what you might think. These people are *not* historical Israel! Remember that we are dealing with a symbolic set of descriptive images written by a Christian who viewed the Judaism of his day as aligned with

Satan (cf. Rev 2:9; 3:9). The images of the twelve tribes may seem to refer to Israel, but the list is strange. It does not start with Reuben (the oldest son) but with Judah (the tribe of Jesus). And it has two references to Joseph (Joseph and Manasseh). Such might be acceptable except that Levi is also included, when that tribe was replaced by a second one from Joseph. All of this means that one tribe is missing. It is Dan, who was historically viewed as a heretical serpent (Gen 49:17; Judg 17:14-20) and whom the early Christians often linked with antichrist figures. (The term "antichrist" refers to a powerful persons who represent the demonic and is used only in the Johannine epistles.) The image of the twelve tribes here is not a symbol of ancient Israel but refers to the whole people of God, which becomes apparent later at Revelation 14:1-5, where the 144,000 are said to be the redeemed of God and the Lamb.

As the first segment of this interlude closes, a second one appears. It is a numberless crowd from around the world who are dressed in the white robes of victory (cf. 6:11) and proclaiming their acclamation of God and the Lamb, lauding them with a sevenfold doxology (7:9-12). When questioned concerning the identity of this huge group, one of the elders reveals that they are the authentic people of God throughout history. Indeed, they have been part of the "great tribulation," suffering throughout the ages. They have also been marked by the blood of the Lamb, just as Israel experienced delivery when the blood of lambs was splattered over the door frames of their homes before the first Passover. Here again readers must be careful not to temporize this statement of the tribulation as being a specific future event not yet experienced; this picture is *supra-temporal* (or above a specific time; the great tribulation was already beginning for some in John's day, so be careful with arithmetic thinking). It is a proleptic picture of heaven similar to the one detailed later when hunger and thirst are ended and sorrowful tears are no more (7:16-17; cf. 21:4-6).

With this preliminary vision of heaven introduced, the first cycle reaches its conclusion as the powerful Lamb breaks the seventh seal. But to our surprise, instead of a cataclysmic finish, silence ensues (8:1). The result is a dramatic shock. Awesome silence is one of the most powerful dramatic devices in theatrical presentations. It is similar to what Elijah must have experienced in his flight from Jezebel after he witnessed the terrifying storm, the shattering earthquake, and then God's visit in eerie silence (1 Kgs19:11-12). In such a dramatic presentation, we (the audience) wait breathlessly for what is about to happen next.

In Revelation, the angelic trumpeters of the second cycle appear next and with them another angel who is dispatched from God and who flings a golden incense burner containing the combined prayers of God's people on the earth. John knows that in this act, God is about to unleash a great divine reckoning, especially since the event is accompanied by a catastrophic display of thunder, lightning, and a quaking of the earth (8:2-5). Accordingly, four of the trumpeting angels dispatch their judgments, and, as John indicates, a third of the earth is generally devastated (8:7, 8, 9, 10, 11, 12), with the exception of the grass, which is completely consumed (8:7). The repeated use of "third" here is undoubtedly intended as a signal that the judgments of this cycle are only a preliminary stage in the process of righteous vindication over evil—similar to the plagues of Egypt before the exodus.

These four judgment segments are then followed by a flying eagle announcing that three severe woes are coming upon the people of the earth (813). Thus, when the fifth trumpeter sounds, the first woe begins as the bottomless pit, like a black hole, opens. Instead of sucking everything in, it spews out ghastly, locust-like creatures that for a short time (five months) are allowed to attack humans. There is no doubt of their evil nature and mission since they resemble terrifying armored scorpions and are directed by *Abaddon/Apollyon*, the Satanic-like figure whom the ancients call "the Destroyer" (9:7-11). Evil is here being unmasked, and it is an ugly picture.

But the evil portrait gets worse in the second woe as the sixth trumpeter blows his horn. With John's fastidious sense of exactness for time (a four-fold designation) and his intimidating description of the large, dragon-like cavalry,[32] the forces of evil are brought on the scene from Mesopotamia.[33] Their task is to judge and kill a third of condemned humanity in their mission of destruction. That evil mission, John realizes, is in the control of the Lord because the intention is to bring about the repentance of rebellious humanity, but even such destruction does not lead to a change in human behavior. Tragically, humans persist in their idolatrous worship practices and in their immoral, evil activities (9:20-21). John's portrait of Jesus (and of God) is here becoming precisely defined because, although the Lord is the *pantocrator* ("the Almighty," 1:8), he does not control human response. Yet he is still the judge of humans!

The second woe is concluded, but as in the previous cycle an interlude is inserted before the seventh trumpeter arrives. On to the stage or screen comes a mighty angel from heaven that would have dwarfed the ancient Colossus that stood in the harbor of Rhodes. In contrast to many interpreters, this theophanic angel knows what is about to happen, and in a deafening voice he summons the seven thunders to announce their message. But even though John hears it, he is not permitted to write its content, undoubtedly because God does not reveal every mystery to humans (10:1-7). But this angel has an open scroll in his hand, and he makes John eat it and proclaim its bittersweet message to the world (10:8-11; cf. Jer 15:16; Ezek 2:8-9).

The message is revealed in a moving action scene in which God sends two witnesses to proclaim the coming judgment with the power to perform miraculous deeds under divine authority, even as Elijah shut down the rain and Moses turned the waters into blood (11:1-6; cf. 1 Kgs 17:1; Exod 7:17-19). But even this last-ditch effort fails to bring repentance to the world—represented by a combined image of Sodom, Egypt, and Jerusalem that crucified Jesus. And, instead, the witnesses are killed and desecrated by the evil powers (the beast) as the people celebrate the demise of the witnesses (Rev 11:7-10). But the rejoicing is short-lived because the God of heaven responds by raising them to life and answering their defilement with a catastrophic judgment on earth that mirrors again the end of time like the sixth seal (11:13; cf. 6:12-17).

But what about the third woe and the seventh trumpeter? It is probably not what you expected. John loves to surprise the reader, and instead of an even more severe judgment, he presents in dramatic fashion the announce-ment that "The kingdom of the world has become the kingdom of our Lord and of his Christ, and he shall reign forever and ever" (11:15). I am sure that if you are familiar with Handel's famous *Messiah*, you will prob-ably respond immediately with "Hallelujah!" Yes, we have another vision of heaven: the wrath of God is here viewed as finished, and the future has been merged by John into the present since the almighty God has begun to reign (11:17). Indeed, the "lost ark" of the covenant is presented as having been returned to the temple (11:19), even though we will discover later that there is no longer any need for a temple in heaven (21:22).

The Second Cycle has thus been completed, but rather than moving directly to the Third Cycle, in a similar pattern to the Gospel organization, John inserts a new introduction to the second half of this book in chapters 12 and 13, which focus on the evil trinity as the beginning of the end of the created order. This second introduction involving the enemies of God serves as an appropriate contrast to our portrayal of Jesus, the Lamb of God, and his mission, which is the focus of chapter 14.

This introduction begins with John using an ancient international creation myth well known from Greece to Egypt[34] that involves a hungry, jealous dragon bent on eliminating heroic figures. John uses the earlier imagery and brilliantly transforms the myth into a vehicle for the proclamation of the gospel. Thus, in this picture or sign (*semeion*), he redesigns the People of God (God's agents for confronting the problem of evil) as a cosmic pregnant woman wearing a jeweled tiara or crown with twelve stars and ready to deliver her offspring (12:1-2). She is then vividly contrasted in a second sign with a gigantic super-powerful (ten horned) Dragon ("the Devil") who has seven crowned heads (symbolic of superhuman authority) and a viciously destructive tail (12:3-4a). I pause for a moment to point out that when the reader encounters a mixture of ten and seven, as here, it should be a signal that the figure represented is *not* divine like God but nonetheless strong and verging on being semi-divine.

The stage is set for a cosmic face-off between the Devil and God through God's agents. When the woman delivers her child (Jesus) who is to rule the cosmos, the Dragon seeks to consume the child—just as Herod tried to kill the baby and the Jewish authorities and Roman forces of evil sought to eliminate Jesus in the crucifixion (12:4b-5). The heroic son, however, is snatched (resurrected/ascended) to heaven. But it means that the followers of the son will be pursued by the Devil/Dragon, although God will sustain them (12:6).

As the cosmic picture unfolds, there is a switch made in the scene to introduce a cosmic battle. Enter Michael, the warrior archangel, who is given the task of defeating the Devil—also known as Satan, the ancient deceptive snake (12:7-9). I suspect that John may purposely use Michael here as a surrogate for God to ensure that his readers would *not* regard the Devil and his associates to be on the same level of power and authority as the Creator. By contrast, the Mesopotamian dualistic literature pictures their gods like Ahurimazda (Light) and Ahriman (Darkness) as being virtually equals, set against each other in a cosmic battle. But in Revelation it is absolutely clear that the forces of evil are no match for the "authority" of God and Christ. Here the Devil is definitely dethroned by the "blood of the Lamb" and the testimony of Christ's faithful witnesses who are willing to die for him. But John is aware that the situation for Christians is hazardous because, even though God provides support for his people who are in danger, the Dragon is still bent on pursuing the woman—the people of God—even into the remotest protected areas of existence (12:10-17). The warning for Christians who bear the testimony of Jesus therefore is unmistakable: be ready for the attacks of the Devil/Dragon!

But the Devil is not alone in his destructive mission. John pictures him as having tremendous support in his evil work, epitomized in two powerful evil servants, along with countless unidentified minions. The first associate serving the Dragon/Devil is portrayed as a terrifying multi-animal Beast that has ten horns (power) and seven heads with ten crowns, and since it is associated with the sea and the whole earth is under its control, it is undoubtedly to be identified with earthly political power, here understood as Rome (13:1-3). The one mortally wounded head likely represents the hated Nero (one of the eight emperors from Augustus to Domitian) whom many speculated may not have actually died but, being so evil, was reincarnated as the evil Domitian (13:3). This designation helps us understand why John has the eighth emperor related to the earlier seven (cf. 17:9-10). For John, this political Beast blasphemously claims divinity, just as Rome expected its citizens to worship *Dea Roma* (13:1, 5-6) and severely persecuted non-compliant Christians (13:7). In the light of such hostility on the part of mighty Rome, John calls the believers to recognize they are secure in the Lamb (note the Book of Life; 13:8) so they should be prepared for captivity, avoid violent reaction, and endure suffering as people of faith (13:9-10).

The second associate of the Devil/Dragon appears like a horned "lamb," but his voice betrays him as being in the service of the Dragon (13:11). Although he can perform mighty acts like the true Lamb, the purpose of this wonder-working deceiver is to entangle people in the false worship of political power and strength (e.g., Rome) by means of complete economic control of peoples' lives (13:12-17). Accordingly, John warns his readers not to be confused by such a fraud but wisely understand that the nature of this figure should be recognized through his Hebraic numerical code as none other than *Nero redivinus* (Nero reincarnated as Domitian), namely the triple six (666) of superhuman incompleteness.[35] Thus, by detailing these three brief portraits of what I call the evil trinity, John has in fact emphasized the authentic portrait of Jesus as the Lamb of God as he returns to the "unveiling" of the mission of Jesus in the last half of his book.

In contrast to the enemies of God who are associated with the unstable sands of the sea (e.g., 12:17 b; cf. the two houses of Jesus in Matt 7:24-27), the Lamb and his saints (144,000) appear on the solid rock of Mount Zion (Rev 14:1). But note that John does not say Jerusalem here because for him there are two cities by that name—a heavenly one (21:2) and the place of the unhappy memory of the crucifixion that he has already linked to Sodom and Egypt (11:8). These *144,000* who follow the Lamb, as indicated in the discussion of Revelation 7, are not to be viewed simply as Jews but are the true people of God who are able to sing the new song of redemption (14:1-4) and have rejected the lying pattern of the Devil (14:5; cf. John 8:44). John also inserts a comment here that has troubled some interpreters when he adds that they are "chaste/pure" and "have not been defiled (*emolunthesan*) with women" (Rev 14:4). This idea is rooted in the two concepts of (1) "Holy War" in which sexual activity at such a time was regarded as unholy activity or blasphemous (cf. the story of Uriah and David in 2 Sam 11:8-11) and (2) the worship of other gods being regarded as adultery. The authentic Lord is here portrayed as surrounded by his people of integrity, ready for the final face-off between the forces of good and evil.

John does not keep us waiting for a hint of the outcome as he provides a quick summary of what is on the horizon before he presents the third cycle of the seven bowls of judgment in chapter 16. The overview starts with the announcements of three angels. The first represents the universal (fourfold) good news addressed to the whole world to "Fear God" and glorify the Creator of the universe because the time for judgment has arrived (14:6-7). The second is identified as Babylon, the evil city that has been conquered (14:8). And the third is that judgment awaits all those who have been committed to the Beast (received his mark) and engaged in the false worship of the world (14:9-11). So the call for God's people is to remain faithful in persecution and remember that "blessing" will follow (14:12-13).

With these announcements, the Son of Man takes center stage, but this time he is portrayed as the powerful, eschatological cloud-rider with a judgment sickle in his hand (14:17; cf. Dan 7:13), and as he swings his powerful sickle other angels enter the scene and execute the anticipated judgment so that the blood of the condemned flows for about 180 miles (the rough length of Israel; Rev 14:19-20). What follows then is a great choral refrain that literally explodes on the pages of our book as another Johannine sign (*semeion*), taking the form of a joint song to Moses and the Lamb and introducing the final seven-fold cycle of the terrible Judgment Bowls (15:1-4). With that song ringing in our ears, the seven angels exit the Temple in Heaven (the presence of God) bearing the seven last plagues, a reminder of the earlier ten plagues of Egypt (15:5-8; cf. Exod 7:14–12:36), and no one can enter that temple until the plagues are finished.[36]

The final Cycle of Seven Bowls is a fascinating collage of plagues and judgments as the future is merged into the present and past (note the lack of the future at 16:5). The first five angels pour out their bowls, which involve (1) terrible sores; (2 and 3) bloody seas, rivers, and springs; (4) scorching sun and blistering heat; and (5) consuming darkness. While these plagues are devastating in their results, humans choose to curse God rather than taking God's warnings seriously and understanding that the cries of the saints from the altar have finally been heard (16:1-11; cf. 6:10). Then the sixth angel empties the next bowl, signaling that the "evil trinity" has initiated their concluding attempt at confusing the nations with their blasphemies and powerful signs while they prepare for the final battle at Armageddon (the mountain of Megiddo). But they hardly realize who they are up against because the Lord will soon arrive "like a thief" in the night, and the faithful will be "blessed" (16:12-16).[37]

The seventh and final bowl is then discharged as a thunderous voice from the temple reechoes Jesus' words from the cross: "It is finished!" (16:17; cf. John 19:30 and Rev 21:6). With those emblematic words ringing down the corridors of time, the final cataclysmic destruction of the world takes place as islands and mountains completely disappear while humans curse God as they are inundated with huge hailstones from heaven (16:18-21). Thus ends the three great dramatic Cycles of Revelation.

We turn now to the last two major sections of this book, which mirror the last two sections of the Gospel of John.[38] The Final Judgment account begins with the doom of Babylon, the Great Prostitute. For John this finely bedecked woman who is enthroned on many waters represents none other than Rome, the ruler of the Mediterranean world with the clearly mixed seven heads and ten horns of evil (17:1-3; cf. 13:1). This Babylon has caused the death of many Christians (witnesses for Jesus; 17:5-6), and her power is mirrored in the threefold expression that she "was, is not, and will soon be" (17:8; cf. the threefold description of God at 1:4, 8). Her identity is revealed in the secret code of the seven heads that "are seven hills" (the well-known description of Rome) as well as "seven kings" that are epitomized in the "eighth" king (undoubtedly Domitian; 17:9-11). These emperors along with their understudies that follow them into battle are then contrasted with their sworn enemy, the mighty Lamb, who is their conqueror and who is "Lord of lords and King of kings" (17:12-14). John correctly foresees that although Rome controls its world (note the four-fold designation of people, 17:15), the subject ten heads (subordinate kings) will ultimately turn on Rome and devour her because evil is by nature self-destructive (17:16-18).

As John envisions Babylon (Rome) falling, he records a series of seven poetic responses beginning with a taunt song in which Babylon is viewed as a deserted haven for demons and foul creatures (18:2-3; cf. Isa 14:1-23); then he moves to a great warning in which the faithful are told to flee the city as she is judged and consumed with fire (Rev 18:4-8).[39] These taunts and warnings then issue in a series of laments on the part of the nobility and wealthy who wail over the burning of Rome and fear for their lives (18:9-10), as well as merchants who bemoan the fact that their luxury goods no longer have any value (18:11-16), and shipping moguls and their sailors who grieve over loss of job security from the great international trade industry that relied on Roman protection and has just come to a screeching end (18:17-19). Indeed, rejoicing as well as meaningful labor and even the delights of marriage have ceased as the memory of the martyrs is being avenged by divine judgment (18:21-24).

These poetic responses receive a kind of antiphonal answer in a series of great Hallelujahs ("Praise to God"; 19:1, 3, 4, 5, 6) that obviously inspired Handel in drafting his magnificent "Hallelujah Chorus." Like Handel, John earlier must have been drawn into the heights of ecstasy as he reflected on the salvation of God (19:1), the righteous judgment of God (19:2-3), the vastness of the multitude of God's people (19:5-6), and finally the marriage of the Lamb in which the bride (Christ's followers) is/are dressed in the finest white linen—namely, the wonderful deeds of his people (19:7-8). No wonder the "unveiling" angel tells John to record the fourth great Beatitude at this very point: "Blessed are those who are invited to the wedding celebration/dinner of the Lamb!" And the angel adds that these words are certified as authentic from God (19:9)! Wow! That is about all John can take, and he falls down before his angelic messenger in worship. Quickly the messenger reminds him, however, that angels here are just servants, delivering the witness of Jesus. Worship belongs only to God! And did you also note that the angel (19:10) twice says that this message is the testimony/witness (*marturia*) of Jesus? Do not forget that this book is/contains the Revelation of Jesus Christ (1:1). You are about to meet him again!

A few items still need to be finalized. What about evil and the viperous trinity? You guessed it. They are next on the agenda. Onto the stage of reality comes the Great Warrior on a white horse, who represents absolute authenticity (faithful and true), whose name is "The Word of God," and whose robe is dipped in blood (19:11, 13; cf. John 1:1, 14), and inscribed with "King of kings and Lord of lords" (19:16). The portrait is obviously one of the Mighty Jesus, the Victorious Christ. No one fights him and wins! Indeed, have you noticed that, unlike in most of our movies and videos, there are *no battle scenes in Revelation*? You may see an enemy army, but the next thing you discover is that the fighting is over, and all you learn is that the evil forces have been destroyed.

Consequently, there is no fighting here. The birds are simply invited to come and pick the carcasses of the enemy in a different supper of God (19:17-18) than the one described earlier (19:9). The allies of the Dragon— the powerful political beast and the false prophet (fraudulent lamb) are quickly captured and summarily propelled alive into the torturous fiery lake (19:20), while those who have been aligned with these demonic forces (have the mark of the Beast) are dispatched speedily by the sword that issues from the mouth of Mighty King Jesus (19:21; cf. 1:16).

Are you ready for the termination of the Dragon? Sorry! You will have to wait a little longer because John wants you to have a more dramatic climax to our story. Let the Devil be restricted (bound) in his all-out efforts of recruiting his worldly forces while the gospel is being proclaimed during his millennium (a thousand years; 20:2). Let the saints who have died be given new life and be blessed (the fifth Beatitude; 20:6) in the assuring presence of Christ during/in the first resurrection for a similar millennium (a thousand years; 20:4-5). No worry—those saints will not suffer condemnation, for they are now in the arms of Jesus, safe from the wiles of the Devil. What a marvelous story! It really communicates with those in this growing biblically illiterate era. But, sadly, the Devil still reigns in many of our churches as Christians fail to understand the beauty of this picture and instead argue over the meaning of the millennium. Friends, do you not think that it is time to give up our arguments over the millennium? We are not in control of time! Jesus, the emissary of God, the Mighty King, understands the divine plan. Let God be God. Let us as Christians not fuss with one another on the pretense of knowing the future. It does not help us communicate with those who are being wooed by the Devil.

The Devil's opportunity for enticing the world will continue to grow and indeed explode as his forces multiply. But Satan is not ultimately in control of time, and God will decisively act according to the divine will. And when God acts, the Devil will be summarily defeated, and he will also be propelled into the fiery lake forever, where his cohorts in evil have already been consigned (20:7-10). But that is not all that takes place in the conclusion to this temporal age; there is still the fearful judgment throne awaiting the people of this world.

In the final scene of this Judgment section, John makes it evident that facing the supreme tribunal will be an intimidating experience because, at the sight of this judge, even the earth and sky will scatter (20:11). Before this divine judicial bench, the dead from all ages must appear. Then the records concerning their lives will be opened and the actions of each person will be revealed (20:12). Hiding one's deeds from this court is impossible, and authentic judgment on what one has done is guaranteed. And who could escape such a judgment? But wait a moment! There is one more book—the Book of Life—and that book is crucial; if one's name is not inscribed in it, that person will follow the Devil into the eternal fiery lake along with its conclusion of death and the grave (20:14-15). The verdict of condemnation to the great lake of fire is none other than the second death (20:14), which John has mentioned in the discussion concerning the millennium (cf. 20:6).

But what about those whose names are written in this strategic book? They have already experienced the resurrection! Do you see? Those who experience the first resurrection with Christ will have no fear of the second death (20:6). Do you understand the marvel of God's graciousness? In the midst of judgment, there is the amazing work of Jesus, the reigning Christ! Evil is finished; death is no more. Yet there is life beyond the grave! The book of Revelation is in truth a message of hope in the midst of suffering, pain, and persecution. What is next?

It is the Final Vision—the New Heaven and the New Earth. A new Earth? Oh, yes! Everything is new (21:5)! There is even a new Jerusalem given by God like a bride (21:2, 9; 22:17), reminiscent of an earlier bride—the church (see for example Eph 5:25, 29 and the pictures in Isa 61:10; 62:5). Then, the great goal of God will finally be achieved when God will dwell with his people (Rev 21:3) as Jesus earlier "tented" on earth (see John 1:14, *eskenosen*). Death will be gone; mourning and crying and pain will have disappeared (Rev 21:5). Indeed, the words of Jesus on the cross that have echoed through the ages—"It is finished"—have come to their ultimate fulfillment (21:6; cf. John 19:30). He is the one who was from the beginning (cf. John 1:1) and is the end as well—the Alpha and the Omega. At the end of time he provides "living" water freely from the divine fountain for his people who have lived on the edge of the desert (Rev 21:6; cf. Jesus' earlier words at the Feast of Tabernacles in John 7:37-38).

To make sure his readers take seriously their calling to sonship and daughterhood with God, John reminds them of their responsibility for a correct lifestyle. They must not forget that in heaven there is no evil and that those who engage in such practices have been condemned to the fiery lake—which includes all liars (21:7-8). Why did John emphasize "all" liars? It is because the key to understanding the Devil is that he is a liar (cf. John 8:44).

But now it is time to reflect briefly on the new Jerusalem. Of course, the city of God is on a mountain (21:10) because that is where encounters with God have traditionally taken place—for example, Mount Sinai, Mount Horeb, Mount Carmel, the Mount of Beatitudes, the Mountain of the Transfiguration, and an unnamed mountain in Galilee where the Resurrected Lord appears to the disciples and commissions them with the gospel (Matt 28:16-20). Naturally, you would expect this city to be radiant, shining like a brilliant jewel (21:11). And since in John's day cities still had walls, so this Jerusalem has walls. But you may think that it is strange historically that the gates of those walls are linked with the twelve tribes and the foundations with the twelve apostles. Yet this city is the "new" Jerusalem, and the tribes have already been redefined.[40] Likewise, the foundations of this city are laid in the gospel of Jesus Christ (21:12-14).

The shape of the city, however, is a bit odd because it is in the form of a huge cube with each dimension being twelve thousand (Roman) stadia, but be careful in recalculating the numbers in terms of miles, as some translations do, because it is easy to lose the significance of the number 12, which stands for the people of God. God has perfectly designed the people's city. And even though cities are hardly cubes, do not lose sight of the fact it has a perfect shape (21:16). The walls likewise are intended to proclaim the divine hand in planning because they measure 144 cubits—12 x 12 (our 216 feet). So here again, be careful not to lose the significance. And the foundations of these walls are laid with twelve beautiful jewels, while each of the twelve gates is constructed from a magnificent pearl (21:19-21). But please do not ask about the size of the oysters that produced such pearls. Give your imagination a chance to conceive of such a city. Then reflect on the fact that the city, including the street system, is made of pure gold, but it is nothing like any gold we know because this gold is transparent (21:18, 21). Can you imagine such a sight? Earthly Jerusalem even today is built from a yellow colored limestone and can be breathtaking in the setting sun. Yet it would hardly compare to John's vision of the heavenly Jerusalem!

But wait! As I have indicated several times earlier, we are in for a surprise. There is *no temple* in this divinely planned city! The reason is that God and the Lamb are present in this city (21:22), so there is no need for a sanctuary—the Most Holy Place. Do you remember that in his account of the cleansing of the temple, John already indicated that Jesus is the *naos*—the sanctuary, the very site of God's presence (John 2:19)? Likewise, there will be no need for the earthly luminaries such as sun and moon in the new Jerusalem because God and the Lamb are the light of this new reality (Rev 21:23; cf. John 8:12; 9:5). Once again, John reminds his readers of the difference between this reality and our world when he adds that the gates of the new city will never be shut because the old realities of night and evil patterns and practices no longer exist. These inserts into John's visionary descriptions of the new reality are obviously intended to challenge his suffering readers not to abandon responsible living for Christ.

Then he returns to his final description of the new reality as he synthesizes the garden of Eden story, with its blessings and temptations in Genesis, and Ezekiel's picturesque vision of the future in which he describes the fruitful river that flows from the throne of God and the life-giving tree on both sides of the river that continually supplies its fruit to the people of God while its leaves are for the healing of the nations (22:1-2; cf. Ezek 47:1, 12; Gen 3:22). In this new reality, we have already been made aware that God and the Lamb are intimately united in their purpose and that the terrible curses that followed the great garden disobedience of humanity (cf. Gen 3:16-19, 22-24) have been lifted since God's people (God's name is on their foreheads) will finally see his face and live forever (Rev 22:3-5; contrast Exod 33:20; Isa 6:5).

The book is thus finished except for the epilogue in which Jesus, the Spirit-leading Lord even of the prophets, (1) promises again that he is coming soon (22:6-7; cf.1:1); (2) provides the sixth Beatitude of blessing upon the obedient (22:7); (3) reminds John to worship only God (22:8-9); (4) forbids sealing up this prophecy but allows people the choice to continue their current actions while warning them that they will be held accountable (22:10-12); and, in the seventh Beatitude, (5) blesses those who remain faithful with the promise of access to the tree of life and entrance to the new city of God, which is not for the disobedient (22:14-15).

This profoundly moving drama concludes with a magnificent three-fold invitation to "Come" enunciated by Jesus—the promised Davidic King and the spectacular morning star—and to "receive" freely the water of life (22:16-17). But to this encompassing invitation he also adds a terrifying warning that anyone who dares to tamper with the contents of this "unveiling" will be subject to its curses (22:18-19). Then, to Jesus' personal promise of a soon return, John adds his own testimonial *maranatha* prayer—"Amen! Come, Lord Jesus!" (22:20; cf. 1 Cor 16:1)—as well as his benediction on behalf of all Christians (22:21).

With these incisive words, the book of Revelation is finished and the New Testament is completed. The Christian canon is thus beautifully concluded. But the closing invitation to "Come" remains open for all who read its message. Indeed, the invitation continues to beckon the current generation, which wrestles with a growing biblical illiteracy and may not even be aware of this invitation. It is our job to present it to them in ways that they can understand.

Questions for Reflection

1. After reading the author's analysis of the Gospel of John and Revelation, do you think that the portraits of Jesus in both books might be related? Could one author have possibly written two such different books? Explain the reason(s) for your view.
2. What pictures of Jesus are the most captivating for you? Why?
3. What pictures of Jesus do you find the most unlikeable? the most encompassing?
4. How would you evaluate Dr. Borchert's organization of the book of Revelation? Is it helpful?
5. How did you react to the way he treated the Seven Churches of Revelation?
6. What is your opinion of the way he handled the issue of the millennium?
7. What did you think of this author's treatment of Revelation as a dramatic presentation? Have you been able to recognize its dramatic features?
8. Are you comfortable with the idea of using your imagination to interpret the various sections of Revelation? Does such a methodology help or detract from your understanding of Scripture? Explain.
9. As you now reflect on the book of Revelation, how has this treatment of the book enabled you to read it with more (or less) confidence?
10. How does the treatment presented here compare with what you have heard/studied previously? With what you have experienced in your church?
11. Finally, are you prepared to meet this Jesus *today*?

Notes

1. Please see R. Alan Culpepper's book, *John, The Son of Zebedee: The Life of a Legend* (Columbia SC: University Press, 1994). Concerning the authorship of these books, it is important to note that the Gospel itself (like the other Gospels) does not indicate who wrote it, although the traditional view that it was written by John, the son of Zebedee, the one whom Jesus loved (13:23; 19:26), the unnamed "other disciple" (20:4) and "witness" (21:24), is probably—after all the arguments—still the most likely. The dating of the book could be any time from the fifties to the nineties, but I see no reason to reject the traditional view that it was written after the other Gospels and probably during the early reign of Domitian. The second century dating by Bultmann and others makes no sense in the light of the discovery of the Roberts Fragment found in Egypt. The place of writing was probably Ephesus, where tradition indicates that John was residing. Likewise, you will sense that I see no reason to reject the same John as the writer of Revelation and the traditional dating later in the time of Domitian for the book of Revelation. I do not, however, wish to focus attention on these issues.

2. For some representative views on the Gospel of John see George Beasley Murray, *John*, Word Biblical Commentary (Waco TX: Word, 1987); Gerald L. Borchert, *John 1–11* and *John 12-21*, New American Commentary (Nashville: Broadman and Holman, 1996, 2002); Raymond E. Brown, *John i-xii* and *John xii-xxi*, Anchor Bible (Garden City NY: Doubleday, 1966, 1970); Gary M. Burge, *John*, NIV Application Commentary (Grand Rapids MI: Zondervan, 2000); D. A. Carson, *The Gospel According to John* (Grand Rapids MI: Eerdmans, 1991); Craig R. Koester, *Symbolism in the Fourth Gospel: Meaning, Mystery, Community* (Minneapolis: Fortress, 1995); J. Ramsay Michaels, *The Gospel of John*, New International Commentary on the New Testament (Grand Rapids MI: Eerdmans, 2010); Leon Morris, *The Gospel According to John* (Grand Rapids MI: Eerdmans, 1971); Gail R. O'Day, *The Gospel of John*, New Interpreter's Bible, vol. 9 (Nashville: Abingdon, 1995) 491–865; Rudolph Schnackenburg, *The Gospel According to John*, 3 vols. (New York: Cross-road, 1987); Ben Witherington, III, *John's Wisdom: A Commentary on the Fourth Gospel* (Louisville: Westminster John Knox, 1995). For other views on the Gospel of John see Rudolf Bultmann, *The Gospel of John* (Philadelphia Westminster, 1971); R. Alan Culpepper, *Anatomy of the Fourth Gospel* (Philadelphia: Fortress, 1983); C. H. Dodd, *The Interpretation of the Fourth Gospel* (Cambridge: University Press, 1958); Ernst Haenchen, *John 1* and *John 2*, Hermeneia (Philadelphia: Fortress, 1984); John Paul Heil, *Blood and Water: The Death and Resurrection of Jesus in John 18-21*, CBQ Monograph Series 27 (Washington, DC: Catholic Biblical Quarterly, 1995); Martin Hengel, *The Johannine Question* (London and Philadelphia: SCM and Trinity, 1989); Brooke Foss Westcott, *The Gospel According to St. John* (Grand Rapids MI: Eerdmans, 1954).

3. Gerald L. Borchert, *John 1–11*, New American Commentary (Nashville: Broadman and Holman, 1996) 11.

4. This Greek phrase is difficult to render in English and is usually translated poorly as something like "with God."

5. For my extended discussion of the Cana Cycle see Gerald L. Borchert, *John 1–11*, New American Commentary (Nashville: Broadman & Holman, 1996) 151–222.

6. Some commentators have problems with the word "believe" here and try to find distinctions in the Greek, but such efforts are pointless.

7. For information related to the Baptismal Liturgy of Dead Sea Covenanters see R. Eisenman and M. Wise, *The Dead Sea Scrolls Uncovered* (New York: 1992) 226–28.

8. For information on the Taurobolium see C. K. Barrett, *The New Testament Background: Selected Texts* (New York: Harper & Row, 1961, etc.) 96–97.

9. See Gerald Borchert, *John 1–11*, 223–368.

10. I have been convinced for many years that chapter 5 of John is about Sabbath and not out of place as Rudolf Bultmann argued (see his wrongly conceived plan to rearrange the chapters of John in *The Gospel of John: A Commentary* [Philadelphia: Westminster, 1971] 209, 237). But I wondered why the Festival Cycle in John begins with a Sabbath controversy. That question was answered when in 1995 I met with my colleagues in Old Testament while I was at Southern Baptist Seminary. I remain greatly indebted to them because they helped me work out the strategic importance of Sabbath in the Jewish Festival Calendar. Together we agreed that in Leviticus 23 each of major Jewish festivals can be understood as containing or equivalent to a Shabboth celebration. For me, the problem was solved. John perceived the nature of the Jewish festivals much better than Bultmann. I also reject Ernst Haenchen's contention that the festival references in John "are without historical or chronological value" (see his evaluation in *John 1: A Commentary on the Gospel of John, Chapters 1–6* in Hermeneia [Philadelphia: Fortress, 1984] 243). For my other comments on the issue of the festivals see Gerald Borchert, *John 1–11*, 224–27, 230.

11. Segments of this statement have been used by many who separate "truth" from Jesus. Because the search for truth is the goal of most academic institutions, this statement concerning the relationship of truth to freedom is an inviting idea and has been used even in school charters and on institutional seals with little relationship to the Johannine context.

12. Many Jews in the Second Temple period believed that the spirit of a person hovered around the corpse for up to three days, but thereafter it was consigned to *Sheol*—the place of the dead.

13. Unlike Raymond Brown (*The Gospel According to John XIII-XXI* [Garden City NY: Doubleday, 1970]) and others, I believe that the major break in the logic of John's Gospel comes at the end of chapter 11. The second volume of my commentary begins appropriately, I believe, with chapter 12, which roughly parallels the role of chapter 1 in the first half of the Gospel. Brown begins his second volume with chapter 13. For my organization of this second half, see Gerald L. Borchert, *John 12-21*, New American Commentary (Nashville: Broadman & Holman, 2002).

Some scholars [see for example Leon Morris, *The Gospel According to John: Revised* (Grand Rapids: Eerdmans, 1995), 542], designate this section of John as Farewell "Discourse(s)." I have not done so, because it involves much more than speeches.

14. For a fuller discussion and pictorial representation of this cycle as a target see Gerald L. Borchert, *John 12-21*, 72-75. Many scholars prefer to designate such a format as a chiastic structure. The term comes from the Greek letter "Chi" which is similar to our

letter "X." Whatever one may call it, the Johannine construct here is a magnificent literary piece of writing.

15. The concept of "the Way" is directly related to the Hebrew idea of "walking" (*halak*) that I have discussed several times earlier. The Qumran Covenanters also placed their hope in following "the way" and their Teacher of Righteousness with his rules or interpretations of the Torah (cf. 1 QS 9:17-21) as they prepared "the way of the Lord" in the desert (see Isa 40:3-5; cf.1 QS 8:11-16). Note also that the "Followers" of "the Way" was a designation used of the disciples/followers of Jesus before they were consistently called Christians (cf. Acts 9:2; 19:23; 22:4; 24:14). For further interpretation on these verses from John, please see Borchert, *John 12-21*, 107–15.

16. It is imperative for readers to be able to hold in dynamic tension the terrible suffering of Jesus in the Marcan cry of dereliction (Mark 15:34; cf. Matt 27:46) and this statement of utter confidence by Jesus in John 16:32. Both are true!

17. For further details on the structure see Borchert, *John 12-21*, 185-211, and "The Prayer of John 17 in the Narrative Framework of the Johannine Gospel," *Gemeinschaft am Evangelium* (Leipzig: Evangelishe Verlagsanstalt,1996) 7–18.

18. Six of the seven petitions in this prayer include the word *pater* ("Father"). They are 17:1, 5, 11, 21, 24 and 25. The seventh, which does not have "Father," is at 17:17.

19. It has been argued that since Pilate was an equestrian and perhaps may have been sponsored by Aelius Sejanus who was a "friend of Caesar," he may have longed for such a title. For a longer discussion on this topic, please see my extended notes with references in Gerald Borchert, *John 12-21*, 255, notes 97 and 98. What can be said here in brief is that the Jewish establishment was aware of Roman politics and used their knowledge to advantage.

20. Tradition is strong that John resided in Ephesus and lived there to be a very old man before his death. Visitors to Ephesus can still see the "traditional" site of Mary's house, which lies a short distance from the center of the great ancient metropolis.

21. For further discussion on the development of the traditions concerning Mary please see my brief excursus in Gerald Borchert, *Jesus of Nazareth*, 223–24. I would also plead that those who in their reactions to church theories of elevating Mary refrain from degrading her. She was the Mother of Jesus, and the New Testament affirms her as "Blessed" (Luke 1:42; 2:42).

22. Please note that this statement is reasserted at Revelation 16:17 and 21:6 when evil is finished and the new heaven and new earth are introduced.

23. Eight days later according to our calculations would be seven days later because in our contemporary culture we do not count the starting day. The worship implications are obvious because the church met on Sundays in celebration of Jesus' resurrection.

24. "The book is finished, superbly finished!" See *Le quatrieme evangile* (Paris: Emile Nourrey, 1921) 514.

25. I tell my students that knowing a little Greek can lead to making big mistakes. *Agapao* is not just God's self-giving love and *phileo* is not just human love. If you check John

5:20, for example, you will discover that in the statement "the Father *loves* the Son," the verb for "love" is *philei*.

26. Since the book of Revelation is the subject of differing opinions as well as much questioning and debate, I have included a rather long list of representative works on the nature of apocalyptic literature and the book of Revelation itself. See for example David E. Aune, *Revelation 1-5, Revelation 6-16, Revelation 17-22* (Dallas/Nashville: Word/Thomas Nelson, 1997–1998); Gerald L. Borchert, "Revelation," in the *New Living Translation Study Bible* (Wheaton IL: Tyndale House, 2008) 2160–99; C. Marvin Pate, K. L. Gentry Jr. et al., *Four Views on the Book of Revelation* (Grand Rapids MI: Zondervan, 1998); Leon Morris, *Apocalyptic* (Grand Rapids MI: Eerdmans, 1972); Mitchell Reddish, ed., *Apocalyptic Literature* (Peabody MA: Hendrickson, 1996). See also George R. Beasley-Murray, *The Book of Revelation* (London: Oliphants, 1974); James Blevins, *Revelation as Drama* (Nashville: Broadman, 1984); M. Eugene Boring, *Revelation* (Louisville: John Knox, 1998); John W. Bowman, *The Drama of the Book of Revelation* (Philadelphia: Westminster, 1955); G. B. Caird, *A Commentary on the Revelation of St. John the Divine* (New York: Harper & Row, 1966); Robert G. Clouse, *The Meaning of the Millennium* (Downers Grove IL: InterVarsity Press, 1977); Adela Yarbro Collins, *Crisis and Catharsis: The Power of the Apocalypse* (Philadelphia: Westminster, 1984); Philip E. Hughes, *The Book of Revelation* (Grand Rapids MI: Eerdmans, 1990); Craig Keener, *Revelation* (Grand Rapids MI: Zondervan, 2000); George E. Ladd, *The Revelation of John* (Grand Rapids MI: Eerdmans, 1972); C. S. Lewis, *The Great Divorce* (New York: Macmillan, 1946); Bruce J. Malina, *On the Genre and Message of Revelation* (Peabody MA: Hendrickson, 1995); John Newport, *The Lion and the Lamb* (Nashville: Broadman & Holman, 1986); Christopher C. Rowland, *The Book of Revelation*, The New Interpreter's Bible, vol. 12 (Nashville: Abingdon, 1998) 501–743; H. H. Rowley, *The Relevance of Apocalyptic* (New York: Harper and Brothers, 1963); Steven S. Smalley, *The Revelation to John* (Downers Grove IL: InterVarsity, 2005); H. B. Swete, *The Apocalypse of St. John* (New York: Macmillan, 1909); Arthur Wainwright, *Mysterious Apocalypse: Interpreting the Book of Revelation* (Nashville: Abingdon, 1993); J. F. Walvoord, *The Revelation of Jesus Christ* (Chicago: Moody, 1989).

27. The seven Beatitudes are at 1:3; 14:13; 16:15; 19:9; 20:6; 22:7, 14.

28. The suggested route would involve the north-south highway that began south of Ephesus through Smyrna (modern Ismir) to Pergamum (and on to ancient Troy and the inland passageway to modern Istanbul), then southwest to Thyatira, Sardis, Philadelphia, and Laodicea and finally back to Ephesus on the east-west highway. Concerning the question about more cities and churches than these seven and my response above, there were for example the tri-cities at the southwest corner of our group: Colossae, Hierapolis, and Laodicea.

29. In the early period, Christians often attended and were attached to synagogues in Asia Minor, but after the Jamnia Councils and the declarations of Christians as heretics, the Jews often reported Christians to Roman authorities as non-loyal Roman subjects. For the addition of the Jewish curse on the "Nazarene" heretics to the Twelfth Benediction see C. K. Barrett, *The Background of the New Testament: Selected Documents* (New York Harper & Row, 1961) 167.

30. Note here that in contrast to Revelation 1:4 and 8, the statement concerning the God of time by the four living creatures is made at 4:8 in the typical human pattern of past, present, and future ("was and is and is to come").

31. The fourfold designation of "tribe, language, people, and nation" is meant to include the entire world.

32. John hardly intended for readers to multiply the Greek number of twice myriads (our ten thousand) times myriads as Westerners tend to do. Instead, his goal was undoubtedly to shock readers with the vast forces of evil that would challenge the Lord. Moreover, modern attempts to identify these dragon-like cavalry forces with contemporary weapons like helicopter gunships are exercises in futility. John was painting a ghastly word description of the nature of evil and the fact that these terrifying forces of evil serve God in his judgment of destroying humans who stand under God's condemnation.

33. Even though John was writing in the Roman era, his perspective as a typical Jew was that destruction would come from the north (Mesopotamia) since the fall of Samaria and the loss of the so-called ten tribes was inflicted by Assyria in 722 BCE, and the fall of Jerusalem and the exile came at the hands of Babylon shortly thereafter in 586. These experiences were seared into the Jewish mindset. Continuing attempts by modern interpreters to contemporize the area across the "Euphrates" (Rev 9:14) with countries like China, Russia, Iran, or the region of Syria, Iraq, etc. are part of the endless struggle by Westerners to predict the arrival of events leading to the end of time.

34. For example, in the Greek culture the myth involved *Gaea* (earth) and *Chronos* (time), the dragon, who tried to gobble up the male offspring but failed in his attempt through *Gaea's* quick action. In Egypt (the Semitic culture), Isis saved her son Horus from the jaws of the jealous dragon.

35. Standing between five (the number of human completeness) and seven (the number of perfection or ultimate completeness), the number six became the number of failure or evil. The tripling of the six falsely suggests that it is a divinely oriented three, but such a suggestion is only to be viewed as a charade. If you are interested in further information concerning the main symbolic numbers that carry major significance in the Bible, see Gerald Borchert, "Symbolic Numbers" in "The Book of Revelation," *NLT Study Bible*, 2173; or my longer excursus in *John 1-11*, 254–56.

Since in Hebrew the letters also carry numerical value, the number 666 intriguingly can be assigned to NERON CAESAR. Omitting the pointed vowels (e, ae, a) and including the textual "o" of Hebrew, the letters and their value are n, r, o, n, c, s, r, or 50, 200, 6, 50, 100, 60, 200 = 666. There is a variant in some Greek manuscripts of Revelation that reads "616," which was an attempt on the part of later scribes to correct what they viewed as an error, and they omitted the last "n" of "Neron" valued at 50 and read "Nero" instead. That variant, however, is not likely the original reading.

Because Nero was viewed as epitomizing evil and reportedly disappeared, a myth concerning him developed that he really did not die but would come back to life reincarnated as another evil tyrant. Some even suggested that he was reincarnated as Domitian, enhancing this *Nero redivinus* myth.

36. As I indicated earlier, the book of Revelation must be treated as a series of visions or scenes and not pressed to conform to Western standards of logic. Accordingly, one should not be concerned and seek a modern rationalized distinction if John says that there is no Temple in Heaven/the new city in one place (e.g., 21:22) and can speak of a temple in other places (e.g., 11:19; 15:5-8). Let John present his visions and let us try to understand their meanings.

37. This text contains the third of seven blessings (Beatitudes) in Revelation. They are at 1:3; 14:13; 16:15; 19:9; 20:6; 22:7, 14.

38. Just as the Gospel has three cycles and concludes with the Death Story and the Resurrection Stories of Jesus, the book of Revelation concludes with the Final Judgment account and the Vision of the New Heaven and the New Earth.

39. This warning text became the theme for John Bunyan's famous *Pilgrim's Progress*.

40. See my comments above at Revelation 7:4-8 concerning the twelve tribes.

Chapter 7

Conclusion: Our Living Portraits of Jesus

Thank you for walking with me through some of the most significant pages of the New Testament—the collected accounts of the greatest story ever told! When God sent Jesus into the world, God shocked humanity with the climax to the divine plan for correcting the tragic state of the created order. This provocative climax, which came in Jesus, was necessary because humans had rejected responsible living through the loving free choice that God gave to them.

In brief, the result of this determined rejection—which in the Bible is forthrightly called sin and rebellion—is that humans are under the righteous judgment of God. Yet the Creator of all things was not willing to abandon humans and the creation *en masse* to condemnation and destruction. Instead, into this tragic situation on Earth God has injected a recovery plan for disobedient humans through the redemptive/saving work of Jesus. This infusion focused directly on the decadent condition of humanity that needed to be corrected or recreated so that people could represent as much as possible the image and likeness of their Creator.

In the course of this present work, therefore, I have taken seriously the fallen state of humanity and its need for renewal. I have also recognized that such a renewal or transformation is not within the limited capacity of humans. The problem is deep in mortals, and, in addition, there is a powerful enemy who has consistently mobilized his servants against the positive work of God and Jesus (the Son). Their evil goal is to undo the divine work of humanity's transformation and renewal. The combination of enemies under the devil is forcefully engaged in attracting humans to the dark side of existence while opposing the positive efforts of the Godhead. To counteract human rebellion and the efforts of the devilish enemy required the personal work of God through the Son. Jesus, God's Son, gave his life to effect the amazing re-creation that we call salvation in humans who respond, accept God's divine gift, and seek to walk in God's ways.

Nevertheless, since the Creator has not withdrawn freedom of choice from earthlings, it means that God and Jesus have been in a constant super-human struggle to confront the error-prone wills of people and challenge them to walk in trusting obedience with God in Christ. Indeed, Luke (Acts 4:12) indicates that it is the genuine way[1] for humans to experience a personal, radical, life-altering acceptance by God. It is the way to life fulfill-ment—even though it may be a painful, suffering journey. Moreover, it is clear from the New Testament that accomplishing such a transformation of the human will necessitates more than supplying people with informa-tion over against the ancient Gnostics, who focused on providing secret knowledge. Such misdirected approaches continue even today. Instead, transformation of life is required, which has been made possible only through the sacrifice of Jesus and in the gift of God's personal presence in the life of the believer through the *persona* of the Holy Spirit.

The core of this majestic story of God's work among humans involves God's only Son, and that is the reason I have focused this work on the portraits of Jesus in the New Testament. Some of the word pictures of Jesus that I have discussed include the powerful Son of God, the Divine "Word," the Suffering Messiah, the Resurrected Lord, the Second Adam, the Model for Humanity, the Visible Image of the Invisible God, the "I am" before Abraham, the New Mountain Man who is superior to Moses and Elijah, the sinless High Priest, the Apocalyptic Son of Man, the Warrior on the White Horse, the "Standing" Lamb of God, and the long-anticipated Davidic King, to identify only a few symbolic images. This Jesus whom we regard as the Savior of the World "tented" (*eskenosen*, John 1:4) among humans for a few brief years while revealing the loving heart of God and seeking to bring divine reconciliation and forgiveness to the mortals who have repeatedly rebelled against their Creator.

Pondering the meaning of the portraits of Jesus and the other word pictures I have discussed concerning the Lord's person and mission can be a rewarding experience for Christians as they seek to enter into a more dynamic life with God. Especially for those in our era who long to be more biblically literate, some of these images will assure them of their walk with God while other pictures will challenge them to remember that God was not playing games with mortals when Jesus gave his life to bring wholeness to humanity.

In our era of growing uncertainty, economic insecurity, outright hostility, political disruption, and biblical illiteracy, the hope of drawing closer to God though Jesus is fraught with increasing frustration. Easy answers and quick-fix programs are *not* adequate treatments for bewildered people who are bombarded with quick solutions to personal traumas and worldwide upheaval. The church does have the answer in the magnificent story of God through Jesus! But too often our faith communities resemble more of the frustrations and upheavals in our twenty-first-century world than the promise of the new heaven and the new earth in the world to come.

The message of Jesus in the New Testament has not been altered, but I wonder, do we know it? Would we recognize the Son of God if he came into our midst? Or would we be like his hometown people of Nazareth who wanted to throw him over the cliff when he proclaimed the coming of God's long-anticipated "Jubilee" (Luke 4:16-30)? We may have many Bibles in our homes, and we may be carrying the biblical texts on our smart phones, but has this good news been integrated into our lives? Or is it just "the sweet old-time religion" that may have sufficed for some of our grandparents?

I have asked myself repeatedly, *does our Jesus shake us up?* Does he wake us up? Or have we neutralized him and his message of reconciliation and the promise of the new creation? Could we be like the sleeping or dead church of Sardis in which our Christianity lies in a state of suspended animation (Rev 2:12-17)? In my travels, I have learned that there are places in our world where Christianity is wonderfully alive and vital and where miracles are actually occurring. How about in our faith communities? Are people anxious to learn more about our Jesus, or are we too polite to join Peter in calling people to be saved from this crooked or unscrupulous (*skolias*) generation (Acts 2:40)? Do you not agree that Peter's words in that passage are tough? He must have been convinced that the Jesus he knew could change the world. And what about Paul? Luke tells us that the residents of Thessalonica were troubled because they fully believed that Paul's Jesus could upset the entire inhabited world (*oikoumenen anastatosantes*; Acts 17:6).

In the next few moments, will you join me in reflecting on the situation as the early church with its new believers faced the task of living authentic, Christ-like lives in an unfriendly and even hostile environment?

Paul and other leaders had already suggested to the early Christians the beginnings of a critical strategy with his thematic idea of "living in Christ" (*en Christo*). That strategy implied living with the vision of Jesus the Christ through the realization that the continuing presence of the Holy Spirit as one's constant companion who reminds us of the model or vision of Jesus (note especially John 16:13-15).

Do you understand why I have chosen the "portraits of Jesus" as the theme of this book? If the early believers were going to get their strategy correct, the model of the living presence of Jesus would have to be front and center in their lives at all times. If this strategy was crucial for the early church, would it not be a wise one for us to adopt—we who are living in the twenty-first century with our growing biblical illiteracy?

What did the early Christians set out to do in this regard? Because the first witnesses were dying, these early believers needed clarity on who Jesus was—their model. Accordingly, they made a concerted effort to collect and preserve the genuine portraits of Jesus. Did they have only *one* authentic portrait of Jesus? The answer of course is no. These early, post-apostolic Christians jointly agreed that there were four authentic portraits/testimonies concerning the life and work of Jesus (namely, the Gospels known as Mark, Matthew, Luke, and John).

The early followers of Jesus recognized that these four testimonies were all slightly different and had specific emphases that related to them in different ways. One second-century Christian by the name of Tatian, however, from his defensive perspective, was not happy with the variations he saw in the four testimonies, and he tried to harmonize the four into one witness.[2] Did the early Christians accept his attempt? I am sure that by now you have surmised that the answer is no—because most people in our church pews do not even know his name. The early Christians rejected such tampering with these four special witnesses to Jesus.

These early believers also agreed that there were authentic instructions on how to live the Christ-like life. These instructions were not a new set of rules or laws but guidelines on how best to walk with their Lord Jesus. Therefore, these instructions needed to be collected and preserved as well. Do we have all of these early documents? We do not.[3] But what we do have are important examples of how they and we should seek to live authentic lives in Christ.

The next question is, were there other portraits of Jesus that were not considered to be authentic? Of Course! We have a number of them. Some are rather fantastic and even magical, such as (a) the one that presents the boy Jesus making mud birds along with his friends, but Jesus' bird is able to fly! You can judge such a portrait. And what about (b) the one where a neighbor boy dies when he falls off a roof and his parents charge Jesus with pushing him off? In defense, Jesus restores his life so that he can testify to Jesus' innocence. The picture asserts the truthfulness of Jesus, but in the authentic portraits of Jesus he rejects the temptation to use miracles for his welfare (cf. Matt 4:5-6; Luke 4:9-12). And what about (c) the one where a teacher is instructing Jesus, and Jesus in turn instructs the teacher concerning the minute significance of the mere letters in his lesson? I am sure that Jesus was knowledgeable, but I doubt that he used his knowledge for show. These and many other stories hardly represent the authentic Jesus.[4]

Some writings about Jesus, however, are badly skewed and in fact present a Jesus that contradicts the portraits in our four authentic witnesses. These works would have been regarded as Gnostic, inauthentic, or even heretical by second- and third-century Christian writers like Irenaeus and Tertullian.[5] The existence of such writings has been known for centuries, but more recently copies of a large number of them have come to light in discoveries from Nag Hamadi, Egypt. Among the documents uncovered are works such as the Gospel of Thomas, the Gospel of Philip, and even one designated as the Gospel of Truth, which may have been written by Valentinus, a candidate for the bishopric in Rome before he was rejected as a deviant/heretical leader.[6]

These documents attest to the fact that Christians have struggled from the beginning with those who would skew and falsify the model or portrait of Jesus for their own ends. Indeed, even Paul in his earliest letter (Galatians) bears witness to people who would distort the message of Jesus and the implications of the gospel. In his anger and frustration with these people and their views, he twice called down an *anathema* (an intense curse) upon them and their perversions of Christ and the gospel (Gal 1:8, 9). Indeed, he repeated such a curse in his extended instructions to the self-centered Corinthians as he prayed for the quick return of the Lord (1 Cor 16:22). Paul understood that living the Christian life was serious business, and he was committed to living the truth. He knew that truth does not need labels. It is neither conservative nor liberal. Truth is truth, and, as John indicated, Jesus embodied the truth! Christians are, therefore, called to follow Jesus who is the emancipating truth (cf. John 8:32; 14:6).

The quest for authentic/truthful portraits of Jesus was the goal of the early Christians because of their strong desire to walk with their risen Lord.

That quest should likewise be the goal of every sincere follower of Jesus today, especially in this era of growing biblical illiteracy.

Walking by the Spirit (Gal 5:16) with a vision of the risen Lord before us may seem like a simplistic strategy for living and dealing with a complex, confused, and misdirected world. Yet it is one of the most profound concepts in Scripture. Many sophisticated humans on planet Earth would prefer a neat "set of rules" or laws to order their lives. Or they may desire to have some neatly devised and constructed "program" with precise, easy-to-follow "how to" instructions packaged on their smart phones. Instead, humans are offered a freeing "way" of life—a "walk" that encompasses a call by the Spirit to follow and obey the vision of Jesus the Christ day by day.

This biblical way is hardly an easy one like joining a dinner club by walking down the aisle of a church, attending regularly prescribed meetings, paying weekly dues, and then proceeding with life as one did before the induction service. This way of "walking"—living with the portraits of Jesus that are ever present in life—however, is intensely focused. Yet it is the way to hope and liberation in a world divided by race, gender, and socio-economic, political, and religious differences. It is the way of relatedness and community that is now preparing humans for a future with the Lord and with each other. This walk in a sense may recapitulate the intended walking with God that should have taken place in the garden of Eden. The ever-seeking God still calls to humans, "Where are you?" (Gen 3:9), and longs for them to respond in obedience to the divine model for life.

As should be obvious, then, this work on the portraits of Jesus has not been concerned with drawing or painting word pictures about a heroic figure who lived on this planet for a few short years. It has been about recapturing a vision of the one who embodied the way of God for mortals and who provided for them in his self-giving life and sacrifice the way to immortality, which they could never attain by their own power.

For Christians, Jesus must become the crucial factor in formulating our personal perspectives, in developing our churches' goals, and in the future of Christianity. So the questions for us to ask might be, how are we perceived by those who need to meet Jesus and find new life in him? Are we viewed as gathering around his tombstone while we celebrate our "remembrance" of him at the Lord's Supper? In reflecting on Jesus, how do we connect his self-giving sacrifice and his resurrection? We readily proclaim that he is the victor over the devil and his agents, but how does that affect our daily lives? Indeed, how does his sacrifice play out in the way we relate to others? And are we as Christians viewed as meeting behind shut doors for our comfort and protection? Or are we meeting in order to go into the world with the powerful good news of forgiveness? Since Jesus is assumed to be actively transforming us, how can the people we meet in the world recognize that change? These questions are tough for us, but we need to ponder them because they may tell us important facts about who we really are. We might as well face them realistically because God already knows the answers.

Friends, I realize that not many academics write about these matters. But I think they need to be treated when we think about the portraits of Jesus. The way we view Jesus is crucial. Our sharpness of the portraits of Jesus will determine the way we live, the way we worship, and the way we witness!

So, as I opened this book by welcoming you to view, study, and proclaim to others the portraits of Jesus, now in closing this final chapter I welcome you to live and share these portraits with others as you await the *parousia* (the coming presence) of the Lord in power and glory.

God bless you in living with the Living Jesus!

Notes

1. The text of Acts 4:12 asserts that there is salvation in no other name than that of Jesus. There is no question, then, that this and other texts in the New Testament are intended as forceful missional statements and that there is an exclusive sense in them that can and has led to unfortunate instances of human triumphalism among some Christians and even in some mission strategies. Such patterns of triumphalism can be judged as part of human frailty, which can also be seen in some forms of Judaism, Hinduism, etc., and is currently being exhibited in some tragic forms of Islam with murderous results.

The true God in Jesus did not and does not take away from humans the right of a free will. Humans who violate the free will of others hardly represent the authentic God in Christ who not only did *not* create humans to be robots/automatons but also gave his life for humans and who continues to give them the right to choose and even to disobey the divine will, while reminding them that they are ultimately accountable to God for their choices. Following the mission of God in Christ is a critical calling for Christians. But forcing others to conform to one's view of God is to pretend to be God and is to succumb to the fateful temptation that has been present among humans since the story of the garden of Eden (cf. Gen 3:5).

2. The second-century Tatian, in an attempt to remove any variations in the Gospels, combined all four into one and omitted or altered any concerns he had in constructing his "harmony," which is called the Diatessaron. For copies of Tatian's work see J. Hamlyn Hill, *The Earliest Life of Christ Being the Diatessaron of Tatian* (Edinburgh: T. & T. Clark, 1894)

or A. S. Maemajdji, *Diatessarin De Tatian* (Beyrouth: Imprimerie Catholique, 1935). For some of my comments on Tatian see G. Borchert, *Jesus of Nazareth: Background, Witnesses, and Significance* (Macon GA: Mercer University Press, 2011) 4, 75, 238–39.

3. For example, we do not seem to have two of Paul's letters to the Corinthians. See 1 Cor 5:9 and 2 Cor 2:4.

4. For a collection of these documents see Edgar Hennecke, Wilhelm Schneemelcher, and R. McL. Wilson, *New Testament Apocrypha* (Philadelphia: Westminster, 1963). For some of my further comments see G. Borchert, *Jesus of Nazareth*, 185–88.

5. For my brief summary of the views of the Heresilogs see Gerald L. Borchert, "Insights into the Gnostic Threat to Christianity as Gained through the Gospel of Philip," in Richard N. Longenecker and Merrill C. Tenney, eds., *New Dimensions in New Testament Studies* (Grand Rapids MI: Zondervan, 1974) 79–93.

6. For a collection of these and other documents see James M. Robinson, *The Nag Hamadi Library* (San Francisco: Harper & Row, 1981). See my further comments on the gospels in G. Borchert, *Jesus of Nazareth*, 175–84.